Male Impersonators

*Over the streaky urinal, crude obscene drawings, pleading
messages jump at you. Someone has described himself glowingly,
as to age, appearance, size. Beneath the self-glorying description,
another had added: 'Yes, but are you of good family?' Another
scrawled note – a series: 'Candy is a queen.' 'No she isn't.' 'Yes I
am ...' And in bold, shouting black letters across the wall:*

IN THE BEGINNING GOD CREATED
FAIRIES & THEY MADE MEN

John Rechy, *City of Night* (1963)

Male Impersonators

Men Performing Masculinity

Mark Simpson

29 West 35th Street
New York NY 10001

© Mark Simpson 1994

Published in the USA in 1994 by

Routledge
29 West 35th Street
New York, NY 10001

Published in the UK in 1994 by Cassell, London

Library of Congress Cataloging-in-Publication data
A catalog entry for this book is available from the Library of Congress.

ISBN 0-415-90991-0

Typeset by Fakenham Photosetting Limited, Fakenham, Norfolk
Printed and bound in Great Britain by Mackays of Chatham, plc

Contents

Acknowledgements

I would like to thank Nick Haeffner, who initiated me into the world of cultural studies and psychoanalysis and whose private library of hard-core theory has kept my habit well supplied. Without him and his constant encouragement even through my most despondent and self-pitying periods and his unflagging ability to appear eager to read each new draft I proudly produced, this book would not have seen the light of day. I am also very much in debt to Alan Sinfield, who not only wrote the combative foreword but also took the time to read drafts and make detailed suggestions; moreover his stimulating talk at the 1992 Gay Studies Conference in York, 'Should there be gay intellectuals?', provided part of the inspiration for this project.

Thanks also to: Simon Audley and Kate Searle for their keen-eyed proof-reading and invaluable advice; Imanol Iriondo for his insight, indefatigable humour and wit; Michael Blighton for his comments, support and patience at my moods, poverty and a kitchen table overflowing with notes, books and newspaper cuttings; Adam Briggs for his thoughts on 'Narcissus Goes Shopping'; Dick for his interest and the steady supply of books and cuttings from his jaunts to the USA; Peter Cummings for allowing me to rifle through his fabulous AMG collection to choose the cover photo; and all the 'non-practising homosexuals' at No. 42 for their patience with my ceaseless telephone calls.

'Missing the Mark' originally appeared in the *Guardian*; ' "Suede" by Suede' in *Him*; 'Working Class Heroes' in *New Statesman and Society*; and 'Swish That Back End, Bill!' in *Gay Times*. 'Funny Men' is based on an unpublished article written in association with Nick Haeffner, researcher into British cinema and cultural identity at Sussex University; it is included in a rewritten and extended form with his kind permission.

Foreword

TOM entered his late teens in the 1950s. To be male and doing anything gay was illegal – as it still is in the United Kingdom if you are in your teens. As well as the law, Tom had a problem of culture.

> The images presented to me at that time were of gay men playing parts. Some were active, others were passive, just like men and women. If you were labelled 'butch' you were expected to be the boyfriend or the husband in the relationship. Likewise if you were the passive partner you were seen as the girlfriend or wife. It's interesting that if you were classified as 'butch' you had a better standing in the group; if passive, like women in general you had less standing.[1]

Tom experienced his sexuality as circumscribed by 'the images presented'. They made him feel he was acting, subjected him to stereotypical roles, involved him in an unjust status hierarchy.

Yet, even here, today, Tom writes: 'Some were active, others were passive, just like men and women.' Even with his present insight, perhaps through a slip of the pen, Tom writes as if men *as such* are active and women passive: the old ideas have not gone away. First, male homosexuals are, and always were, men, so their supposed activity and passivity have to be included in any definition of how men are. Second, not all men are active, and hardly any are active in all respects, all the time; nor are all women passive, and hardly any are passive in all respects, all the time. Third, what are active and passive anyway? – for instance, which is which in fellatio? The sucking person and the inserting person: aren't they both active and passive?

These questions are intriguing not just for gay men; the

active/passive, masculine/feminine roles and hierarchy that tangled up Tom and his friends are applied in the first instance to women and men in general. One of the exciting features of the present study by Mark Simpson is that it draws together the preoccupations of feminism, men's studies and gay studies. As Tom perceives, the one system is bugging us all. For lesbians and gay men, the situation is indeed perverse: a model of how heterosexual men and women are supposed to be, which is tendentious, inadequate and oppressive in the first place, is twisted into bizarre contortions in order to purport to describe us.

Since any 'failure' in 'masculinity' has always been of crucial concern to the prevailing sex–gender system, we should be wary of the customary ways of talking about it. Simpson, like some feminists, finds virtue in psychoanalysis. As he points out in his introduction Freud indeed says that 'all human beings are capable of making a homosexual object-choice' and that heterosexuality is 'a problem that needs elucidating and is not a self-evident fact'. However, he also endorses, though uneasily, Victorian ideas of masculinity and femininity. To be sure, Freud acknowledges that there is no reliable correlation between male homosexuality and effeminacy. 'In men the most complete mental masculinity can be accompanied with inversion', he says in *Three Essays on the Theory of Sexuality* (1905); while some inverts feel themselves to be women in search of men, others look for what are 'in fact feminine mental traits'.[2] But although Freud says here that masculinity and femininity may be variously distributed, he still thinks he knows what they are, 'in fact', and presents them as normative attributes of men and women respectively. In ancient Greece, he adds, 'what excited a man's love was not the *masculine* character of a boy, but his physical resemblance to a woman as well as his feminine mental qualities – his shyness, his modesty and his need for instruction and assistance' (p. 10). This is what 'a woman' is supposed to be like – shy, modest and in need of instruction. Those are her 'feminine mental qualities', and they are supposed to help us understand homosexuality.

Reading Freud is like reading Marx or the Bible: in such a massive and ambitious body of writing, almost any emphasis can be supported. He does question the idea of masculinity and femininity; yet that idea keeps finding its way back. He tries saying 'active' instead of 'masculine' and 'passive' instead of 'feminine', though that only compounds the problem – as he admits in *New Introductory Lectures in Psychoanalysis* (1973). Yet, a couple of pages later, he is asking himself: 'how does a girl pass from her mother to an attachment to her father? or, in other words, how does she pass from her masculine phase to the feminine one to which she is biologically destined?'[3] Freud needs this kind of formulation to get the 'Oedipus complex' to work. According to that theory, infants identify with mothers and fathers – who are presumptively feminine and masculine. This may be observed in the 'Wolfman' analysis, where Freud records a breakthrough at the point where the boy 'discovered the vagina and the biological significance of masculine and feminine. He understood now that active was the same as masculine, while passive was the same as feminine'.[4]

The reader will decide for herself or himself how far a deployment of psychoanalytic notions of masculinity reintroduces the problem which it aspires to address. But Simpson is surely right to say that current tendencies in the representation of the male body are disconcerting. He terms it 'a crisis of looking': 'Homosexuality, if it is to exist at all, must be *segregated*: it must be the Other which male heterosexuality defines itself in opposition to.' Lately, gay images no longer seem distinct from straight images. In advertising, the cinema and pop music, gay kinds of appearance, and gay kinds of invitations to look, challenge not only the idea that gay men should be invisible, but also the idea that they are deeply different from straight men.

'Traditional heterosexuality *cannot survive this reversal*', Simpson believes. Let's hope so. In many ways, of course, we already don't have traditional heterosexuality. That is why (neo)-conservatives go on about it so much: urgent ideological work usually signals the failure of a system, not its dominance. However, there are two reasons for not being too optimistic.

First, ideologies are amazingly resilient, and they often thrive on contradictions. We have learnt that since the heady days when cultural theorists started on this kind of analysis. To be sure, the sex–gender system is riddled with inconsistencies, and the current cascade of representations may seem hectic, even panicky. But that doesn't mean it is going to collapse. Second, as Simpson shows, the exotic sex–gender jumbles of our time are not necessarily nudging us in progressive directions. They may be reinscribing the system that, at first sight, they seem to undermine. They may be producing unanticipated modes of oppression.

Since Tom encountered oppressive images of masculinity in the 1950s, the apparatus for pushing representations at us has been vastly elaborated. The sophistication of narrative, design and technique in the instances Simpson discusses is exhilarating – but also awesome. How are we to gain any control over our own imagery? One sign of the balance of forces: the critique which you are about to read is in old-fashioned print, whereas a characteristic of many of the texts Simpson discusses is that they are audio/visual (films, advertisements, TV and records) and they have made a great deal of money for international capital. The dispersal of old-style sex and gender assumptions may leave market endorsement as the principal source of personal validation. A freeing up of sexual identities, if that is what we are seeing, may be at the price of other freedoms.

Alan Sinfield

Notes

1. National Lesbian and Gay Survey, *Proust, Cole Porter, Michelangelo, Marc Almond and Me* (London: Routledge, 1993), p. 155.

2. Sigmund Freud, *Three Essays on the Theory of Sexuality*, ed. James Strachey (London: Hogarth, 1962), pp. 7–9.

3. Sigmund Freud, *New Introductory Lectures in Psychoanalysis*, trans. James Strachey, Penguin Freud Library (Harmondsworth: Penguin, 1973), Vol. 2, p. 152.

4. Sigmund Freud, 'From the History of an Infantile Neurosis', *Standard Edition of the Complete Psychological Works*, ed. James Strachey (London: Hogarth, 1955), Vol. 17, p. 47.

For
Michael and Imanol

Chapter one

Introduction

> *The lifeblood of a soldier is masculinity ... and it is
> inarguable that the majority of a fighting force would be
> psychologically and emotionally deflated by the close
> proximity of homosexuals who evoke effeminate or
> repugnant but not manly visions.*
> ● *Bruce Fein*[1]

> *Obviously gays should be banned from the armed forces.
> We have to share eight-man quarters – how would you like
> it if your room-mate got drunk and made a pass at you?
> And you wouldn't know where to look in the shower.*
> ● *Jack, British Army Sergeant*[2]

THE year 1993 may well come to be seen as a watershed
in the study of modern masculinity. After the fashionable chatter
of the 1980s about a 'crisis of masculinity', brought about, it was
said, by the advances of feminism and the gay movement allied
to the economic upheavals of post-Fordism, the switch from
'male' heavy industries to 'female' service industries, there finally
appeared incontrovertible evidence of just such a 'crisis'. The unprecedented furore which erupted in the United States (echoed in
Britain) over newly-elected President Clinton's pledge to end the
Pentagon's ban on lesbians and gays was a crisis so public that no
sociological enquiry was needed to reveal it. Suddenly the final
masculine citadel, the last place where you could be sure that men
were men, was being infiltrated; adding to masculinist anxieties,
women were also admitted to certain combat positions for the
first time in both Britain and the US armed forces. The ultimate

yardstick of 'authentic' manhood was put in doubt: if women and queers could be soldiers too then what was there left for a man to do that was manly; where and how was virility to show its mettle?

If Clinton had failed to anticipate the symbolic importance of the issue, the Christian Right, always more adept at symbolic politics, did not. They immediately saw an opportunity to resurrect their *kulturkampf*, or 'cultural war', launched with calamitous results for the Republican Party by Pat Robertson at their infamous 1992 Convention in Houston, where he called on the faithful to wage a war 'for the soul of America.' In fact what he and other fundamentalists were calling for was a defence of traditional masculinity; a counter-revolution for patriarchy. As Naomi Wolf commented at the time, 'The Republicans have declared war on the war against men.'[3] In the religious Right's *weltanschauung*, America's ills were caused by the increase in godlessness: a lack of respect for Our Father in Heaven. This 'spiritual' concern about 'the soul of America' translated, of course, directly into the need to 'defend the family', i.e. the authority of earthbound fathers. Persecution of those who hindered this project – liberals, feminists, queers – was not just a necessity but a divine mission. 'Free us, Oh Lord, from spineless liberals, lisping queers and women with moustaches,' they cried, 'and our men will be *men* again, the family saved, order restored and America made potent once more!'

In contrast to the mutual suspicion of many gay men and feminists, the necessary connection between homosexuality and feminism has never been doubted by the religious Right. Feminists and queers are both despised for being gender rebels, for resisting the Law of the Father. Moreover they are seen as mutually dependent and symbiotic: feminists are 'mannish' women and therefore lesbians (hence the stories that were circulated during the election about Hillary Clinton's 'lesbian crèches' in the White House if her husband won) whose 'unnatural' and domineering character encourages the development of 'womanish' men – i.e. gay men; likewise, 'womanish' men encourage 'mannish' women. In effect religious fundamentalism is here reduced to sex and gender fundamentalism: *sexual* deviation is merely a metaphor – albeit the most inflammatory – for sex-gender deviation. So the bumper stickers in the car park outside the Houston convention read: 'God created

Adam and Eve – not Adam and Steve!' Against this background it hardly seems surprising that the plan to lift the Pentagon's ban on lesbians and gays – in effect an end to the State's involvement in the Inquisition against gender heretics – resulted in homosexuality replacing abortion as the No. 1 issue in the religious Right's hate hit parade.

Perhaps a more worrying development than this predictable mania was the way in which the current crisis in masculinity has provided the religious fanatics with some unlikely allies in the form of a new group of fundamentalists: the burgeoning men's movement, also concerned with the decline in paternal power and the spread of 'unmanly' men. Unlike the religious fundamentalists the men's movement did not declare its gender fundamentalism openly, and instead claimed to be 'complementary' to feminism. But in the person of their most famous ideologist, Robert Bly, they bewailed the development of 'soft men' as a result of a newly discovered phenomenon called 'absent fathers' and the resulting 'domination' of sons by their mothers. Like many self-serving philosophies, this argument was also used to account for the opposite phenomenon, the development of 'hyper-macho' behaviour amongst young men and their involvement in gang culture, dovetailing nicely into the moral panic about youth crime on both sides of the Atlantic and blaming it all on single mothers again (this idea reached Hollywood in 1993 in films such as Steve Anderson's *South Central*, a morality tale about black youth gang violence in Los Angeles with a paternalist message). The upshot of both usages of the absent father formula was the same: families without men at their heads will produce unsuccessfully masculinized men and thus the ruin of society.

The men's movement also began to make the connection between homosexuality and feminism in the cultural war. Its main advocate in Britain, Neil Lyndon in his comically mis-titled book *No More Sex War*, railing against the evil 'incubus' of feminism and the lack of 'paternity rights', imagined an alliance between the 'gay movement' (meaning gay men) and 'the sisterhood', describing it in a typically martial metaphor as a 'Treaty of Brest-Litovsk' (the First World War peace treaty between Germany and newborn Soviet Russia that allowed the Germans to devote their attention to the Western Front).[4] This evil alliance was secured because gay men (the Soviets?) 'offered their penises to one another' and were thus considered 'safe for women [the Germans?] who themselves distrusted penetration and its consequences.'[5] This is what the new wave masculinists are most angered by, and what their talk about paternity rights is really about: the way in which the penis, the virile organ, has become a plaything. Like the religious Right they fear that the phallus has lost its power (this is also the basis of the Right's opposition to abortion – that it robs the phallus of its dominion over female bodies; in part this is itself a displaced anger at contraceptive technology which gives women even more power over their own bodies but which is not usually attacked as it is economically useful to men).[6]

The fear of the trivialization of masculinity and the revelation that it might, after all, have no substance, no core and no dignity is a growing concern of many men who are not involved in either the religious Right or the men's movement. And they have good reason to be concerned. Everywhere they look they see naked male flesh served up to the public on billboards, magazine covers and television screens. Men's bodies are on display everywhere; but the grounds of men's anxiety is not just that they are being exposed and commodified but that their bodies are placed in such a way as to passively invite a gaze that is *undifferentiated*: it might be female *or* male, hetero *or* homo. Traditional male heterosexuality, which insists that it is always active, sadistic and desiring, is now inundated with images of men's bodies as passive, masochistic and desired. Narcissism, the desire to be desired, once regarded as a feminine quality *par excellence*, seems, in popular culture at least, now more often associated with men than with women. Sexual difference no longer calls the shots, 'active' no longer maps onto 'masculine', nor 'passive' onto feminine. Traditional heterosexuality *cannot survive this reversal*, particularly because it brings masculinity into perilously close contact with that which must always be disavowed: homosexuality.

Heterosexuality as it has been understood in countries like the United States and Britain can co-exist but cannot co-habit with what is designated 'homosexuality': 'how would you like it if your mate made a pass at you?' Virility is what men value above everything else and virility is, to all intents and purposes, precisely *that which is not queer*. This is why the debate about gays in the military has focused so obsessively on the idea of gay men sharing quarters with straight men and the image of two men dancing together at military balls, and why the position of women has been consistently ignored.[7] Homosexuality, if it is to exist at all, must be *segregated*: it must be the Other which male heterosexuality defines itself in opposition to. But the manner in which the Right tried in 1993 to defend this segregation actually points up how much times have changed and how hopeless their task is: posters of men kissing were pasted up outside US military bases. No doubt this was intended to provoke disgust with the unmanly, unnatural image of two men being tender towards one another and impress upon military men and the public alike the impossibility of such 'men' being admitted into the ranks of the armed forces. But ironically, set against the increasingly high profile of lesbians and gays in the media and the proliferation of the undifferentiated, 'queer', imagery of men, the posters seemed to depict not so much an outrage as merely the latest advertising ploy.

The increasing difficulty of trying to enforce or even depict a demarcation between homosexuality and heterosexuality became even more apparent when TV news programmes attempted to illustrate the 'problem' of gays in the military by showing endless footage of GI's taking showers: the hetero male's terrible anxiety that his best pal might make a pass at him was depicted in shots of acres of ripe, naked young male ass. The attempt to depict the heterosexual male world of buddiness and virility, innocent of the taint of queerness, collapsed into voyeurism of the queerest kind: a televised military Mr Hot Buns contest.

Homosexuality is a genie that is out of the bottle. Long considered somehow 'inauthentic' men, gay men have succeeded, by their visibility, in bringing into question the whole category of masculinity, 'queering' the image of what should be the very archetype of all-American virility. Of course, as openly gay US Representative Barney Frank has said, 'We don't have ourselves dry-cleaned. We've been taking showers for a long time.'[8] But now homosexuality is a *public* issue; the argument about whether the military ban should be lifted is an argument not about whether lesbians and gays should serve (they can and do serve now, so long as they remain closeted), but about the maintenance of public/private distinctions that have been the mainstay of the toleration/control of queers and queerness in Britain and the United States. In demanding their official acceptance in the military, gay men are demanding their right to a place in the most public masculine institution; they are marching out of their darkened bars and bedrooms into a transparent world where, we are continually reminded, there is no privacy, a world where men are required to be *intimate* with one another.

This is to say not merely that gay men can be just as macho as straight men, which is banal and anyway hardly commendable, but that the problem of gays in the military, the problem of desegregating homosexuality from a private ghetto into a heterosexual world that depends on homosexuality remaining invisible, encapsulates the problem faced everywhere in popular culture today by this frail phenomenon we call masculinity – the problem of *looking*, that is, how to prevent the 'deflation' of 'manly visions' by the proximity of homosexuality. Thus the public does not wish to have to look at the queer in uniform and the soldier does not wish to have to look at the queer *out* of uniform. The soldier's fear that he will become the object of an unashamedly queer gaze in the shower is not just the fear that he will suddenly know his nakedness, but also that he will *know the nakedness of his buddies* – that he 'won't know where to look'. The barracks' showers will have become as (homo)sexualized as the billboards, TV and cinema screens. The policy guidelines issued by the Clinton administration to the Pentagon in July 1993 (dubbed 'Don't ask; don't tell') attempted to resolve the 'crisis of looking' by keeping queer desire invisible. Thus, 'Sexual orientation will not be a bar to service unless *manifested* by homosexual conduct' (emphasis added).

Male Impersonators examines the crisis of masculinity as a crisis of looking and looked-at-ness, a puncturing of 'manly visions' in film, rock and roll, pornography, advertising and sport. These diverse essays have as their aim the enhancement of all that is abhorred by those who declared 'war on the war against men', and subjecting men to that queer gaze that makes them so anxious about dropping the soap in the shower. The title, *Male Impersonators*, was chosen to emphasize the crisis of identity that faces men today in a world where 'man' and 'manly' appear to have become freely floating signifiers with no referents – and also to *exploit* it. These essays, I am not ashamed to admit, take great pleasure in celebrating the fragmentation of that which has always wished to be seen as a monolith; they have at their heart a fervent wish to denaturalize masculinity, which has in the past tried to pass itself off as unaffected, spontaneous and effortless in order to keep the mechanisms of patriarchal power secret. Homoeroticism occupies centre stage not just because I am gay (although this is a major factor, of course), but also because, *when revealed*, it is the greatest challenge to virility and thus masculinity's claim to authenticity, to naturalness, to coherence – to dominance.

In effect what I hope to achieve is something equivalent, albeit on a more modest scale, to those men who wish to serve in the armed forces as open, *visible* gay men: a desegregation of homosexuality and heterosexuality – in this case in the public world of popular culture. As noted, this desegregation requires a transformation of that thing we call heterosexuality, but as homosexuality is itself defined in relation to heterosexuality, this desegregation also implies a transformation of homosexuality – in other words, nothing short of a revolution in the 'common-sense' notions of sexuality on both the gay and straight side of the bedroom.

Modesty requires me to admit that this project of 'desegregation' is not entirely novel. It began, many gay readers may be surprised to discover, with the work of Sigmund Freud.

> Psychoanalytic research is most decidedly opposed to any attempt at separating off homosexuals from the rest of mankind as a group of special character. By studying sexual excitations other than those that are manifestly displayed, it has found that all human beings are capable of making a homosexual object-choice and have in fact made one in their unconscious. Indeed, libidinal attachments to persons of the same sex play no less a part as factors in normal mental life ... than do similar attachments to the opposite sex.[9]

The significance of Freud's refusal to assign homosexuality to a 'third sex', to designate homosexuals a 'race apart', has yet to be fully realized. By insisting that 'homosexual object-choice' was something that all men were capable of and had made, albeit unawares in most cases, and something that played 'no less a part in factors of normal mental life' than heterosexual object-choice, Freud overturned the idea that heterosexuality and thus masculinity was non-complex or unproblematic; by bringing the unconscious into play Freud was able to analyse what appears unanalysable since it is culturally dominant.

As Freud himself suspected, his 'discovery' of the unconscious was a rebellion against common sense at least as momentous as Copernicus' discovery that the sun did not revolve around the earth, or Darwin's that man was descended from apes. Freud's work was a culmination of the process of *decentering* that began with the discovery that man was not at the focus of the universe and was then hastened by the discovery that he was not specially created. Freud abolished the idea, carefully maintained since the Renaissance, that man was a free, conscious, independent agent, his ego reigning supreme, replacing it instead with the notion of subjectivity; something neither free, nor fully conscious – and therefore not independent. And just as the discoveries of Copernicus and Darwin took some time to effect their revolution, so it is with Freud: only now, almost 90 years after the publication of his *Three Essays on Sexuality*, are we beginning to see the full impact of his ideas in mainstream life.

Freud's theory of infantile sexuality is at the centre of the radical potential of his ideas. According to this we are all born in possession of undifferentiated desire, or polymorphously perverse – able to respond erotically to all and sundry: breasts, thumbs, bowel movements, even rattles, all offer opportunity for erotic pleasure. During this period infants have no understanding of sexual difference and little girls are unaware of their 'castration' and are 'masculine' in behaviour. Only later does the knowledge of sexual difference set in; this is the beginning of the Oedipus complex where the child resolves the incest taboo and learns to separate desire into identification and object-choice. Thus, within the terms of this system, heterosexuality, the differentiation of desire according to sexual difference, is not an inborn natural condition but rather something that is imposed through the Oedipus complex – that is to say, heterosexuality is a *cultural* phenomenon. Freud's ideas about infant sexuality suggest that in a sense we are all born perverts and that heterosexuality, so-called mature sexuality, has to be acquired, that it is a human artefact rather than a biological given – i.e. 'unnatural'. The value of this approach is not that perversion (the turning away of sexual drive from reproduction) is revealed as natural, or less unnatural than so-called mature sexuality, and therefore good, but that heterosexuality is *de*naturalized and opened up to analysis.

> Thus from the point of view of psychoanalysis the exclusive sexual interest felt by men for women is also a problem that needs elucidating and is not a self-evident fact based upon an attraction that is ultimately of a chemical nature.[10]

Of course, this 'problem' of heterosexuality has not been elucidated by those who came after Freud, nor even particularly by Freud himself. Instead, homosexuality, monarch of the perversions (although, due to its frequency, Freud hardly thought it worthy of the name), has invariably been characterized by psychoanalysis in the English-speaking world as the problem. Indeed psychoanalysis has often joined forces with psychiatry in the determined medicalization of homosexuals and their torture/treatment, something which has stigmatized Freud's ideas amongst them for most of the twentieth century.

While it is not the purpose of this book to vindicate psychoanalysis or save it from its past, I hope that by employing it in the way that I have, in the way that has been meticulously avoided for so long – to 'elucidate' the problem of heterosexuality and masculinity – its usefulness as a critique of 'common-sense' notions which segregate homosexuality and heterosexuality, masculine and feminine, will become apparent.

This critique, particularly of the masculine/feminine opposition, is not always apparent in psychoanalysis and is very much a matter of interpretation. Indeed, in 'A Case of Homosexuality in a Woman' Freud admits that 'psychoanalysis cannot elucidate the intrinsic nature of what in conventional or biological phraseology is termed "masculine" and "feminine": it simply takes over the two concepts and makes them the foundation of its work.'[11] But psychoanalysis, if it shows anything at all, shows in the tortuous and sublime complexity with which it is forced to elucidate 'masculine' and 'feminine' traits in men and women just how *inadequate* these categories are and how foolish and desperate – and indispensable – our faith in them is. Freud confesses: 'When we attempt to reduce them further, we find masculinity vanishing into activity and femininity into passivity, and that does not tell us enough.'[12]

The value of Freudianism has already been appreciated by some representatives of that other group traditionally most hostile to psychoanalysis – women. In her classic text *Psychoanalysis and Feminism* Juliet Mitchell reclaimed Freud for the radical tradition. Through the work of French poststructuralist Jacques Lacan who interpreted psychoanalysis as a branch of semiotics (i.e. the Oedipus complex is symbolic and a problem of language), Mitchell concluded that 'psychoanalysis is not a recommendation *for* a patriarchal society but an analysis *of* one.'[13]

This formulation contains, I believe, an especially important message for the gay movement, which threatens to be seduced by 'third sexers' like Dr Simon LeVay, gay author of *The Sexual Brain*, who propound a biological basis for homosexuality as the key to social toleration[14] (and an antidote to anti-homosexual crude Freudianism). LeVay claims that the area of the hypothalamus believed to be associated with the 'sex drive', INAH3, is the same size in gay men as in heterosexual women, in effect reviving the German sexologist Karl Ulrichs' notion of homosexual men as 'Uranians': 'a class of individuals who are born with the sexual drive of women and have male bodies'. In this kind of strategy, the answer to the problem of homophobia and the threat that the homosexual represents to patriarchy is not to attack patriarchy but rather to try to *accommodate homosexuality to patriarchy* by showing that it bolsters rather than threatens the orthodox notions of masculine and feminine. With his discourse of 'masculinized' and 'feminized' brains and biologically determined sexuality LeVay takes it as given, as much as any religious bigot, that heterosexuality is the universal law that governs desire, that gender is reducible to biology, that masculine and feminine follow on from male and female and that these are categories outside of culture, history and politics – as real and as discoverable as male and female genitalia. The notion of a 'third sex' is in fact not a third sex at all, but rather an exception that *enforces* the rule of the other two: gay men only *appear* to be gender/sexual rebels – rather, since they are born with feminized brains, when they desire men they are obediently following the patriarchal/heterosexual imperative that gender and partner choice must follow on from sex (albeit brain sex rather than genital sex).[15] 'Leave us alone!' LeVay begs Pat Buchanan and Jerry Falwell, 'we are not the enemies of patriarchy that you take us for.'

Since gay men are homosexual because they have 'feminized' brains, they are not 'men' at all. The Otherness of homosexuality is reinforced by biology, the dreadful contagion of homosexuality is locked up in the congenital homosexual's body; common-sense ideas about homosexuality as gender confusion – *anima muliebris in corpore virili inclusa* (a woman's soul trapped in a man's body) – are elaborated, not challenged by this kind of science. This is a strategy that brings to mind the events in a London science college a few years ago when members of the rugby club were so angered/threatened by the presence of a Gay Society on their campus that they decided to join it *en masse* and vote for its disbandment. Now a *gay* male scientist attempts to remove the threat of homosexuality from the masculine world and the masculine body. LeVay illustrates very well the way in which straight and gay men often have as much invested in keeping their difference as rigidly defined as possible as each other. Homosexual men understandably terrified of the consequences of *embodying* the gender conflict that is raging in society, and looking to the security of far-off Uranus, and heterosexual men terrified of the consequences of being forced to co-habit with homosexuals, of their bodies being infected by homosexuality (in fact their own repressed desires), are *both* desperate for confirmation of their separate authenticity/ identity, and look to biology to tell them who they are. Sartre's famous maxim in *Saint Genet, Actor and Martyr* seems to hold more true than ever:

> The homosexual must remain an object, a flower, an insect, a dweller of ancient Sodom or the planet Uranus, an automaton that hops about in the limelight, anything you like except my fellow man, except my image, except myself.

For a choice must be made: if every man is all of man, this black sheep must only be a pebble or must be *me*.[16]

In contrast to psychoanalysis, biological explanations of homosexuality, however 'well-intentioned', will always tend to set it apart as something at best problematic and at worst pathological, and heterosexuality as something natural by default. In the teleological world of biology the only 'real' function of sex can be to pass on genes; homosexuality, the very definition of non-reproductive sex, can only ever be *degenerate*. As Foucault observed in *The History of Sexuality*, it is science which first characterized that species called 'the homosexual', creating a discourse of disease where the church had maintained one of sin. LeVay attacks Freud in *The Sexual Brain* as the author of the suffering of homosexuals – but it was ironically the most biological ideas of his day that Freud had imbibed, such as the idea that the function of sex was to pass on 'germ-plasm' (genes), that encouraged him to regard any sexual activity that was not reproductive as dysfunctional and thus Oedipalization as something desirable. It is the least 'scientific' ideas contained in his work, the interpretation he offers of the symbolic order (as elaborated by Lacan and Mitchell), which offer most potential for homosexuals and any other victims of patriarchy because they examine how meaning is arrived at rather than simply distribute it in the clinically arrogant manner of science.

There are other reasons, besides his anti-segregationist and anti-common-sense position, that have made Freud's work so useful to my project. His ideas on the super-ego and the phallus help to elucidate not just the problem of heterosexuality and to point up the centrality of (implicit) homosexuality in any understanding of masculinity, but also to show the *unconscious* relation of contemporary phenomena such as those identified at the beginning of this introduction: the crisis over gays in the military, the demonization of homosexuality by the religious Right, the panic about absent fathers and the explosion of images of men's bodies.

According to Freud, the super-ego, the individual's social conscience, the internal policeman, is formed from the boy's desire for his father; that is to say he takes as a substitute for the forbidden desire for his father *his own ego* in which he sets up the image of his father. So the whole Oedipus complex and the creation of social feeling, which both depend upon the operation of the super-ego, is based on *homo-desire turned inwards*. As Norman O. Brown has observed, this turning inwards that the boy must perform to achieve identification and manhood involves a certain amount of *impersonation*: 'We make the identification with the lost object by introjecting or incorporating it, not really incorporating it, but passively by making ourselves like it.'[17]

The particular loathing and contempt that many men feel for homosexuality, especially those who exhibit highly patriotic or religious impulses (both are characteristics of an over-rigorous super-ego), are a function not just of their fear of their own homosexuality, but also of the strength of their affection for the 'father' that they have set up for themselves in their ego. Explicit homosexuality represents a threat to the maintenance of the very fraught identification with/impersonation of the 'father', and thus their whole sense of self. This explanation suggests that anxieties about homosexuality will always saturate any discourse about fathers, and that the current panic about the *absence* of fathers is really about the *presence* of homosexuality – if the boy has no father to love and introject how will he be successfully masculinized? What, in other words, is to prevent him from being/remaining a queer? This is the spoken agenda of the religious Right and the largely unspoken one of the men's movement. The gays-in-the-military issue raises the same hackles. As a place where traditionally boys become men, the military acts *in loco parentis*; out gay men make explicit the implicit homoeroticism of that institution.

The increasing use of naked men to sell products outlined in 'Narcissus Goes Shopping' is, it almost goes without saying, evidence of the discovery of the male body's desirability. And yet it is often forgotten that this is a *re*-discovery; that what we are witnessing is a 're-paganization' of society, where the male body rather than the female body is coming to be regarded as representing 'sex'. The resistance of the religious Right to this phenomenon is absolutely correct: this is very much a 'cultural war for the soul of America'. What Christianity brought about and what patriarchal power has relied upon in Western civilization since the time of the Holy Roman Emperors is the symbol of male power – the phallus –

remaining hidden. For as long as it is hidden it cannot be challenged; as Michel Foucault put it, the success of power 'is proportional to its ability to hide its own mechanisms ... for its secrecy is not in the nature of an abuse; it is indispensable to its operation.'[18] The phallus in psychoanalysis is not just the penis; it is the patriarchal signifier, the symbol of male power. Psychoanalysis in its exploration of the unconscious reveals man not to be the independent conscious agent so beloved of liberal philosophy, and instead reveals the operation of the phallic signifier, the phallocentrism of all men, and opens it up to critique. In Roman times the phallus' power, and thus male power, was openly acknowledged; a phallus worn on a necklace was said to bring good luck, representing as it did the god Fascinatus. Everyone was in agreement that the phallus was literally *fascinating* – able to enchant and draw the eye.[19]

The modern-day 'fascination' with homosexuality is very much bound up with society's attitude towards the phallus. The increasing visibility of homosexuality, whether in the media or masculine institutions like the armed forces, 'draws the eye' ('I wouldn't know where to look'), symbolizing the increasing visibility of the phallus and making explicit *all* men's desiring relationship to it and giving them the knowledge of their *own* nakedness. Thus Juliet Mitchell describes psychoanalysis as an exploration not of relations between men and women but of *both* to the phallus.

The increasing explicitness of male narcissism that has also resulted from this nakedness is a preoccupation of these essays. Narcissism, like homoeroticism, is a pre-Oedipal libido; in fact the polymorphously perverse condition of infantile sexuality is, according to Freud, largely a narcissistic or autoerotic state. The peculiar position of narcissism is that it seems to operate both explicitly as the mechanism of homosexuality and implicitly, via the boy taking his own ego as his love-object, the route by which the boy child is successfully Oedipalized – i.e. escapes homosexuality.

Freud claimed that the most essential characteristics of homosexuals 'seem to be a coming into operation of *narcissistic object-choice* and a retention of the erotic significance of the *anal zone* ...'.[20] But he was careful to add, 'What we find as an apparently sufficient explanation of these types can equally be shown to be present, though less strongly, in the constitution of ... those whose manifest attitude is normal.' In these essays, particularly 'Big Tits!', 'Narcissus Goes Shopping', 'Top Man' and 'Marky Mark and the Hunky Bunch', I attempt to show how male narcissism is becoming more and more 'manifest' in popular culture and the manner in which this tends to blur the distinction between homosexuality and heterosexuality rather than maintain it. The function of anality, that other autoerotic libido that must be kept secret, is examined in 'Active Sports'. Anality, like the desire for the father, has to be given up to achieve Oedipalization, designating the anus, like homosexuality itself, something that must remain private and hidden. The fear of the soldier in the shower about dropping his soap is the fear that he will rediscover his anality (Freud argued that it was never completely sublimated), make his anus 'public', and with that lose his masculine phallic identity.

I am keen to suggest that male narcissism, once made explicit and separated from the imperative to disavow homoeroticism, might be a model for a 'new type' of masculinity. Too often taken to be synonymous with selfish individualism and solipsism by the Left and decadence by the Right, narcissism, intimately connected to the dependent mother/child relationship, is a libido that is almost never acknowledged for its non-aggressive and quite literally 'nurturing' characteristics. As long as narcissism in men is regarded pejoratively, homosexuality is likely to receive the same treatment; e.g. Norman Mailer's famous description of homosexuals as 'narcissists who occasionally collide with one another and then realise their mistake' (in fact Mailer is a classic example of the *implicit* narcissist, in swooning love with his own ego and thus rabidly disavowing homoeroticism). Many gay men, also accepting that narcissism is something necessarily pejorative, have taken exception to Freud's conception of how narcissism operates in a type of homosexuality: 'proceeding from a basis of narcissism they look for a young man that resembles themselves and whom *they* may love as their mother loved *them*'.[21] This formula has been taken to result in both a stigmatization of homosexuals as narcissists and mothers as the authors of their sons' homosexuality. Actually it strikes me as a rather attractive vision of both homosexuality and narcissism. Is it really so awful that men should love one another in a maternal fashion? Surely it is only in a deeply misogynistic culture that the (unconscious) attachment of an adult male to his mother should be regarded as so distasteful; Freud's formula could only be insulting to gay men and place the 'blame' for homosexuality on mothers if it is accepted that this kind of narcissism, the desire to re-enact in adult life the joy of infantile 'oneness' with the mother, is something contemptible of itself. Of course, in science and in psychoanalysis there are no purely selfless actions, and yet I find this pattern of nurturing love between men in a world of violence and cut-throat competition strangely beautiful. (So did Freud: his 'Leonardo Da Vinci: A Memory of His Childhood' is a moving tribute to the role of the great artist's attachment to his mother, from whom he was separated at an early age, in his staggering creativity and the bountiful care and largess he bestowed upon his apprentices.)

There have been others, in addition to Juliet Mitchell, who have attempted to realize Freud's idea that heterosexuality was also a problem that needed to be elucidated, and their work has signposted my journey – most notably, Guy Hocquenghem's *Homosexual Desire*, Mario Miele's *Homosexuality and Liberation*, and, more recently, Anthony Easthope's *What A Man's Gotta Do: The Masculine Myth in Popular Culture*,[22] which is one of the best available introductions to Freudian thought and its applications in the field of men's studies. But the text that I found myself turning to most frequently and quoting from most profusely was a work of literary criticism; Leslie Fiedler's *Love and Death in the American Novel*, published in 1959, remains a work of startling insight which caused a scandal at the time because of its use of Freudian ideas, in particular the role of homoeroticism in the American literary tradition, most famously – and to most outrage – queering the relationship of buddies 'lighting out for the territory', buddies like dark-skinned Queequeg and Ishmael in *Moby Dick*, who leave civilization behind in search of a wilderness romance. Fiedler's work was breathtakingly courageous for its time, refusing to allow the homoeroticism he reported to be sublimated out of existence, kept implicit rather than explicit, private rather than public, insisting instead that the emphatic denials of it only served to underline its significance.

There is an almost hysterical note to our insistence that the

> love of male and male does not compete with heterosexual
> passion but complements it; that it is not homosexuality in
> any crude meaning of the word, but a passionless passion,
> simple, utterly satisfying, yet immune to lust – physical
> only as a handshake is physical, this side of copulation.
> And yet we can never shake off the nagging awareness that
> there is at the sentimental center of our novels ... nothing
> but the love of males![23]

Fiedler's value to me has been twofold. Not only did his work on
American literature trailblaze for one such as this on popular culture, but he plays for me the role that Queequeg and the other
'dark-skinned' characters did for the heroes of American novels: a
guide and a companion in a vast unknown continent; where Queequeg was Ishmael's guide to America's fearsome wilderness, Fiedler
is my guide to America's fearsome civilization.

Why the concentration on American popular culture? First,
born on the 4th of July slap-bang in the middle of the last truly
American decade, the 1960s, I have been fascinated by it since I
was old enough to watch *Star Trek* and *Mission Impossible*. Second, because my own subjective interest is here a reflection of an
objective condition: popular culture in both the West and now the
emergent East is increasingly dominated by Hollywood (even as
American political and economic hegemony wanes). I neither
lament nor applaud this in my analysis, but the effects of the American domination of images of men on a British male audience, and
the way in which male role models are now doubly distant (not
only 'unreal' but also foreign), are interesting areas worthy of
study.

Finally some words of caution. While these essays were written by a queer with the stated intention of queering the way we look
at masculinity, their purpose, unlike that of works such as Miele's
Homosexuality and Liberation, is not to recommend homosexuality or even polymorphous perversity. Very often these essays take
a view of homosexual men that is as critical of them as of heterosexual men. I have endeavoured to be non-partisan and I hope I
have not shirked from making observations and putting forward
theories simply because they portray gay men in an unflattering
light. So, for example, in 'Dragging It Up and Down' gay male

misogyny is confronted, even if this means giving space to ideas about gay men's loathing of the female body that have reinforced prejudice in the past (and perhaps to some of the ideas behind Neil Jordan's *The Crying Game*, for which I take him to task in 'A Crying Shame'). In several other essays, including 'A World of Penises' and 'Marky Mark and the Hunky Bunch', the close relationship between both gay and straight male homoeroticism and phallocentrism is discussed, as well as the investment that gay men have in virile – i.e. 'heterosexual' – masculinity. Like the counter-revolutions for patriarchy, I see a connection between male homosexuality and feminism and would very much like gay men and the women's movement to go beyond Lyndon's 'Treaty of Brest-Litovsk' non-aggression pact, but I suspect that such an alliance may continue to prove elusive.

It is important to bear in mind that this is a collection of essays that take one or two ideas as their central theme and develop their argument more or less independently of each other. They lend themselves to browsing and can be read in any order that appeals to the reader, but they are arranged in such a way as to follow a line of development which should aid those unfamiliar with the theory invoked. But whichever method is employed, either patiently chronological or unashamedly dilettante, I ask the reader to remember that I do not claim to be offering in these essays definitive truth, *just a way of looking*.

To this end I quote from the inside front cover of the fall 1957 issue of *Physique Pictorial*, a publication of the notorious Athletic Model Guild (whose handiwork graces the cover of this book), a US underground magazine which featured young male toughs, often fresh out of prison or AWOL, persuaded without too much difficulty by appeal to their narcissism to bare their midwestern corn-fed bodies for the delectation of American queens. AMG pioneered a certain way of looking at men which enjoyed the spectacle of virility and yet ironically framed what was being admired – a way of looking at men's bodies which has become mainstream:

> We hope this book offends no one, though we realize the mere portrayal of any part of the body disturbs some whose minds have been pitifully warped by improper

training. A little gentle humor has been included, and here and there we have poked a little fun at some of our 'antagonists' who take themselves too seriously. It is hoped that all who take the trouble to study the book will get a message of hope and inspiration from it, and will be the better for the experience.

Notes

1. *USA Today*, September 1990.

2. *Independent on Sunday*, 31 January 1993.

3. Naomi Wolf, 'Battle on the Home Front', *New Statesman and Society*, 6 November 1992.

4. Neil Lyndon, *No More Sex War: The Failures of Feminism* (London: Sinclair-Stevenson, 1992), p. 195.

5. *Ibid.*

6. Perhaps the main tenet of Lyndon's book is that the gains that women have made in the last thirty years are entirely the result of advances in contraceptive technology (i.e. the gift of men).

7. Mark Simpson's interview with Tanya Domi, 'Coming out in the wash', *The Guardian*, 21 June 1993.

8. *The Advocate*, 20 April 1993.

9. Sigmund Freud, *Three Essays on Sexuality*, The Penguin Freud Library, Vol. 7 (London: Penguin, 1977), pp. 56–7 (footnote).

10. *Ibid.*

11. Freud, 'A Case of Homosexuality in a Woman', Vol. 19, p. 399.

12. *Ibid.*

13. Juliet Mitchell, *Psychoanalysis and Feminism* (London: Penguin, 1975).

14. Simon LeVay, *The Sexual Brain* (London: The MIT Press, 1993).

15. Genetic explanations for homosexuality were also in vogue in 1993 due to claims by the American National Cancer Institute to have found evidence of a gene passed down the mother's side that was implicated in male homosexuality. This is the same discourse as LeVay's: men who desire men have *maternal* genes/ 'feminized' brains/sex drives of women; thus queer desire is just an illusion brought about by a 'cruel trick of nature' which masks heterosexuality.

16. Quoted in Guy Hocquenghem, *Homosexual Desire* (London: Allison and Busby, 1978), p. 38.

17. Norman O. Brown, *Life Against Death: The Psychoanalytical Meaning of History* (London: Sphere Books, 1967), p. 49.

18. Michel Foucault, *The History of Sexuality, Volume 1; An Introduction* (London: Penguin, 1990), p. 86.

19. Anthony Easthope, *What A Man's Gotta Do: The Masculine Myth in Popular Culture* (Winchester, MA: Unwin Hyman, 1990), p. 12.

20. Freud, *Three Essays on Sexuality*, p. 57.

21. *Ibid*.

22. Hocquenghem and Easthope are cited above; Mario Miele, *Homosexuality and Liberation* (London: GMP Publishers, 1981).

23. Leslie Fiedler, *Love and Death in the American Novel* (New York: Stein and Day, 1975), p. 368.

Chapter two

Big Tits!
Masochism and Transformation in Bodybuilding

One of the ways boys get interested in other boys is by building up their own bodies. Young men are often much interested in advertisements for bar-bells or similar exercisers which promise big muscles and strong arms and legs. Boys who have inferior physiques are intrigued by the ads which describe how seven-stone weaklings are transformed into musclemen. . . . In some respects this is all well and good. I'm in favour of boys being strong and muscular and healthy. But the trouble is that some get so interested in their own bodies while they are preoccupied with building themselves up that in time they can think of little else. Inevitably, too, they compare their bodies with those of other boys, and they both admire and envy those with better bodies than their own. This admiration can take the form of being sexually aroused by the others, and out of this comes the desire to have sex with the body of another person.

● Wardell B. Pomeroy, *Boys and Sex*[1]

THE young, almost exclusively male, crowd is in a state of palpable excitement. Many are jumping out of their seats, faces shiny and expectant with joy. On stage, a man completely nude except for a pair of briefs that appear, like his orange 'sun tan', to have been painted on offers up his body to their rapacious gaze. On his face a strangely disturbing look of pleasure and pain, expressed in a tight, laboured grin, that stays immobile as he turns first this way and then that in a routine that has been rehearsed a thousand times in front of his bedroom mirror. His movements are vaguely in time to Bon Jovi's 'The Final Countdown' which is huffing and puffing over the PA. Preposterous rock meets preposterous body. Each movement flows into a new pose, framing his body in a fresh way, offering the wide-eyed audience more stained and strained flesh to feast on. They yell encouragement, egging him on; compressed air horns shriek; amidst the clamour a friend shouts 'Do it Dave!' The huge veins on his neck throb with the exertion and rush of it all and his whole body flexes and pumps like one enormous, grotesque organ. The throb gets under his skin and extends across his whole body, galvanizing his skin like some kind of demented wiring alive with electricity. The throb seems to drown out Bon Jovi, also reaching his own inflated climax, and the man brings his huge frame round to face the audience, bends forward, still grinning at the now completely berserk boys in the auditorium, and brings his arms half-way out from his body, bent at the elbows, hands clenched into fists and pointing at one another, flexing his whole upper torso, doubling the size of his shoulders, chest and neck, swelling the muscles and veins to the point where it seems he will at any moment explode into 16 stones of bolognese sauce. This is the 'most muscular' pose and the final frightening flourish of his routine. The boys in the audience recognize the finale and are beside themselves now: the cry goes up from a hundred lusty lungs, 'Beef! Beef! Beef!'

This is the bizarre world of competitive bodybuilding.

The music ends and the vast mound of muscle and gristle leaves the stage punching the air with his fists to whoops and cheers. Now the women bodybuilders take the stage. The young men begin to yawn and chatter amongst themselves; many wander out of the auditorium to the foyer to buy some of the various high-protein snacks and dietary supplements on offer that feature pictures of physique stars personally endorsing the product and promising 'enormous gains'. Others peruse the glossy muscle-mags and 'how-to' literature with such titles as *Rip Up!*, *Muscleblasting!*, *Posing!*, *Big Legs!* and *Big Chest!*, the mandatory exclamation marks hysterically advertising the shots of exciting, naked male flesh on offer.

Pomeroy's fears, expressed in 1968, when bodybuilding was in its infancy, would appear to have been borne out. Bodybuilding seems to have led to a cult of the male body that brings about obvious homosexual behaviour in young men. The preoccupation with their own bodies, the comparing of them with other boys, the admiration and envy that this entails must lead to sexual arousal and inevitably to 'the desire to have sex with the body of another person.'

Except this is almost certainly not the case. In fact, bodybuilding does not interest boys in other boys – that interest is palpably already there. What bodybuilding does, ironically, is to allow them to direct that interest in a way that is socially acceptable. Since Pomeroy, bodybuilding has come to be seen as a means by which boys can turn desire into identification. Most of the boys who take up bodybuilding are almost certainly motivated by the same wish to avoid homosexuality that so concerned the sexual 'liberal' Pomeroy. The vast majority of the boys attending bodybuilding competitions like the one described above are heterosexual-identified and few, if any, of their friends consider their antics queer; quite the reverse: they are taken as the quintessence of virile heterosexuality.

It is easy to see where (besides projection) Pomeroy's concern came from. In his day bodybuilding was regarded as something indecent, something rather perverse. It was associated with sleazy Athletic Model Guild and 'physical culturist' magazines; a world of irresponsible young drop-outs and hustlers in Venice Beach, living off generous older 'patrons', who described themselves as enthusiastic admirers of the male form and collectors of Graeco-Roman sculpture. For a man of Pomeroy's generation, to draw attention to the male body in anything but gladiator movies (the licence of exoticism, the justification of historical edification) was considered improper, so it is easy to understand how an interest in the male body would be construed as deviant. Unlike 'proper' sports, bodybuilding does not displace the interest in the male body into activity: instead it focuses unabashedly on the *corpus virile*. Pomeroy's concern that an interest in their own bodies would lead boys to homosexuality is revealing: it shows how in his time the male body was considered so attractive that it had to be denied, even by those who possessed one; boys had to look away from their bodies or else, before you knew it, they would have their hands down their best mate's trousers.

But that was before Arnold Schwarzenegger. Through films like *Pumping Iron*, this five times Mr Universe and seven times Mr Olympia popularized bodybuilding and brought it into the main-stream by exorcizing some of its unpleasant and unwholesome associations. With his Republican 'Mr Clean' image of upright, responsible heterosexuality Schwarzenegger taught America that it had nothing to fear from bodybuilding, that it would not lead its boys along the path mapped out by Pomeroy. Instead it became apparent that bodybuilding could be an *adaptation* of masculinity to the radical changes that had occurred in sexual politics and attitudes towards the male body in the 1960s and 1970s that left the essentials – heterosexuality and patriotic conservatism – more or less intact. The bodybuilder in the shape of Schwarzenegger, rather than ignore or blindly resist change, mobilized a new narciss-istic but fiercely heterosexual masculinity in support of reactionary formations. In effect, the bodybuilder was the fleshy representation of the New Right regressive revolution: in tune with developments in popular culture but deploying them for a right-wing agenda.

Arnie's murderous antics in films such as *Conan the Bar-barian*, *The Terminator* (1984), *Predator* (1987) and *Commando* (1985), along with those of Sylvester Stallone in the *Rambo* and *Rocky* series, portrayed the bodybuilder to young male America as a fantastic warrior/patriot, a role that legitimized gazing at his body at the same time as disavowing any suggestion of passivity: the most active Hollywood stance being, of course, that of the killer. And since bodybuilders had the most passivity to disavow they were invariably the most prolific killers, taking the average body count in the Hollywood war/action film into the realms of a tactical nuclear exchange. The more exaggerated the musculature, the more it had to explain and justify itself in mounds of dead bodies. The psychopathic individualism of the Hollywood bodybuilder-killer neatly fitted into the Reaganite discourse of personal responsibility and individual liberty and the retreat from public space into the most private space of all – the body (one area where the individual was sure to be in control). This was especially attractive to men who had felt challenged by the advances of feminism and the gay movement. The genre of bodybuilder-killer films represented an attempt to restate masculinity in terms of the most hysterically exaggerated 'masculine' signification, a signification that would have been regarded as 'camp' a decade earlier.

So in *Commando*, directed by Mark Lester, Schwarzenegger waddling around barely able to walk due to the over-development of his quadriceps (leg muscles), his rumpsteak body smeared with camouflage paint and carefully always on display, either through cute cut-off combat jackets or helpfully denuded by high explosives, is presented to us as a 'crack' soldier. On top of his foppish muscle drag he dons even more macho accessories; putting on a flak jacket laden with munitions and slinging an armoury of weaponry around his torso until he resembles nothing so much as a walking advertisement for the insecurity of 1980s man. Then we witness him dispatching an entire South American army single-handedly with his – inevitably – enormous gun. As the bodies of the South American soldiers pile up, the American bodybuilder-killer proves his racial and sexual superiority over the wop weaklings. All this is done ostensibly to rescue his little daughter from an enemy who wears leather pants, a moustache and a tight net vest. Thus the enjoyment of the spectacle of Schwarzenegger's sweating muscles is drawn into a heterosexual plotline, one that nicely emphasizes the boundless power of the heterosexual male body next to the helplessness of the female, its virtue next to the homosexual, as well as illustrating the fantastic, phallic killing machine's touching human capacity for 'tenderness'.

The breathtaking gall, and the astonishing achievement, of films like *Commando* is that men's bodybuilding – the obsessive interest of men in men's bodies – and the appropriation of gay macho drag by heterosexual men became both a reassertion of the masculine body's 'natural' superiority over the female and a disavowal of homosexuality.

The paradoxical heterosexual reassurance/homoerotic enjoyment that the muscular male body offered popular culture had been a mainstay of comic strips for boys since the 1940s. But Spiderman and Superman were *closeted* bodybuilders: they wore bodysuits that decently covered their flesh and masks that disguised their identity; their lives were rigidly divided between body-less bourgeois respectability and muscular super-hero fantasy; they led a 'double-life' that no one knew about and were never to be seen at the gym. In the 1980s the body suits and the masks were discarded and the bodybuilder was presented naked and shameless, flaunting his private vice to the world.

Hollywood got in on the act with *Masters of the Universe* (1987), directed by Edward Pressman, a film version of *He-Man* cartoons. Dolph Lundgren in the title role, wearing a posing pouch and leather thongs, battles for control of the universe with the evil Skeletor. Right comely muscular manliness, He-Man, is thus contrasted with wrong repulsive unmuscular unmanliness, Skeletor/skeleton (whose body is never shown). As with *Commando et al.* the female character, in the form of She-Woman (not a bodybuilder), helps both to heterosexualize the muscle man in the leather thongs and to further exaggerate his manly attributes. And again the baddy is coded as a queer threat to He-Man's heterosexual virility: 'I'll have He-Man kneeling at my feet!' he vows and plots to steal He-Man's gigantic sword; when He-Man falls into his clutches he has him flogged with an electric whip. He-Man, the upright hetero bodybuilder, refuses to kneel before this parody of a man (in fact he seems to almost enjoy the whipping) and breaks free for the fight finale, in which he and Skeletor battle over the outsized sword – the key, need it be added, to control of the universe. He-Man wins the day and thrusts his sword into the air, shouting, 'I have the power!' as white lightning squirts out of its tip. This was kids' entertainment in the 1980s.

In Britain in the 1990s the adult and childish interest in bodybuilding came together in a TV programme called *Gladiators* (based on *American Gladiators*). With names like Hawk, Wolf, Warrior and Saracen, the cartoon mythology of the bodybuilder-as-hero was translated into prime-time TV with real rather than fantasy flesh on display.[2] And like the bodybuilder films of the 1980s *Gladiators* was a stage for the male bodybuilder. Unlike its American equivalent the British version's first season did not employ female gladiators who were obviously muscular; instead feminine glamour was, once again, cast to flatter the phallic power of the male bodybuilder.

By the beginning of the 1980s the 'out' bodybuilder was so acceptable as a role model that the killer/warrior disavowal was no longer so necessary. Thus Schwarzenegger played a guardian angel role in *Terminator II*, protecting a mother and her child, in contrast to his original 1984 bad guy role (significantly, the baddy in *Terminator II* is not a bodybuilder). In less than ten years the bodybuilder had gone from demonic alien threat to self-sacrificing angel. Now he launches 'Arnold's Fitness for Kids' and merchandises a hero myth to explain his life-long love affair with his own body:

> Young Arnold watched helplessly as his best friend in class was beaten up by a thug of 13. ... 'At that moment I made up my mind that I, too, would make myself fit. I would work hard to develop a body like our school bully's – but I would use it very differently.'
>
> *The Sun* (7 April 1993)

In keeping with this trend the bodybuilders of *Gladiators* are promoted to their young fans as upright citizens (the bizarre is used to shore up the mundane again) with an anti-drugs, pro-decency stance. Like the appointment of Schwarzenegger to health spokesman by the Bush administration, this demonstrates the key importance of bodybuilding, once regarded as something distinctly deviant, in socializing young people – young *boys* – into acceptable paths of development. As Tom Green writes about Venice Beach and gymnasia in his biography *Arnold*, 'Two decades ago, most of the people who today flock to box offices to buy tickets to an Arnold Schwarzenegger movie wouldn't have thought those places very savoury.' Two decades ago these same people would have been shocked if they caught their boy with a magazine with a picture of Arnold in it; now they think nothing of their son's plastering posters of him on his bedroom walls, reading his *Education of a Bodybuilder* religiously and spending all his pocket money on gym membership and food supplements.

But while the appropriation of bodybuilding to buttress the image of an increasingly unstable masculinity appears to have been phenomenally successful, it is itself inherently unstable, its unsavoury past always threatening to gatecrash its new-found respectability and expose masculinity's own scandalous secrets. As Corinne Sweet and Peter Baker wrote, in an article on steroid abuse and violent crime:

While the English Federation of Bodybuilders estimates
that there are 200,000 bodybuilders in Britain, *Bodypower*
magazine puts the figure at closer to 500,000 – and 80 per
cent of [those at competition level] are believed to be on
steroids. Several needle exchange schemes have found that
up to half their clients are bodybuilders.

Guardian (6 August 1992)

That serious bodybuilding and drug abuse go hand in hand is
widely accepted – but this reality is conveniently forgotten in the
deployment of the bodybuilder as super-hero. It is a testament to
the tremendous disavowal at work in bodybuilding (and masculinity) that the terrific, not to say unnatural, muscular development
of the modern bodybuilder image used to promote Truth, Justice
and the American (and now also the British) Way is largely dependent upon the abuse of anabolic steroids. Once this disavowal
breaks down and the phenomenon is opened up to enquiry, psychopathic tendencies emerge. According to one Detective Inspector
interviewed in the same *Guardian* article, steroid abuse is frequently associated with rape and murder as a result of what is
termed 'roid rage':

> 'One man told me he was a pussycat before steroids and a
> monster with a permanent erection after. In my opinion,
> there's strong evidence that steroid abuse can directly relate
> to sexual and violent crimes.'

The heroic image of modern bodybuilding is so volatile that
it always threatens to invert itself. Presenting a picture of health,
clean living, personal cultivation and conservatism – a modern
religion for kids – it contains within itself the potential to topple
over into its opposite: madness, sleeze, self-abuse and criminality.
Like masculinity, it advertises a superficial strength which turns out
not to bear close examination.

But there is something much more pervasive and even more
dangerous than drugs that bodybuilding always threatens to tip
over into.

I couldn't let this go on any longer. 'Is this a gay gym?' I asked.

'Look honey,' he replied. '*All* gyms are gay.' I examined the men by the machines. There Austin seemed right. 'But what about them?' I asked, pointing to the free-weight lifters.

Austin laughed out loud. '*Especially* them,' he said. 'They just don't know it yet!'[3]

Although Pomeroy's suspicion of bodybuilding is certainly out-moded it has not disappeared, nor is it likely to. While the efforts of Arnold and Co. have done much to convince the world that body-building is impeccably heterosexual it cannot erase the fact that its use as a way of socializing young males into heterosexuality *is utterly predicated upon its homoerotic appeal.* This is the contra-diction which no clean-up campaign will ever dispense with because if it did there would be no bodybuilding.

Pomeroy was right to suspect that bodybuilding involves the eroticization of masculine attributes, but wrong to believe that this leads necessarily to homosex. In fact it employs the desire for the manly body *against* homosexuality. For the masculine attributes to be eroticized, in other words for them to remain masculine, it requires the banishment of homosexuality (although its *potential* remains like a spectre haunting the proceedings).

In his autobiography *Muscle: Confessions of an Unlikely Bodybuilder*, undoubtedly the best account of the world of serious bodybuilding, Sam Fussell attempts to clear the air in his descrip-tion of his very first visit to a gym. By putting the queer suspicion in the mouth of the swish fag Austin, Fussell slyly discredits it, making the queer suspicion something innately queer itself. Also deftly introduced is the presumption that gay and straight bodybuilders can be easily distinguished: 'I examined the men by the machines. There Austin seemed right.' The gays are easily spotted, both by their appearance (unmanly) and their activity (sissy machines instead of butch weights). The real bodybuilders, and hence the real men, are equally easily spotted, and, of course, they are also instantly recognizable as straight. Fussell leaves nelly Austin for the free-weights men. But the unwitting irony in this is that Fussell, in rejecting homosexuality (unmanly men) and its association with bodybuilding, does so on the grounds that it does not provide *the manly men/masculine attributes he is seeking*. Thus in his first visit to a gym Fussell succeeds in vanquishing fags but not the *fag thing*.[4]

His own tale reads like a Pomeroy nightmare made *flesh*. A pigeon-chested 26-year-old Oxford graduate discovers bodybuilding through a picture of Arnold, 'every muscle bulging to the world as he flexed, smiled and posed.' Inspired by admiration and envy to possess a body like Arnold's, he immerses himself in a world where male bodies are ceaselessly displayed and compared to other male bodies. For four years he has what he calls 'the disease', without even a girlfriend to chaperone him and only one recorded (failed) attempt at sex with a woman.

But Fussell's story, rather than illustrating Pomeroy's anxiety that bodybuilding might lead to homosex, actually demonstrates how bodybuilding might work to *prevent* the translation of interest in men's bodies into sexual activity with them, and yet shows how problematic that process actually is and, more importantly, illustrates the wider problem of what it means to be a man.

The point of the following investigation is not to pathologize bodybuilders or bodybuilding – which as an activity has, I'm sure, plenty to recommend it – but to show how every time men try to grasp something consolingly, sturdily, essentially masculine, it all too easily transforms into its opposite. Bodybuilding gives an insight into the *flux* of masculinity right at the moment it is meant to solidify it in a display of exaggerated biological masculine attributes.

Make me a man!

The bodybuilder by definition is someone intent on creating a body that he desires (and often escaping from one that he loathes). The 'science' of bodybuilding, through its apparatus, regimes and drugs, can work the magic of giving a man the flesh he desires to possess.

'Here's the Kind of NEW MEN I Build!'[5] announces Charles Atlas over a picture of a desirable young man with a perfect physique. Then the homosexual appeal is converted into one of narcissistic identification: 'Do YOU *Want to Be One?*' Just send off the form '... And I'll PROVE in Just 7 DAYS I Can Make YOU One!' Alas, Mr Atlas' science, unlike Frank N. Furter's in the *Rocky Horror Show*, is not powerful enough to actually *make* NEW MEN for you, it can only turn YOU into one. The heterosexual bodybuilder must hammer homo-desire into identification and make do with a diet of narcissism.

> But whenever I locked the door behind me and quickly peeled off my shirt, I had to stifle a wolfish whistle. How my beanpole figure had changed in the last year![6]

> He stopped a foot from me to point at his legs and scream: 'Look at those fuckin' gams, Sam! These are manly gams, goddamnit!' He quickly flexed them in the mirror and caressed them with a loving hand ...[7]

The heterosexual bodybuilder, in contrast to Frank N. Furter with his creation Rocky, makes himself his own love object in lieu of another man.[8] Hence the vital importance of mirrors and posing in bodybuilding; hence the loneliness of the 'sport'; hence the unashamedly sexualized descriptions of the personal pleasures of bodybuilding: as Arnold puts it, 'A pump is better than coming' (with whom?).

Freud outlined four possible types of narcissism; a person may love:

(a) what he himself is (i.e. himself),
(b) what he himself was,
(c) what he would like to be,
(d) someone who was once part of himself.[9]

Type (c), 'what he would like to be', is very close to a type of homosexuality, especially since it suggests a narcissistic desire that may attach itself to others who represent 'what he would like to be'. Freud argues that it is through social conditioning and upbringing, specifically through the effect of the critical voice of his parents, teachers, public opinion and fellow men, that 'large amounts of homosexual libido are drawn into the formation of the narcissistic ego ideal and find outlet and satisfaction in maintaining it.'[10] The ego ideal, or super-ego, thus comes to *stand in for* homosexual libido; in other words, the subject's sense of social responsibility/ respectability is founded on the turning around of homosexual desire into the ego.

This is the purpose that Arnold and the Gladiators appear to serve: they become living representatives of the ego ideal (hence the fantasy/mythological element so often associated with them), which are shared by thousands of other boys.

> The ego ideal opens up an important avenue for the understanding of group psychology. In addition to its individual side, this ideal has a social side; it is also the common ideal of a family, a class or a nation.[11]

The homoerotic power the bodybuilder super hero represents to young boys, by encouraging identification with him and the emphasis on social virtue, functions to redirect their homosexual libido into narcissism in which their own ego comes to substitute for the 'lost' love-object; narcissism, regarded as the precursor to homosexuality, is actually deployed *against* homosexuality to socialize young boys. The super hero becomes the super-ego:

> 'Arnie rules. If he picked up his Conan sword and took over the country tomorrow I swear to God I would fight for him. It *sucks* that he can't be president.'[12]

And so Arnold, the 'ultimate male',[13] is firmly established in the psyches of millions of young American boys, their desire for him becoming the prohibition against it. In his biography we learn that large crowds turned up every day on the set of *Commando*, just to catch a glimpse of his lens-lovely physique in the flesh. 'Most are young men,' admits Green. 'No surprise. Who loves Arnold most? They stand behind the crew rather attentively, almost reverentially, and try to compare their builds to the bare-chested Schwarzenegger.'

And so we find Fussell living alone in a flat unfurnished except for an exercise machine and 'A cardboard cut-out of Arnold with loin cloth and sword as Conan the Barbarian'. Thus the heterosexual bodybuilder's relationship to homosexuality is revealed as a sad kind of insubstantial shadow of it, a kind of mourning, a ghostly kind of love. This is the lovelorn marriage of bodybuilder to ego ideal: 'With this ring I thee wed. With my body I thee worship.'

Not permitted to desire another man's penis, the bodybuilder phallicizes that which he is permitted to desire: his own body. The old adage 'big muscles: small dick' is without foundation, but the implied phallic substitution is spot on. The body is 'pumped up', 'rock hard' and 'tight'; the fashion for 'vascularity' calls for minimal skin fat (often special drugs are taken for this purpose) so that the road map of veins is clearly visible, standing out from the flesh in a fashion alarmingly reminiscent of an erect penis. After a successful appearance on stage at a competition, Fussell's training partner compliments him: 'like a human fucking penis!'[14]

As with the phallus itself, size is the overriding issue and everything is constantly subjected to measurement and the tyranny of the tape-measure: necks, calves, chests, arms, legs; the inches measure the man. Extending ordinary male aspirations from between his legs to his whole body, the 'human fucking penis' entertains fantasies of infinite growth that merge with the ceaseless desire for ever more 'male' attributes (the ego ideal is by definition unattainable and this encourages ever greater efforts to reach it). 'I saw my chest growing to such gargantuan proportions that no shirt on earth could contain it ...'.[15] As the bodybuilder's chest swells, so, quite literally, does his ego: the more manly the man's body the more he can direct his homosexual libido towards himself.

Of course fantasies of infinite growth cannot be sustained. But the science of bodybuilding does its level best to maintain the illusion that it can be. Through the use of anabolic steroids, or artificial growth hormones, the bodybuilder is encouraged to believe that he can continue his swelling and stave off his fear of failure to satisfy the ego ideal (failure to satisfy the ego ideal has the tendency, according to Freud, to 'liberate homosexual libido and this is turned into a sense of guilt').

The serious bodybuilder will often use steroids as a matter of course. Those entering competitions have little chance of winning without recourse to drugs. Unlike in the world of athletics where the benefits of steroids are debatable, bodybuilding has long *depended* on them. They promote increased strength and offer remarkable increases in the rate at which the body can metabolize nitrogen into muscle. But the pressure of competition is not responsible for the deepest appeal of these drugs. Their most powerful attraction to the bodybuilder resides in the nature of them, and the symbolism of that 'nature'.

Most of the steroid class of drugs were designed to emulate the effects of natural anabolic agents like testosterone, for administering to those who are deficient in male hormones. Thus steroids are used to combat the lack of physical 'manliness' – precisely the condition that the bodybuilder always finds himself in. Because of the unattainability of the ego ideal, a man already weighing 16 stone and with a 53-inch chest can, like a reverse anorexic, look in the mirror and see himself as chronically deficient in manliness.

Again, this has an interesting parallel with the sex lives of gay men. C. A. Tripp, an anthropologist opposed to psychoanalysis, explains the dynamic of the eroticization of manliness by other men in *The Homosexual Matrix* in a way that sounds remarkably familiar: 'Eroticization always tends to raise the value of the items it touches, not only by exalting them, but by keeping a person's aspiration level soaring ahead of his own attainments, between what he has and what he would like to have.'[16] This *perceived* distance is the standard by which everything is judged, it is 'the contrast implicit in this distance which determines a person's appetite for same-sex attributes and, consequently, his readiness to admire them, to eroticize them, and to import still more of them.'[17]

One of the ways in which the homosexual male 'imports' these attributes is through sexual intimacy and affection.[18] The avowedly heterosexual male, however, is only permitted to import them in a non-sexual fashion, through identification and sublimation: e.g. bodybuilding. So the appeal of steroids to the bodybuilder is not just that they help the process of building muscle but that they represent an *actual* importation of same-sex attributes, a direct route rather than the indirect one of lifting weights. (The appeal of steroids as a means of importing same-sex attributes and further evidence of the wide-reaching importance of bodybuilding as a young male phenomenon is provided by the revelation that an estimated twelve per cent of all American senior high-school boys have tried at least one cycle of steroids.)[19]

The 'importation' of the masculine attributes in the form of steroids takes on a telling symbolism. Tagged 'the juice', Fussell describes two friends receiving its benediction:

> Nimrod withdrew the needle from the vial, slapped Bamm Bamm's naked ass once, then plunged the syringe an inch and a half deep into Bamm Bamm's flesh.
> 'Jesus, Nimrod, it feels like a fuckin' garden hose. Are you sure that's a new one?' Bamm Bamm asked querulously. ... When he pulled the steel dart out of Bamm Bamm's ass, the tiny hole spurted forth a stream of blood which landed with a splat on the plastic covered sofa.[20]

When Fussell's turn comes to receive 'the juice' he discovers that his fear of 'needles' results in him reflexively tightening the muscles in his backside (perhaps indicating that at least one part of Fussell knows full well what all this signifies), making the injection extremely painful. But he soon learns the best way to take it: the 'only proper way to receive the syringe was to relax the ass cheek and jab the needle in quickly, all the way to the base. ...' The bodybuilder finds that 'taking it like a man' enables him to acquire more quickly those characteristics which will make him more like a man; he finds himself echoing, albeit pathetically, the gay male's sexual importation of masculine attributes.

This is a ritual that will not be unfamiliar to anthropologists. David D. Gilmore, drawing on the work of Gilbert Herdt, describes a ritual enacted by the Sambia, a tribe in New Guinea 'obsessed with masculinity':

> ... the youngsters are forced to perform fellatio on grown men, not for pleasure, but in order to ingest their semen. This then supposedly provides them with the substance or 'seed' of a growing masculinity. As one ... Sambia ritual expert instructs, 'If a boy doesn't "eat" semen, he remains small and weak'.[21]

Here, overt homosexuality as opposed to the symbolic 'homosexuality' of steroid injections, is considered to be the normal route to manhood and is later superseded by an adult life of 'full heterosexuality'.[22]

But the most remarkable and instructive scene that the body-building anthropologist Fussell reports is that of a father who acts as trainer to his son, Lamar, injecting him with the 'juice'. Lamar 'offered his enormous white ass to his father. ... Despite the jolt of the needle, Lamar looked up at his father in tenderness.'

Male masochism and bodybuilding

No pain: no gain!
● *A bodybuilding slogan*

In 'A Child Is Being Beaten', a text that has been at the centre of the 'return to Freud' movement in cultural studies, Freud expounds his theory of masochistic fantasy through a child's account of a common dream in which he/she is being beaten by the father. Freud attributes this to a need to be punished for incestuous guilt (desiring the father) but the child also finds this fantasy pleasurable and may substitute the experience of punishment for incestuous desire. In males, Freud analyses this beating fantasy as being based on the negative Oedipus complex, and in girls on the positive. The negative Oedipus complex for boys consists in identification with the mother and desire of the father and corresponds to the positive complex for girls.

But Freud states elsewhere that the 'simple Oedipus complex is by no means its commonest form'; instead he posits a *'more complete'* Oedipus complex which is essentially *bisexual*, including *both* the negative and positive forms:

> That is to say, a boy has not merely an ambivalent attitude
> towards his father and an affectionate object-choice
> towards his mother, but at the same time he also behaves
> like a girl and displays an affectionate feminine attitude
> towards his father and a corresponding jealousy and
> hostility towards his mother.[23]

Thus in 'The Economic Problem of Masochism' Freud describes the wish to be beaten by the father as 'standing very close' to the male's desire to take a passive sexual relation to him and characterizes it as only 'a regressive distortion of it'.

As we have already seen, the heterosexual male body-builder's desires 'stand very close' to that of the homosexual (the negative Oedipus complex). In fact in his undevelopment of the homosexual libido he could be said to represent 'a regressive distortion', bringing bodybuilding, with all its terrible goading and punishment by the super-ego, very much into the realm of male masochism.

In her influential book *Male Subjectivity at the Margins*, which sheds much needed light on the phenomenon of male masochism, Caja Silverman argues that up until now the significance of Freud's assertion that the super-ego is always 'a substitute for a longing for the father' has been missed.[24] She suggests that the implications of this are 'staggering'. Essentially this is because the dissolution of the male Oedipus complex, the origin of the super-ego and the lynchpin of a man's adult character, is now seen to be about 'the male subject's homosexual attachment to the father.'[25] (This is the personal aspect of the super-ego discussed earlier in its social context).

But as Silverman points out, the only way of overcoming this incestuous desire – *becoming* the (symbolic) father – is precisely what the super-ego forbids: 'You cannot be like your father in all respects', it says, 'some things are his prerogative'; this is the unattainability of the ego ideal again.

The super-ego ends up promoting 'the very thing that its severity is calculated to prevent, a contradiction which must function as a constant inducement to reconstitute the negative Oedipus complex [identification with the mother and desire of the father].' The prototypical male subject wants both to love the father and to *be* the father but is prevented from doing either.

This impasse produces a fascinating outcome. The 'morally masochistic' male gives up altogether on the paternal ego-ideal and turns to his mother, identifying with her instead. 'However,' writes Silverman, 'he burns with an exalted ardour for the rigours of the super-ego. The feminine masochist ... literalises the beating fantasy, and brings this cruel drama back to the body.'

The gymnasium is the stage on which this 'cruel drama' is

brought 'back to the body' on a daily basis. It is a hi-tech dungeon where the weak flesh is punished by the willing/willful spirit. Gleaming machinery and neatly arranged racks of free-weights have replaced the instruments of torture. But the agony and the ecstasy do not end with the four-hour work-out infernos Fussell and his brothers-in-sorrow joyously inflict on themselves. Apart from the fear and pain of the injections, the terrible piles that result and the horrific poundages squatted (more anal punishment?), there is the endless discipline of a merciless diet (combined with *forced* feeding, an ingenious innovation of modern masochism), and, come competition time, devout fasting (to reduce skin fat) which leaves them barely able to walk. The literature celebrates the suffering: 'Hardcore Bodybuilding: the blood, sweat and tears of pumping iron.'[26]

But Fussell's strict and uncomplaining observation of the iron law of 'The Three D's' (Dedication, Determination, Discipline) which bodybuilders must live by earns him the respect of those around him, especially his mentor/surrogate father Vinnie: ' "Like a freight-train from hell, baby! Oh yes!", he screamed, "I got myself a real training partner!" ' A 'real training partner' is one who relishes punishment. Before attempting a heavy squat, Vinnie urges Fussell to 'Do the right thing!' – which turns out to be bodybuilder code for a fist in the face: a common technique, apparently, for encouraging that little bit extra sacrifice. ('Do the right thing!', is this not the voice of the super-ego?)

Steroids enhance the masochistic pleasure. 'When you're doin' the juice,' one American teenager tells *Sky* magazine, 'it actually feels good to get hit. That whole part of your body goes "*Ahhhh* ..." '[27] On these drugs the masochistic pleasure can reach giddying heights. In an *Esquire* article on Ray Michalik, winner of Mr Universe 1975, we learn how:

> He invented a training regime called 'intensity insanity' which called for 70 sets per body part, instead of the customary ten. This entailed a seven hour workout and excruciating pain, but the steroids, he found, turned that pain into pleasure: 'a huge release of all the pressures built up inside me, the rage and the energy.'[28]

The tricks that male masochism can play on you! Fussell claims he took up bodybuilding because he no longer wished to be 'a victim'. But in order to achieve this he became a victimizer: 'Without being fully aware of it myself I became the kind of man I once feared and despised. I became, in fact, a bully.'[29] But he was his *own* victim.

As Theodor Reik argues in *Masochism in Sex and Society*, masochists become both their own victims and victimizers, dispensing with the need for an external object.[30] This is the meaning of the bodybuilder's narrative of refusing to be a weakling who gets sand kicked in his face. 'I would work hard to develop a body like our school bully's,' says Arnold, 'but I would use it differently' – that is to say he would *use his body on himself*.

This may go some way to explain the origin of what has been called 'Roid Rage', where bodybuilders on steroids have been known to go into mad binges of assault and rape. These bouts of sadism are, perhaps, nothing more than unsatisfied masochism spilling over into its projected variant, sadism, providing an equivalent pleasure to the more usual one offered by the most rigorous workout ('a huge release of all the pressures built up inside me, the rage and the energy'). Or as Fussell puts it: 'I wasn't just aching for a fist-fight – I was begging for one.'

The theory of masochism also sheds light on the pronounced show-business aspect to bodybuilding. Exhibitionism or 'demonstrativeness' is an indispensable feature of all masochism, according to Reik. The terrible litany of suffering that the bodybuilder inflicts on his body, real enough in its private pain, is always intended for public consumption, whether in the gymnasium with roars and yells, or at contests, sweating and posing with a silent beatific smile. 'In the practices of masochists, denudiation and parading with all their psychic concomitant phenomenon play such a major part that one feels induced to assume a constant connection between masochism and exhibitionism.'[31]

Fussell's aptly named 'Confessions' are as much a part of that process of 'denudiation and parading' as any bodybuilding contest. Although the world of bodybuilding is renounced, that renunciation itself is transformed into part of the same process of exhibitionism. Here also is the key to understanding the obsession the bodybuilding world has with exclamation marks: 'I Can Make You a Man!', 'Arnold!', 'Posing!' This big-tent showbusiness style is a hysterical demonstrativeness.

The masochism of the committed bodybuilder is without doubt the modern-day equivalent of the religious zealot who flogged himself in the street. *The Life of Fussell: His Confessions!*, having become a best-seller, is a more public scourging than any medieval masochist could dream of.

Born into an ivy-league family and with a comfortable academic future mapped out for him, Fussell turned his back on the world and his parents – especially his father – and set about mortifying his flesh. Most alarmingly, like all those using serious quantities of steroids, he was threatening himself with liver cancer and heart-disease. This quasi-religious, self-destructive urge was elucidated by Freud when he wrote that to provoke punishment from the super-ego the masochist must 'act against his own interests, must ruin the prospects which open out to him in the real world and must, perhaps, destroy his own real existence.'[32]

In Arnie's perhaps most popular films, *The Terminator* and *Terminator II*, the male masochistic logic of self-annihilation is starkly obvious. In the first he plays a cyborg, a seeming-human robot, that takes fantastic punishment: gunshots, explosions, fireballs, speeding articulated trucks, and yet keeps coming for more, with a look of bright, fierce joy in his inhuman eyes which remains undimmed until those he pursues oblige him by crushing him to nothing in a hydraulic press. But before this compacted climax can be reached we *see* his 'suffering' strip away his human appearance (and sex) altogether and 'he' is reduced to a ghastly array of gleaming pistons and electrical innards. The sequel (aptly subtitled *Judgement Day*) provides more of the same, but this time Arnie plays the 'good guy' and another cyborg is drafted in to provide scenes of appalling mutual mutilation even more destructive than the first (expensive special effects provide the audience with new ways to enjoy the human body's miseries). 'At last!' you can almost hear Arnie declare, 'A *real* training partner!' At the film's climax Arnie achieves complete corporeal dissolution, hurling his body into a vat of molten metal.

In a similar vein, the frenzied yells of 'Beef!, Beef!' at bodybuilding contests summon up the ultimate image of sacrifice and the primal myth. Cannibalism, noted by Freud as being closely related to sadism/masochism,[33] provides the most extreme and yet the most descriptive metaphor for the consumption/mortification paradox of bodybuilding: the bodybuilder wishing to consume male-ness/the father *and be consumed by it*. Freud points out that 'as a substitute for longing for the father, it [the ego ideal] contains the germ from which all religions have evolved'.[34]

Transfiguration

'Here's the kind of NEW MEN *I build!'*

It should be clear by now that in building up the male body the bodybuilder is in fact attempting to shatter it. Nothing less than transfiguration is what the committed male musclebuilder is after. Through the religious magic and science of bodybuilding he hopes to effect a resolution of the conflict that the super-ego has imposed on him. As we have seen, unable to either be *or* love the father, the feminine male masochist tends to abandon the paternal ideal and to turn to an identification with the mother instead. The science and religion of bodybuilding can make this identification *corporeal*.

Jokes about bodybuilders needing bras for their chests are common enough, but in fact the jokes contain a certain truth. The prolonged use of steroids causes a condition known as gynecomastia, or 'bitch tits', the growth of a bulbous swelling under one or both nipples as a result of the body's oestrogen level rising to counteract the massive dose of what it takes to be testosterone. But this is perhaps the least important of the transformations that the steroid user can look forward to. With prolonged steroid use testicles atrophy, penises shrink and erections become infrequent or cease altogether. In other words, the bodybuilder using steroids *is effecting his own castration*.

This is the unavoidable logic of the bodybuilder's long-term scourging of his masculine body. After years of abuse with drugs and 'intensity/insanity' routines 'Mr Universe' Michalik found his body finally taking the hint and effecting the final transformation:

> His testosterone level plummeted, his sperm count went to zero and all the oestrogen in his body, which had been accruing for years, turned his pecs into soft, doughy breasts. Such friends as he still had pointed out that his ass

was plumping like a woman's and tweaked him for his
sexy, new hip-switching walk.[35]

Of course, the bodybuilder reacts with horror to this development,
but that is just the horror of the caterpillar finding itself pupating: it
knows not that this is what was meant to be and what its whole life
so far has been working towards. The bodybuilder does not understand that he was destined all along to be a transsexual butterfly.

Suddenly, the painstaking removal of all body-hair by daily
shaving, the use of depilatory creams and electrolysis makes sense.
In Fussell's own words, musclebuilders are 'illusionists' and 'the
decorating of the body to such an extreme' is 'essentially a feminine
exercise'.[36] And so the contents of Fussell's gym-bag before a competition read like those of a tranny's handbag: Professional Posing
Oil, Muscle Sheen, Pro-Tan Instant Competition Color, sponge
applicator tips, matte black competition briefs, and mousse.

Women bodybuilders have traditionally been ridiculed, especially by male bodybuilders, for rebelling against their 'natural'
sex characteristics, for being 'mannish' and 'unwomanly'. But now
the secret can be told: this is merely projected anxiety. In the female
bodybuilder, overcoming in her own way her social designation as
'lack', the male bodybuilder, the kids' super-hero, sees his own fate.
As Fussell remarks:'She wasn't quite a woman and she wasn't quite
a man, but she was, unmistakably, a builder.'

The male bodybuilder dramatizes in his flesh the insecurity,
the uncertainty, the enigma of masculinity. He is a living testament,
not so much to the capabilities of the male body, its phallic power,
its massive irresistible virility ('I saw my chest swelling to such
gargantuan proportions that no shirt on Earth could contain it'),
but rather to the sacred mystery of sex and gender, the fluidity of
the categories male and female, masculine and feminine, hetero and
homo and the fabulous, perverse tricks they play.

Pange, lingua, gloriosi
Corporis mysterium.
(Sing, my tongue, of the mystery of the glorious Body.)

● *St Thomas Aquinas*

Notes

1. Wardell B. Pomeroy, *Boys and Sex* (London: Pelican, 1968), p. 59.

2. Comparisons made in the press with the 1970s TV game show *It's a Knockout* only serve to demonstrate how California-ized Britain has become. Eddie Waring on steroids with a UV bed tan and in skimpy lycra? I think not.

3. Sam Fussell, *Confessions of an Unlikely Bodybuilder* (London: Abacus, 1992), p. 38.

4. The imperative to keep homosexuality away from bodybuilding to preserve its manly visual pleasures for its heterosexual disciples is shown later in the book in Fussell's account of the professional bodybuilder Bob Paris' posing programme at the 1989 Arnold Classic: 'Paris concluded his posing program with "The Dying Gaul". . . . It was met with an uncomfortable silence and angry suspicion, the latter confirmed months later when he revealed his marriage to his "husband", male model Rod Jackson, and the joy they shared in their "children", two dogs and a macaw named Barney' (p. 195). Bob Paris is the only out professional bodybuilder.

5. *Picture Post*, advertisements.

6. Fussell, p. 65.

7. *Ibid.*, p. 114.

8. Is it merely coincidence that the bodybuilder boxer fantasy that Stallone created for himself a few years later also had the same name?

9. Sigmund Freud, 'On Narcissism: an introduction', Penguin Freud Library (London: Penguin, 1984), Vol. II, p. 84.

10. *Ibid.*, p. 90.

11. *Ibid.*, pp. 96–97.

12. 'Teenage roid heads', *Sky* magazine, December 1992.

13. Tom Green, *Arnold!* (London: W. H. Allen, 1988).

14. Fussell also chose the soundtrack to the film *Shaft* for his accompaniment: ' "Shaft!" Isaac Hayes sang on the soundtrack, as I made my final counterclockwise turn, crunched my abs, flexed my legs, and pointed at my calves' (p. 212).

15. Fussell, p. 49.

16. C. A. Tripp, *The Homosexual Matrix* (New York and Scarborough, Ontario: Meridian, 1985), p. 78.

17. *Ibid.*

18. The gay man is, of course, also very often a bodybuilder: this exemplifies the way in which desire and identification are not discrete categories and the way in which gay men can 'import' male attributes via *both* routes.

19. 'Teenage roid heads', *Sky*, December 1992.

20. Fussell, p. 120.

21. David D. Gilmore, *Manhood in the Making: Cultural Concepts of Masculinity* (New Haven and London: Yale University Press, 1990), p. 147.

22. *Ibid.*

23. Freud, *The Ego and the Id*, Penguin Freud Library, Vol. 11, p. 372.

24. Caja Silverman, *Male Subjectivity at the Margins* (London: Routledge, 1992), p. 194.

25. *Ibid.*, p. 194.

26. Robert Kennedy, *Hardcore Bodybuilding: The Blood, Sweat, and Tears of Pumping Iron* (New York: Sterling, 1982).

27. *Sky*, December 1992.

28. *Esquire*, November 1992. The injection of the steroids themselves can take on the appearance of Nazi torture: 'they filled enormous syringes with a French supplement called Triacana and, aiming for the elusive thyroid gland, *shot it right into their necks*'. This echoes a scene in *Universal Soldier* (1992) in which Dolph Lundgren and Claude Van Damme play zombie bodybuilder soldiers who are regularly injected through the back of the neck to keep up their inhuman strength. Needless to say, the finale of the film requires the two soldiers to inflict horrific injuries upon one another, which they happily endure.

29. Fussell, pp. 24 and 68.

30. Theodor Reik, *Masochism in Sex and Society*, trans. Margaret H. Beigel and Gertrud M. Kurth (New York: Grove Press, 1962), cited by Silverman in *Male Subjectivity at the Margins*.

31. Reik, p. 72.

32. 'The economic problem of masochism', Penguin Freud Library, Vol. 11, p. 425.

33. Freud, *Three Essays on Sexuality*.

34. Freud, *The Ego and the Id*, p. 376.

35. *Esquire*, November 1992.

36. Fussell, p. 140.

Chapter three

Sex Hunters
The 'Homosexual' Male Heterosexual Economy

The meat market

The trade that organises patriarchal societies takes place exclusively among men. Women, signs, goods, currency, all pass from one man to another – or so it is said – suffer the penalty of relapsing into the incestuous and exclusively endogamous ties that would paralyze all commerce. The work force, products, even those of mother-earth, would thus be the object of transaction among men only. This signifies that the very possibility of the socio-cultural order would necessitate homosexuality. Homosexuality is the law that regulates the socio-cultural order. Heterosexuality amounts to the assignment of roles in the economy; some are given the role of producing and exchanging subjects, while others are assigned the role of productive earth and goods.

● *Luce Irigary*[1]

'*We share a lot of things, that's for sure: clothes, experiences – just life in general ... we have a lot of fun together.*'

● *Lee*

46: Male Impersonators

'We come for the surfing, the sun – if we're lucky. But most of all we come for the top-level shagging.'
● *Geordie*

SIX young men from Northern mining communities share a small caravan in Newquay, Cornwall, for the summer. The experience brings them very close. 'We don't really know it but we've become a kind of family,' confides Lee, 26, joshingly tagged 'Al Pacino' by the others for his battered good looks. But this is no ordinary family; this is a boy's dream family: 'I never knew someone could have so much freedom,' says Lee, bursting into tears. He is quickly consoled by hugs from Geordie, 37, the oldest member of the 'family' who acts as mum, dad and zany uncle to 'the lads'.

*The Sex Hunters*², a remarkable fly-on-the-wall TV documentary of these young men's summer together offered the viewing public an inside look at the private world of lads who seem to have built an 'ideal' community for themselves on a campsite in Newquay. They have everything a group of lads could wish for. They have surfing. They have boxing. They have weight-training. They have (sometimes) sun. They have girls. They especially have girls. But even more especially they have *each other*.

These thoroughly heterosexual young men display extraordinary and touching affection and even tenderness towards one another in front of the camera. Nor do they seem afraid to admit that they enjoy looking at one another. David, 28, a tall Chippendale look-alike with long blond hair admits, 'I think we're all vain to an extent – I think everyone is. I think that's the reason we like to keep in shape. In a place like that you see each other and you're bound to think, "Oh, I wish I had a body like that".' We see them boxing stripped to the waist and surfing in sleeveless short-panted wet-suits. And we see Billy, a 25-year-old bodybuilder, stripped completely, wandering around the caravan, curtains open, lights blazing, pretending to dry himself (while expertly keeping the towel out of our line of vision).

Their shared narcissism, like their single promiscuous lifestyle, is singularly 'gay'. We witness David and Billy sharing a ritual 'dressing-up' in front of the mirror before they go to the bar where they work as bouncers and Geordie tends the bar. First they apply Ponds Cream to their shaved muscular torsos. Then come the black, button-fly jeans (bottom button left undone), tight white vests (cut to show off shoulders and back), black bomber-jackets (carefully turned in at the waist to give that perfect shape), and – the final flourish – all set off by a colourful bandana tied around the head.

Confirming the commitment to the 'gay' life-style of these straight boys, we hear Billy tell us that he does not want to get married and admit, 'I don't really want any kids.' Geordie (who does most of the talking and probably most of the thinking for these boys) maintains that he will never get married – 'I'm not afraid of being alone because most married people are alone, even though they're still married' – and proudly displays a strategy for defying baldness that gay men have employed for years: shaving his head.

But if 'homosexuality is the law that regulates the social order' in this community there is absolutely no question but that 'heterosexuality assigns the roles'.

All the tenderness these young men show one another and their interest in each other's bodies is predicated on a ruthlessly, almost 'murderous', heterosexual 'intercourse' or exchange in which women have the status of legs of ham or sides of beef. The room containing the double bed in the caravan is called 'the slaughterhouse' and Geordie boasts of having 'forty victims this summer'. 'You wouldn't believe it,' he says. 'You can get away with murder if you're dressed to kill.'

In this economy the lads 'produce and exchange subjects', the most important of which are women. For them, women seem to represent all other subjects: 'signs, goods, currency'. Girls are a currency of esteem between them, goods to be exchanged, a *sign* of their masculine prowess. The value of these goods, their currency, is determined entirely by what they fetch in the male market, their use-value in the competition between males.

The lads come up with a ritual system to express that value and to award esteem: a toy race-track on which each of them is represented by a car and the name of a Grand Prix driver. Each woman laid represents a point. They hold an awards ceremony at the end of the summer in which Billy, Lee and David win trophies for first, second and third places respectively. Women are 'scores' in a game in which men's respect is the prize. And every woman is only worth one point, no more no less: they cannot have any *intrinsic* value, any value beyond the male market: any differentiation would result in disharmony between the lads. In this race, women are the lubricant that allows these men to associate so intimately without friction.

Billy and Dave share the caravan's only double room/bed. Geordie tells us that whenever one of the lads brings home a girl, no matter how late it is, they are always willing to get out of bed and sleep on the floor. But then they have no choice: sharing the double bed would not be possible in the first place without the primacy of heterosexuality being taken for granted.

'I only chatted her up because I was behind Billy in points,' says Geordie, explaining why he was seducing a girl he found unattractive. He would have backed out, he says, if he had not discovered that Billy had already smooth-talked her tent-mate. Billy and Geordie 'shag' the girls in their tent. 'I didn't even undress her,' jokes Geordie. 'I just cut away the clothes where I thought the parts were.' Coitus is achieved, but the girls' presence is hardly acknowledged: 'I could see Billy's little bottom going up and down ... I finished in about 15 seconds. I looked over and Billy was still going. I thought, I bet he's still going 'cause he thinks I'm still going.'

The interviewer asks Geordie point-blank if he likes women. 'Yes. We all do,' he affirms. 'It's our reason for living. And Newcastle United.' The lads do like women – much in the same way that they like sport. Women are a thing, an activity ('*it's* our reason for living.'), something to bring the lads together, something to share, exchange and collect, like football cards. 'I've only actually liked a couple of the girls this year,' confesses Lee. 'It's a bit strange. We're playing with people's lives and they're just points on a race-track to us.'

We see Geordie reading out to the lads a letter a past 'victim' has written to David. 'I trust you not to show this letter to the others,' reads Geordie and the boys burst into derisive laughter. Geordie tells us that they receive a lot of these letters but they never answer them, they share them with the lads instead. In another scene we see Billy call to a fat girl out of the caravan window; hiding his mouth Geordie makes 'boom, boom' noises in time to her footsteps, while Billy teases her, pretending that they had a date.

The roles assigned in this economy by heterosexuality cannot be blurred. Women have to remain 'things', not just commodities, but split-off, butchered, aspects of the self – the receptacle of the lads' projected 'femininity'. By making fun of the feelings expressed/represented by the foolish girls in their gushing letters, the feminine is ritually routed, kept at bay (giving them the masculine credit to spend feminine feelings on each other). 'I wear condoms to stop my willy smelling,' confesses Geordie. 'Fish', the woman/feminine commodity and the contamination it represents, has to be guarded against. Even the most 'intimate' contact is really no contact at all.

Freud characterized as a 'universal affliction . . . not confined to some individuals' the tendency of men to find that 'Where they love they do not desire and where they desire they do not love. They seek objects they do not love in order to keep their sensuality away from the objects they love.'

As the lads prepare to leave the camp-site and go back to their homes there is much hugging and kissing of foreheads (foreheads are erotically 'safe'). Billy gets a long hug from Geordie, who also grabs Billy's dick through his pants: 'I've almost grown attached to this,' he says, wiggling it for the camera. 'I'm glad someone has,' jokes Billy, 'winner' of the race-track competition.

The film closes with Geordie and Lee singing and playing their guitars (they used to be in a band) in front of a couple of giggling girls with faces hidden by white face-packs. 'Looking for a love of a different kind' the lads croon. Harmonizing the final line, 'I'm sick and tired of all the nice girls', their heads come together in front of the camera, blocking our view of the embarrassed girls, to give each other a mock kiss on the lips.

> *Why then consider masculine homosexuality as an exception, while in fact it is the very basis of the general economy? Why exclude homosexuals when society postulates homosexuality? Unless it is because the 'incest' at work in homosexuality must be kept in the realm of pretense.*
> ● *Irigary*[3]

Notes

1. Luce Irigary, *New French Feminists*, ed. Elaine Marks and Isabelle de Courtivron (Brighton: The Harvester Press, 1981), p. 107.

2. *The Sex Hunters*, a Kim West production for Channel 4's *Short Stories* series, first broadcast 18 December 1992. A bad imitation of it appeared a few months later in BBC2's *Forty Minutes*, which followed the antics of a bunch of young Geordie males on holiday in Spain.

3. Irigary, *New French Feminists*, p. 107.

The Sex Hunters of Newquay are not just a British phenomenon. A report in *Sky* magazine (September 1993, 'Arrested development') tells of a Los Angeles white teen gang called the Spur Posse who 'are committed to one goal – sexual conquest. ... To the Spur Posse ... sex is just another sport, where they score points for every hook-up – Spur slang for sex.' Their top scorer is also called Billy. But there the comparison ends: unlike the appalling-but-lovable Newquay lads, nine members of Spur Posse have been charged with rape.

Haggling

Geordie (real name Alan), the apparent spokesman for the boys, very kindly agreed to discuss the film and what it revealed, if anything, about the way 'lads' relate to men and women. My thanks go to him for his 'sporting' sense of humour, and to *Sex Hunters* producer Kim West and her friend Sebastian for their perceptive contributions (which saved me a lot of work).

Alan: In the weeks before the screening I got worried that we were going to be lynched. The woman that worked with Kim, she really thought that we were going to get it in the neck. I said to her 'you underestimate Northern humour'. But then when the press got hold of it I began to worry about it myself. We went into London the next day and the reaction was just incredible: people were stopping us in the street.

Mark Simpson: Was there any difference between the reaction of women and men?

A: Well, I thought that we were gonna be in trouble over either the reading of that girl's letter or my going 'boom, boom' when the fat girl came up to the caravan window. But this girl behind

the counter in a shop said 'I loved that bit where the fat girl came
up to the window.'

MS: Perhaps the kind of women that would be offended wouldn't
say anything to you?

A: Maybe. But I think that the only people who would have been
offended would be the girl who wrote the letter and the fat girl
who walked up to the caravan. Apart from the typical ones.
Actually, a lot of married people were offended 'cos I was slagging
off marriage.

MS: What did they say?

A: A friend of Kim's was really keen on me *before* the
programme. She even rang me twice on the day. But after the
programme went out – nothing. She said to Kim 'He's never had
children so he's never known what a great feeling that can be.' She
failed to mention that she probably hasn't had a shag for two
years. That's what I was getting at.

MS: From a certain perspective your views on marriage and
relationships are unorthodox, perhaps even radical.

A: I don't think what I'm saying is radical. When people are in a
fuckin' rut and bored with life they don't admit it – they just go
through the motions.

MS: The set-up you have down there, this all-boys-together
alternative family, do you think that a lot of men would like to
live that way if they had the chance?

A: Yeah. A lot of men would like to have the summer we have.
But y'know a lot wouldn't come out and admit it. But the men
working on the film, the camera-man and the sound-man – they
were definitely envious of us, weren't they?

Kim West: Yeah.

A: They let on to Kim more than they did to us about feeling
jealous. But they were certainly getting into it by the time the
filming had finished.

KW: There is a kind of fascination to that male bonding thing –
you just get drawn into it. It happened to me. I found myself
wanting to be a boy while I was there. I've had a similar set-up
with girls, but not to the same degree. I don't know if it's common
amongst all boys, but these ones all had an incredible loyalty
towards one another which we discussed when we were down
there. You just wanted to be one of them by the end of it.

MS: But Alan, couldn't it be argued that although you had this very loyal, very warm and friendly relationship with the other lads in the caravan, it was all based on an 'annihilation' of women: you call the fuck-room the 'slaughter house', women you pick up are 'victims' ...

A: ... but that's just boy's talk ...

MS: But *why* do they talk like that?

A: Because that's how boys are. Why is it when women get together that they say things like 'Oh, it wouldn't go hard, he could only do it once, it was only that big. ...' We're no different. They're just the same as us. What do you think footballers talk about when they're in the shower? It's the same thing. I can't understand why people get worked up about it. I could understand if we talked like that in a pub, 'Ay victim! Come over 'ere, do you want to come back to our slaughter house?' But we don't. That was just our private little caravan, and they were part of our own private sense of humour.

MS: Putting it another way, it seems like you saved all your affection and genuine emotional displays for one another.

A: No, there was lots of affection flying around when you actually got a woman on her own ...

KW: ... for an hour.

A: For an hour – an hour's worth of concentrated affection!

MS: But it seemed like the pleasure of *that* was in the relating of it to the lads an hour after that.

A: Well. ... but it can be humorous ... sex can be funny. You just laugh about it. We don't talk about every woman like that. And don't forget, it is pretty meaningless. Y'know, yer never gonna see these women again.

KW: Some of them you don't know their names and you do it in the dark. Why is that better than a wank? Is it because of the story that you can tell your mates the next day?

A: Well, don't forget that we were entering into the, er, spirit of the race-track – and a wank don't count on the race-track, otherwise I would probably have won it!

MS: The point I'm driving at is that in the film – I don't know what your lives are really like, all I have to go on is the film – in the film it seems as if women are disposable, their only value is in bringing you, the lads, closer together.

A: They were only disposable because they were there for a couple of weeks. I could have fallen madly in love with someone and she would still have been gone by the end of the week.

MS: But that was a situation that you had engineered by being there in the first place.

A: Only because we worked there. It's just better ... knowing that they're gonna be gone at the end of the week. And the reason why we were so free like that is because we didn't have to answer to anybody. The thing that cracked me up was ... going to call me mother on a Monday night you'd see this queue of people waiting to use the phone and they'd only been there *two days*, and they wanted to ring up where they'd just come from! There'd be young lads on the phone going, 'Oh, it's not very good ... the weather's crap', trying to make it sound bad for the whingeing git on the other end of the phone. They consciously can't let go and have a good time. They know that she's upset because, (a) he's gone away on holiday with his mates and didn't take her, and (b) it doesn't matter what the hell he does, she's not going to believe him when he gets home.

MS: Where do you and your mates live when you're not on the campsite?

A: One of them's in Miami at the moment. Matt goes to university in Newcastle, David lives with his Dad and Lee looks after his Old Man's nightclub, and I live in Islington. Winter's like a hibernation period for us.

KW: It's a shame the film couldn't have been longer because a lot of people said 'We want to know more about each character.' Alan was the main character, we focused on him but we could have spent more time on the other characters and it would have all come out, like Lee is unhappy at home, that's why he was getting so upset on film because he'd never had so much freedom.

MS: Well, Lee has these family problems, but then so do a lot of people.

A: But for three months he didn't have those problems. Newquay is amazing, you just lose track of everything down there. You don't even know what's No. 1! You don't watch the telly or nothing. It's like the land time forgot.

MS: But your role in the alternative family down there is interesting. You're the oldest by how much?

A: Ten years.

MS: Do you play Daddy at all?

A: Errr ... they might look up to me a bit because I'm older ... but I don't think it's because I'm older.

MS: It's because you're more articulate than they are?

A: Yeah, I would say. But we all look up to David to be Daddy because he's got the fists. Y'know, so there are like two Daddy's going on there. And we can all look up to Lee as Daddy 'cause he's got the wheels. Y'know we all have our little Daddy moments.

MS: You've all got something that the others want?

A: Well, y'know, we've all got our uses.

MS: Yeah, you're all useful to one another ... but it seemed like in the film, especially towards the end, that you were being very ... very kind of supportive and that Lee was, in particular, looking to you for a lot of support.

A: Well, you see, they all knew Lee, roughly. They all came from the same area and so I think there was still a bit of 'We all know who he is because we have to go to his Dad's nightclub.' I think there's still a bit of that there. I'd never seen him before I met him in Newquay, I knew nothing of his past and we just hit it off instantly. So perhaps that's why he likes me.

MS: Um, you were there for him perhaps in a way that his father certainly wasn't?

A: Maybe.

KW: I would say yes to that.

A: Really?

KW: Yeah.

A: It's his mother who he, er, feels sorry for.

KW: He feels sorry for her but he idolizes his father.

A: I don't know that he idolizes his father.

KW: I think he probably used to.

A: But he doesn't now. Well, we were there at Christmas and his fucking Dad was like a drunken fat little grey-haired midget and he was dancing with an 18-year-old dolly-bird with big tits and right in front of his mother. And his sister had the audacity to come up to me and say 'You're not very popular in this pub because of that programme', and there was her father being far worse than we could ever be right in front of her face.

MS: Lee said something like 'I can't believe that you can have this much freedom', and that's what I think many men and some women watching the film might feel jealous of.

A: Well I never discovered that feeling until I was 35. I'd always been, y'know, stuck in the 'you've got to have a job' mode.

MS: Do you think you'll stay single for ever?

A: Do I think I'll stay single for ever? I hope so.

MS: What about the other boys?

A: Well, Billy, the one who's in Miami, he's the freest of us all. I've only known him two years and he's never *lived* anywhere, he's always been here, & there and everywhere. He's the freest of us all. David ... I can see David and Lee getting married ...

Sebastian: To each other!

A: Yeah, hopefully [laughs]. But I can't see them being happy. I just don't think it works. But y'know people can't look at us and think that we're lucky, because we *chose* this life and everybody can choose that life. I didn't ask people to get married, have babies, have mortgages, get jobs, then lose the jobs, then lose the houses, then lose the wife, then lose the car, then lose the flipping kids and all you're left with is living in a bastard tent with someone's fuckin' cat. What sort of life is that? Life isn't about that. But for some unknown reason they chose a life like that either because they were too weak or too scared of being alone and they thought they were going to be happy out of it and that is *pathetic*.

MS: It seems to me that ... by the way, which one was Billy? I can't remember what he looked like.

A: He was the one with the bandana on, he was the main muscle ...

MS: Oh, right.

A: He was the one whose, er, dick was ...

KW: He came number one.

A: He was the race-track winner.

MS: It seems that Billy has got, well, when I use the word narcissism I don't necessarily mean it in a derogatory way, but you could see that Billy was completely in love with himself. But it seemed like he had his own emotional capital there with him: his body, he can take that with him wherever he goes and he'll get work, and he'll get attention and he'll like himself, and he can go to the gym and make his friends – so he's got his own little world which revolves around his body. But it seems to me that you're the only one that has what you've just been talking about, that kind of independence, that will, er, to be free, to be single, and I would envisage the others, apart from Billy, getting married very soon.

A: But perhaps you can only say that about me because I've actually reached 37 without falling by the wayside.

MS: Well perhaps, but even if I take that out of the equation, it seems like you're the only one that can. .... In a way when you say 'why do people get married' it's a rather self-centred thing to say, because it seems like most of those other boys are going to end up in a situation where they aren't going to be functioning without somebody to wipe their face and do their washing and all that, y'know? And in a way your alternative family, which is very attractive and seems to work very well, depended on a number of things, one of which was you, and the other was that it was ephemeral, it was not *real life* in the sense of a permanent set-up.

A: But what is permanent? It might be easier for me. The reason I can confidently say I'm not going to get married is because I've got my own little place. People say 'when are you going to settle down?' But I'm already settled down – *without a woman*. I don't need a woman to do all those things that a lot of men need. I know how to operate a washing machine. So what does a woman end up being? She ends up being a glorified housekeeper! Except a housekeeper comes in, does the cleaning, does the washing and then bogs off with her wage packet – a wife doesn't get that. All I need a woman for is nice times.

MS: But you've got the character, the confidence and the personality to expect to get and go on getting those women, whereas a lot of men have the anxiety that they won't unless they pay for it.

A: But David still has.

KW: I must say, out of the six of them, there were only three of them that were really interested in sex. The other three were only interested in things like surfing. David, the main catch, was just not interested in picking up women.

MS: What does David look like?

KW: He's the one with long blond hair.

MS: Women seem to like men with long blond hair.

KW: It doesn't matter what kind of hair David has.

A: He's got it cut short now anyway – he's just like the ultimate man. But he lacks confidence.

KW: Some people might think he's stupid, and he's a coal miner's son and all that, but I think he just hasn't experienced life. But he does seem a bit dumb to begin with.

A: But you can't say he's got no brain.

KW: When you get to know him you find out lots of lovely qualities – but he didn't say anything in front of the camera. And the funny thing is that some of the women wouldn't take no for an answer. Sometimes the lads weren't interested and the women just went for them: they'd made up their minds that they wanted them and they were going to get them.

A: And that was mainly with David. And the thing is, that doesn't stop at Newquay. Even down in London with what you would call intelligent, career-minded women – fuckin' border-line right-on feminists – as soon as they've had a couple of leg-openers down them and David walks into the room, that's it, they've gone – they're just hanging on the chandeliers, swinging at 'im vagina first, y'know? And he's there with his baseball bat, whopping them all off because he's looking for something special.

But I know what you're saying: when a man gets a woman he thinks 'Well, I've got one now, I've got to pull myself off the open market and stick with this one.' That's a fuckin' *sad* way of thinking. If you stay single there's always gonna be somebody comes along, y'know, and the older you get the more worldly you get. If you look after yourself there's always gonna be a woman come along – if you become a fat slob then there won't.

MS: It would be very easy for someone watching the film to turn around and say, 'Well, these men are interacting – like perhaps most men do to some degree – at a homoerotic level.' The atmosphere between you was very loving and very ... electric. It didn't seem like there was any actual sex going on between men but there was an erotic charge.

A: What? – suppressed 'omosexuality?

MS: Well, let me explain what I mean by homoeroticism. When you describe something as being homoerotic it relies on the Freudian idea that people are initially open to both hetero and homo attraction but usually the homo component is sublimated, turned into a non-sexual expression. According to Freud this sublimated homoerotic desire is vital to civilization and helps to bond men together, especially in single sex groupings like schools, sports teams and the military – or your caravan. And looking at your relationship to each other in that caravan there seemed to be this very loving atmosphere … you were very physical, very affectionate, and – this is the really interesting bit – unlike other male groups – like rugby clubs for example, where any affection and touching has to be carefully proscribed with drink and aggression – you seemed unafraid of this being read into it. What do you think of that?

A: Well, perhaps we were less afraid. We just didn't have anything to … you see we had this situation where we were all working in a night-club, so all the other lads instantly hate your guts because we had a monopoly on all the decent women, so it was like the last wagon-train in our caravan in the middle of this campsite surrounded by lots of people who hate yer. Like the women who can't have yer, they instantly hate yer; and the ones that you slept with the night before and you're not gonna touch, the next night they're gonna hate you – so that is why we feel you have to …

KW: That was something that struck us really strongly, that they were really affectionate with one another and were unafraid – it didn't seem to enter their heads that people might think that they were gay. Whether they're offended by that at the end of the day is up to them. It wasn't even an issue. They were quite prepared to hold and kiss one another and I was really touched by that. I thought that was quite unique.

A: It's like Kim says, for years women have been buying women's magazines and all they've been doing is looking at …

KW: Other women's bodies.

A: Women are obsessed with all that. And then we come along, to us, acting normal and we get these words thrown at us. Y'know like the 'suppressed homosexuality' one.

MS: The reason why you interest me is not because you're very 'different' or 'weird'. It's because what I could see going on between you was very recognizable. I could see a lot of men in that situation – if they had the opportunity. But I must admit I was surprised by your candidness in front of the camera. I *know* that a lot of men can be very affectionate and fond towards one another and very physical, but only under strict kinds of ground rules, and one is that you don't let other people see you. Or that you have a good alibi, like being 'sooo drunk' that your mate has to hold you up by putting an arm round you and can play a drunken 'joke' like kissing him.

A: Well I don't drink. I don't need all that. I'm not afraid of showing affection.

MS: Well, let me try out my little theory on you. If you weren't fucking all those women, and so ostentatiously telling one another about it and in such great detail, would it have been possible for you to have been so relaxed and so physical with one another?

A: Yeah, I think it would have been. Because not all of us – there were really only three of us chasing the women, the others weren't particularly interested.

MS: Well, amongst you three then.

A: Yeah, because the year before I only slept with one girl. I don't think that had anything to do with it. It's just a part of it, part of being away.

KW: It is a part of it, like the surfing's a part of it, the training's a part of it, the boxing's a part of it ... they do talk as much about surfing as they do about women.

A: Well, they do. And about fuckin' tuna fish and protein. Y'know I don't get involved in all that side of it.

MS: What about that clip which showed you talking about a time when you were fucking a girl in tandem with another lad, Billy?

A: Night manoeuvres.

MS: And you said something like 'I came in three minutes.'

A: No – three minutes! thank you! – no, fifteen seconds – it was a joke.

S: Everyone misunderstood that.

A: Everyone picked up on it.

KW: But then you did admit it was fifteen seconds.

A: Yeah. But fifteen of the best seconds of this here life.

S: No, no, it's a misunderstanding. Alan wasn't saying that it's any bad thing to come in fifteen seconds.

A: Fuckin' 'ell, every man in this pub has come in fifteen seconds.

S: No, no Alan, it wasn't that. You were telling a story.

MS: The story as I remember it, is that you came quickly – fifteen seconds.

A: Normal.

MS: And you looked over and Billy's bum was still going up and down and you said that he must have thought that you hadn't come yet.

A: Well, y'know, I just had the vision of Billy thinking 'I'd better not stop yet in case he's still going.' I didn't want to get into that situation because we knew that we didn't really fancy either of them.

KW: So why were you doing it? For a story to tell.

A: Why were we doing it? Because we could.

KW: For each other. Not for girls, not for your own pleasure. You were doing it ...

A: We were doing it because there were a thousand men on that campsite who would have swapped places with us, but we were the lucky ones.

KW: Why were you lucky? You did it for your mates, admit it.

A: For the hell of it!

KW: For your mates.

A: Not for yer mates, because, er, ...

KW: What, yourself?

A: Yeah!

KW: Oh, 'I shagged a really horrible girl last night' – what thrill do you get out of that?

A: It's nice to shag a horrible one – for a change. We just did it for the hell of it. And we were involved in the race-track, don't forget.

KW: And no consideration of their feelings.

A: No.

MS: You keep coming back to the race-track as if the race-track was this thing that was given from outside – imposed on you – but *you* created the race-track.

A: Yeah, I know, but ...

MS: And the race-track served *your* purposes, which is what we're interested in.

KW: I must say I've not heard Alan mention the race-track as much as I have tonight.

MS: What does the race-track represent?

A: It represents how many women you've shagged.

MS: Yeah, but it represents the competitiveness doesn't it?

A: Yeah.

MS: But what is that competitiveness about?

A: It's just a male thing, isn't it. I'm sure every …

MS: Seems like, to me, a lot of men get a sexual thrill out of the appreciation and esteem of other men and their envy, and that's something that comes through in sport, and even arts and literature, but it also seems to come through in your race-track.

A: But I think that's a female thing as well, isn't it? Everyone looks to winners and admires them. It's not just a male thing. I mean, I'm sure millions of women looked at Sally Gunnell when she won the gold and admired her and thought 'bloody 'ell, I'd like to be standing on that rostrum now.' And we were all looking at Billy thinking we'd like to be standing on that winner's rostrum.

MS: Yeah, yeah, but why do you enjoy the admiration?

A: Well, because everybody enjoys admiration.

KW: Admiration for having sex with sixteen ugly women. Or ten nice ones and six ugly ones.

A: When did they turn into ugly women all of a sudden? I didn't enjoy that particular shag, but then you don't know before you've done it. Each shag could be the shag of your life. We could have gone into that tent, the pair of us, boxing gloves ready, and we might not have wanted to come out of that tent, we might have still been in that tent now. How do you know until you actually unzip it and away you go. As it was, it was a fuckin' nightmare and we couldn't wait to get out. Surely that's the same for a woman?

MS: Well perhaps, but we're not talking about women at the moment and you're not a woman so you can't tell me what a woman might think. It's interesting to explore what your relationship to women is, but in terms of what we're talking about: why you do the things *you* do, to get an idea why men do the things *they* do.

S: How did you get a hard-on that night?

A: How? I've always got a 'ard-on.

S: Seriously.

A: You just get aroused don't you?

S: How?

A: Because you're in a sexual situation.

S: What, with two dogs?

A: Yeah!

KW: Two unattractive women waiting for you?

A: We all get, we all ...

KW: Did Billy give you a hard-on?

A: Billy was nowhere near me.

KW: Was it the thought of him then?

A: No, I can still get a hard-on without Billy being there. Y'know, you can't give Billy the credit ...

S: *That* night, what was it.

A: It's ...

S: You didn't talk to her. You didn't see her body.

A: Well perhaps I just get a hard-on pretty easy then.

MS: Maybe you got a hard-on thinking how powerful you were as you imagined the admiration you would be getting because all the other men wanted to screw these women.

A: No, I said every man on that camp would gladly have swapped places with me. Y'know, the lads who were walking home drunk again without getting what they came on holiday for.

MS: What I'm getting at is that perhaps you got a hard-on because you had an imaginary audience with you, an audience of men and they're cheering you on, and you're on the race-track again, and the male crowd is either going 'yeah!' or 'that fuckin' jammy bastard!'

A: No. I don't think so. Because I could've gone home with them two from Blackburn the other night, no race-track, no audience of men cheering me on.

KW: No point in doing it then – and that's why you didn't.

A: No .... In different circumstances I would've – just for the hell of it. And I would've still got a hard-on.

MS: Well look, the contradiction that I'm driving at is that you say that you are an individualist, you say that you don't care what other people think, but it seems to me that, like most men, you care most of all about what other men think, in the end.

A: Not *all* men – there's only six of us in the caravan.

MS: But it is their admiration that is most valuable to you, isn't it?

A: Well, I don't think that David admired us the next day, and Tony certainly didn't.

KW: But *Billy* admired you ...

S: But there's a lot of things that you don't talk about in that caravan, isn't there?

A: Like what?

S: Like the way that David didn't pull all year.

A: Oh yeah, we talked about it!

S: No you didn't. It was a really taboo subject.

A: It wasn't. I was always going 'What's wrong? What's wrong with you? Just do it for the sake of it!' And he'd go 'No, I don't want to.'

MS: So because he didn't pull you asked him 'What's wrong with you?'

A: Yeah! We used to think that there was something wrong with him, because he didn't want to. But you go through phases in life. The phase he's going through – I have been there. Where you just don't . . .

KW: David wants to meet a girl to settle down with.

A: He wants to meet someone special at the moment because he's having women throw themselves at him left, right and centre, and it all becomes pretty meaningless for him.

MS: But isn't it more interesting to think, not why David doesn't want to have sex with every girl that comes along, or even every other girl, but rather why you immediately thought that there was something wrong with him because he wasn't. It was almost like he'd broken an unwritten rule.

A: Yeah, almost. But he was thinking that there was something wrong with us because we could go with them two.

MS: You were saying earlier that if you weren't all fucking women left, right and centre there wouldn't be any difference in your behaviour, that you would be just as affectionate and relaxed with one another. But it doesn't seem that way, does it?

A: Well yeah, I was still just the same with David because I understood why he didn't want to.

KW: You thought it was just a sorry phase he was going through.

A: Yes – not a sorry phase – I know exactly where he's coming from.

KW: What if he never gets that back, never comes out of that phase?

A: Well, he's got a search on his hands, hasn't he? Don't get me wrong, if I could meet a woman and be happy, and everything remains the same as it was on the day I met her, I would gladly have that. But it just becomes a pain with all the games and rules slapped on us in relationships, and you start to think why the fuck do I bother. So if I actually thought I could meet somebody and it stayed fresh and exciting I would probably be happy with that – for a while.

MS: In terms of the situation in the caravan we were talking a moment ago about David and how he broke the rules.

A: No he didn't break any rules.

MS: Well, he broke an unspoken rule.

A: No, he just didn't enter into the spirit . . .

MS: . . . of the game! What if one of them said 'I don't fancy women any more; I fancy men.' What would happen then?

A: [*Pause*] For me, nothing. Nothing would happen. That doesn't bother me. I don't care what anybody else does with their lives, that's entirely up to them – I do not judge people.

MS: Yeah, that's a general liberal attitude, but in terms of the dynamics of your alternative family in that caravan, if one of the blokes said that he didn't fancy women any more, that he fancies blokes instead . . .

KW: Or he fancied both.

MS: Umm, y'know – wouldn't that be a big spanner in the works?

A: Well that's like . . . we're entering the realms of surmision here. I can't . . .

MS: It can happen.

A: Yeah, but until it actually happens I can't . . .

MS: Well, the reason why I asked you that is because in the case of David – and I'm not saying that David is going to turn round and say he's gay – but David seemed to be sailing close to the wind because it seems – not that you were on the verge of chucking him out – that your relaxed atmosphere and physical intimacy is very much dependent on your attitude towards 'the feminine' on that holiday. By fucking so many women you're proving to yourself and anyone who's watching that you're 'OK', that you're a 'regular guy'. That allows you, that gives you the credit to spend on that affection and tenderness towards one another which otherwise would be very difficult.

A: I think that we all have other things that we gain respect from, y'know, we all respect David because, er, he looks after us in violent situations. He doesn't 'ave to shag thousands of women to earn our respect, we all respect him that way.

KW: I'd be interested to hear what you'd say if one of them came up to you and said 'I had a really good shag last night – *he* was really great ...'

A: But until that situation arises then ...

KW: And for you to say 'Oh yeah, what was he like?' I just can't picture that in that caravan.

A: No, I can't picture it either, so it's pointless.

MS: I mean, c'mon, you say you can't picture it – you don't *want* to picture it, do you?

A: It doesn't bother ... as I've just said ...

MS: It's inconceivable in *that* set-up, isn't it?

A: No – nothing is inconceivable, but what's the point of considering something until it happens? Until that situation arises how do I know how they'll all react? How do I know how Billy would react to David if he came out and said he was gay – I don't know.

MS: I'm not actually asking you to predict how everybody would react, but ...

A: Personally, it wouldn't bother me if *any* of them were gay. Y'know, I've got a ... I've got a gay friend, who was here at the weekend who *openly admits*, *openly admits*, that he wants me. Y'know, and I'm forever fending 'im off, and that doesn't bother me.

MS: Well, that's quite flattering isn't it?

A: Well, I don't look at it as being flattering – that's just him, that's the way he is. So I don't expect him to behave any differently because he's in my company.

MS: OK.

A: But I wouldn't expect the same ... easy attitude off the others, I must admit. Now, looking how they are to Tony because they think he's a bit effeminate – y'know, Tony got a lot of stick.

MS: Doesn't that kinda tie in with what I'm long-distance driving at here?

A: Maybe it does ... but don't forget that we cannot all be totally free of hang-ups and prejudices, can we?

MS: No, no, no ...

A: I think that considering that we're all together in that caravan we all do pretty well.

MS: Yeah, the whole reason why the set-up intrigues me is because it's a mixture of ambiguities for me. I think it's very enviable and at the same time I think it's very unsettling because I suspect that the community you have there, like many all-male communities that get together and talk about common interests, activities – whether that's fucking or surfing – is based on a kind of exultation, a kind of worship, of the masculine and a denigration of the feminine, whether that's the feminine embodied in women, or whether that's the feminine embodied in so-called 'effeminate' men, men who, either in terms of where they put their dicks or how they dress or cut their hair, don't conform to that masculine ideal that you're supposed to worship. It could be argued that your 'butchery' of women, the way in which Tony gets picked on for what the other lads perceive as effeminate behaviour, and the way you are constantly competing with one another to be the top dog, the big man, El Honcho – the winner of the race-track game – we have that worship of the masculine and the denigration of the feminine, the 'monstrous feminine', a thing to loathe, to fear, to hunt down and destroy. That's why I asked about the gay man, because the gay man represents to many men the worst possible embodiment of the feminine – whether or not he's effeminate.

A: [*To Kim*] But I've already said this to you that I found it amazing that I was accepted by them all, by David and them; haven't I?

KW: Yeah.

A: I don't go out drinking.

KW: But they *know* that you're really masculine and that you're really, really into women [*Alan talks over Kim*].

A: They know that Tony has got a steady girlfriend. So what are they talking about? I don't go drinking with the boys . . .

KW: But you're not effeminate.

A: I'm not *hard*. So why did they accept me?

KW: But you're really masculine in the way you talk, and they probably laugh about the way that you talk about women.

A: But, I'm like Dr Ruth down there in Newquay. I'm the one that always feels sorry for the girls.

MS: [*Slightly sarcastic*] You're the sensitive one.

A: [*Challenging*] Yeah.

MS: You sound almost *awed* that they accepted you.

A: Not awed by them.

MS: OK. Not awed by them, but you're surprised.

A: Yeah, and for the very reasons that you're talking about. I stick out in crowds. Like take the rugby mob you mentioned earlier. If I was a good rugby player I wouldn't be standing in the corner with me fuckin' trousers down, pissed and singing dirty songs. I'd be sat in the corner talking to a female about 'femaley' things and you know what rugby players are like, they'd probably go 'look at that gay bastard over there.' But I wouldn't be because. . . . I'm not gay. But I wouldn't have to stand in the corner with them to prove myself. I've never had to go out of my way to be anything other than who I am to be accepted by this lot.

MS: What about at school, what kind of people did you hang out with there?

A: Just like these. When you come from Nuneaton that's all there is, really. Since school-days I've never had friends like these – that's why it was a refreshing change to meet . . . 'cause London's full of the sort of people you get in that pub [*the fashionable Islington pub/bistro we met in*], y'know, they lose the sort of . . . they almost turn into New Men. They're all in there now talking about what they did at work, their new project. But it's nice to go to a place like that campsite with Billy and David and say 'Fwooarr! look at 'er over there!' I think a lot of women in London miss that. It's been so long since they've experienced that approach. There are so many women in London who *haven't had sex for fuckin' donkey's years*. They go out with men who go 'Oh yes, and what project are you involved with at the moment?' And what they really, deep down want is for some fuckin' man to say, 'Look, why don't you come back to my place now?' Women like the caveman approach – [*to Kim*] don't yer?

MS: You like it as well, don't you?

A: Well, that's basically what we've evolved from.

MS: But you seem to like it in other men . . .

A: But I really feel that we have got a bit more. . . . See, the woman who did the programme with Kim, she really hated us before she even came down – she thought we were gonna be what

you described. We just saw this film as a chance to make
something happen, y'know they could have made a programme
about six gits surfing and had me saying 'Oh yes, we sell a lot
of Holsten Pils in 'ere.' And that would have been fuckin'
rivetting ...

MS: And I'd *definitely* be here now.

A: Exactly, discussing *why do we think it is* that we sell such a lot
of Holsten Pils in this area?

Chapter four

Active Sports
The Anus and Its
Goal-Posts

*What you must do, son, is become a fucker and not
become a fucked. It's as simple as that. Boys or girls, up
the pussy or the arse, whichever you prefer, but you've got
to remember there's a cock between your legs and you're a
man.*
● Colin MacInnes[1]

*A mum whose husband is in jail told yesterday of her new
lover ... a 14-year-old schoolboy.*

*Police have quizzed Debbie, but plan no action. Inspector
Terry Lowe said: 'Only a man can be charged with
unlawful sexual intercourse.'*

*The inspector added: 'Basically, the lad has found
something better than football.'*
● Daily Mirror[2]

TWO images of football are offered by two famous photos.
One shows Bobby Moore and Pele at the 1970 World Cup final
with their shirts off, touching each other's faces and embracing
with smiles and relaxed bodies. The other shows Vinny Jones
standing in front of Paul Gascoigne, facing away, his left hand
reaching behind him clutching Gascoigne's groin; their bodies and

faces are rigid and contorted: Jones' with hate, Gascoigne's with pain.

The Pele/Moore image speaks of the sublime fraternity of 'the beautiful game', harmony between teams, nations, races – men. Their bodies, in their openness and nakedness, appear to give us the sexual resolution to masculine conflict that we are often promised but never shown. Strip off those opposing jerseys, cast aside conventions and culture, and underneath are we not the same? The blond English boy and the black, curly-haired Brazilian reach out to one another, dissolving differences with open arms; black and white are united in an equal embrace of hot skin; in a word: Love.

Jones/Gascoigne represent the necessary antithesis. Their 'embrace' is even more intimate than the former but it expresses, through the grotesque parody of the greatest tenderness between men, the greatest hate. Jones's face, a portrait of malice, faces away from Gascoigne, but his hand conveys its message, anonymous-and-yet-personal: the very essence of masculine violence. Here there is no fraternity, no equality; this is a triumphal depiction of domination. Vinny Jones, football's 'Hard Man', the crew-cut castrator, holds cry-baby Gascoigne's soft manhood in his hod-carrier's hand. In this tableau from a male morality play there can be no mistaking the import: in hetero-speak, Jones is 'the fucker', Gascoigne 'the fucked'.

And like the tough on whose right-hand knuckles are tattooed the words LOVE and on the other HATE, the first image of football's beauty depends upon the second's ugliness. The Love of Pele and Moore depends upon the Hate of Vinny and Gascoigne; two views of the game that are in fact a unity. One portrays 'beauty', the other 'beast'; both combine in the myth of football.

> *For every Gary Lineker there's a Vinny Jones, for every David Gower a Curtly Ambrose. But without the ball-breaking bad guys, team sports would lose their terrible beauty.*
> ● *Esquire*[3]

The manly passion of football is permitted because it is predicated on manly violence, without which the passion would no longer be manly. For some, football is 'the beautiful game', a tournament of lyrical bodies, a brotherhood of grace and style, represented by the Pele/Moore photo, in which the ball almost floats through the air supported by the sheer aesthetic wonder of it all. In fact it is the very *brutality* of the game that makes any elan or tenderness so welcome – or possible. In this masculine universe there can be no loveliness without horror; pleasure is circumscribed by pain, gain by loss, love by hate; each goal scored and game won, each and every joy attained, is wrung from the despair of other men.

The final binary of life and death is there in the iconography of football, marking out the boundaries of what is permissible in men's lives. Both in terms of the picture itself and in terms of its recent context, Pele and Moore *have finished playing*, while Jones and Gascoigne have not. The photo of Pele and Moore achieved phenomenal popularity in 1993, appearing in almost every newspaper in the country, *after* Moore's death. The (male) nation went into mourning, tearful tributes to him flooded the media and a shrine of flowers and scarves grew at his home ground of West Ham. Dead and gone, Moore became loss and pain *and* beauty, the object of a torrent of 'feminine' emotion from millions of men, in a way that no man alive could be.

As the universal affection towards football stars like Pele and Moore shows, the appeal of football does not consist of belonging to a place or a club; it is not the tribalism or territorialism of sociologists that attracts men, but membership of the masculine club itself. The grief at the death of a footballer is not just a release of emotion like that at the end of a game. It is also grief at the realization that there is a final whistle for the game of masculinity itself; in other words the ultimate failure of disavowal. Fear of death, which Freud described as a mere shadow of the fear of castration, re-emerges even out of the most vital and vigorous of lives. However successful their performance as a member of the team, however many trophies they win and however much male esteem they earn, men still cannot keep the most prized trophy of all – the phallus.

It is this trophy that is always what is at stake in football. 'Love' in football is man's love for and desire of the phallus; 'hate' is their hatred for and fear of castration. Little wonder that for boys football often becomes an obsession that will stay with them for the rest of their lives. Football teaches them how to be a man through phallic competition; 'love' can only be realized through the 'castration' of other men. But the binary of love and hate in football is sometimes indistinct: the 'love' for the phallus often runs perilously close to a desire *of* the phallus; and homo-desire threatens the love/hate, phallus/castration binary.

'Why has the relationship that began as a schoolboy crush endured for nearly a quarter of a century, longer than any other relationship I have made of my own free will?' asks Nick Hornby in the introduction to his acclaimed autobiography, *Fever Pitch: A Fan's Life*.[4] Unwittingly he provides the answer in his account of his first match at the age of eleven: 'I remember the overwhelming *maleness* of it all – cigar and pipe smoke, foul language (words I had heard before but not from adults at that volume), and only years later did it occur to me that this was bound to have an effect on a boy who lived with his mother and sister; and I remember looking at the crowd more than at the players.'[5]

The 'overwhelming *maleness*' of football is a swooning passion for virility that sweeps boys keen to be men and not at all sure how to become one (except not to be a 'poof') off their feet. Football provides the boy with an answer to the problem of how to reconcile his homoerotic desire, his 'feminine' love *of* 'manliness', with his desire to *be* manly, i.e. not 'a fucked'. If, in the words of Eve Kosofsky Sedgewick, 'For a man to be a man's man is separated only by an invisible, carefully blurred, always-already-crossed line from being "interested in men"',[6] then football blurs it still further but sharpens it at the same time, giving boys and men more leeway to express something approaching an interest in men as well as setting up clear ground rules that reassure the male spectator/player who is quite literally paranoid about overstepping that 'always-already-crossed' line. This is in fact very close to the classic Oedipal trap laid for homosexual men described by Hocquenghem:

The sophism of the 'accursed race', and of homosexual perversion as a whole, lies in the fact that the word 'virile' describes anyone who is not 'queer', while the 'queer' is the

penis lover, and the penis is the phallus, i.e. the organ of
virility; and so the circle of impossible love is closed.[7]

The 'circle of impossible love is closed', keeping gay men inside and
straight men outside. The straight man is required to disavow queer
desire precisely because he so values the penis, 'the organ of virility'. Queer desire, for the straight man, is the 'impossible' love
since it would require the renunciation of that which he loves –
virility.

The basic ground rule of football both closes the circle and
seems to offer some escape from it. It is simply this: interest in men
is permitted, indeed encouraged, but must always be expressed
through the game. A man's love for football is a love of and for
manhood, composed of a condensation of introjected (turned
inwards) homoerotic desire. Boys discover that football places them
in a masculine universe where they can enjoy the company of men
and the spectacle of their bodies – as long as it is framed within
competition, a struggle for dominance: to be 'a fucker'; love is once
again circumscribed by hate. The game itself becomes the phallus,
something to be forever pursued and worshipped, something that
bestows manhood: 'I fell in love with football as I was later to fall
in love with women,' declares Hornby in the first line of his first
chapter.

Like millions of other little boys before him, armed with his
new manly credentials Hornby found instant acceptance at school
where he might otherwise have found painful, sadistic rejection
(especially in view of what he describes as his unprepossessing
physical attributes). He found the key to popularity and plenitude
in his Soccer Stars stickers, swopping 'Ian Ure for Geoff Hirst,
Terry Venables for Ian St John'. By sharing in the boy's love for
football stars, Hornby found that the male club opened its arms
wide for him. The wonder of football: the expression of an 'interest
in men' cements the image of manliness in the eyes of the young
football fan and his peers, rather than shattering it, and provides an
intimate – although mediated – connection to other boys! Boys
from other schools, boys from other parts of town, even *older* boys
are now just as likely to show tenderness to a weaker new boy
where before they would have shown their fist: *so long as they
support the same team.*

The competition imperative means that hate must never be let out of sight of love. On one occasion Hornby found himself supporting the 'wrong' team and trampled into the playground grit. He did not relish the experience: 'I wanted to be with the rest of the class, trampling the hell out of some other poor heartbroken kid – one of the swots or weeds or Indians or Jews who were habitually and horribly bullied. For the first time in my life I was different and on my own, and I hated it.'[8] (It is interesting to note that it appears there were no 'pansies' at Hornby's school, which is unlikely to say the least.) Now humiliated as Other, he found himself wishing that his father had taken him to the usual zoo or deserted dining room instead of that first football match. As indeed he might: what, after all, is the point of football if it does not bring you membership of the male club?

But when the fetishes of football, like Hornby's Soccer Stars stickers, do work their magic and bring forth masculine tenderness, the joy and happiness of the boy are immeasurable. Pictures of hunky footballers, powerful thighs flashing in the sun, become the objects of exchange between boys, giving them status and esteem: in other words the football stars play the same role women will later in their lives; they are objects exchanged in what Irigary would call a phallocentric economy, mediating between the boys and preventing their relations breaking down into 'incest'.

Nor is this position of footballers as objects of exchange something limited to picture cards swopped between boys. They are only imitating the adult world of football itself. 'Player takes field to free soccer "slaves"' reads a headline in *The Guardian*.[9] 'Football players are human beings not inanimate objects to be bought and sold like goods with no say in where they work,' a representative of the soccer trade union is quoted as saying. The transfer-fee system means that a footballer may have to remain at a club even after his contract expires. Players are objects of exchange between clubs and managers, i.e. men, rather than subjects in themselves. Ironically, the game of football offers up star footballers as men that boys will envy and want to emulate, and yet their position in the phallocentric economy is close to that of women.

Another favourite of the young football fan, the team shot, illustrates this further. A group photo of Norwich City in *Soccer Stars* (April 1992) shows all 'the lads' in their strip, flanked by their physio and second team coach, with their manager and assistant manager in the middle of the first row. If the team is a family, as is often fondly suggested by those involved in the sport, then parental connotation of the manager and assistant manager cannot be overlooked. Here we have a family without a mother: women have been abolished in the phallocentric economy of football. The manager is clearly the patriarch; he is the only one to wear a suit and is easily the oldest. The 'strip' that the rest of the team wears, including the assistant manager, represents the 'Name of the Father', marking them as belonging to him. In front of them are the magical objects which have made all this possible: three footballs. Football is an activity *and* an object which literally mediates between the men, taking the place of 'woman'.

The football fantasy of abolishing women is even exploited in adverts. In a promotion of Weetabix we see manager Brian Clough and 'his boys' eating breakfast together in what appears to be a domestic kitchen. The fantasy of a motherless family works both ways: that of an older man having a harem of young bucks/ sons undistracted in their devotion to him, and that of boys enjoying the exclusive attentions of an older man. (Weetabix, it should be pointed out, is a family breakfast cereal aimed primarily at young boys.)

And if the passion for football for boys, like the passion for virility itself, is based on introjected homo-desire, it should be no surprise that it is frequently fathers who introduce their sons to the sport. In the Oedipal family, the son's identification with the father represents the introjection of his desire for him. It is also in this way that the boy learns to separate identification from desire (although this is never completely successful). The taboo on any suggestion of desire between father and son, the result of both the incest taboo and the especially strong anti-homosexual taboo, often leads to a ban on *any* tenderness, a breakdown in communication and dreadful isolation that far too many fathers and sons know.

Hornby knew it, but football provided an escape of sorts. After his parents separated at eleven, he tells us, he would spend weekends with his father which were endured in 'more or less complete silence'.[10] Until, like many fathers desperate for something 'safe' to do with his son (and talking, without ground-rules, is perhaps the most dangerous thing of all for men), Mr Hornby had the idea of taking his son to a football match. This provided them with a 'medium to communicate';[11] in other words, football stood in for direct tenderness between father and son.

> *Like every father I desperately wanted a son – and [on the day of his birth] Shirley had her work cut out to stop me going out and buying his first pair of football boots there and then!*
> ● *Derek Hatton*[12]

Football can be talked about in the most heated fashion without actually betraying anything personal; it is an activity that can be shared, but at a distance, watched over all the time by thousands of other males, whose presence wards off the possibility of anything 'unmanly' – i.e. anything unmediated – entering into the man-to-man relation. Football not only intervenes for the taboo romance between father and son (in its social as well as familial form), it comes to *substitute for it*. The accepted position of players as objects, the fact that they are out of reach and yet never out of sight, and the manner in which they have been substituted, combine with their often superior physical attributes (compared to the boy's father) to allow the boy a slight slippage of the chains of sublimation; allowed an inch or two of libidinal freedom, the young fan directs a hot blast of Eros towards his favourite players.

'I loved Bobby Charlton and George Best ... with a passion that had taken me completely by surprise', confesses Hornby, dazed by the way in which he found himself head over heels with the game and its heroes after his father took him to see his first game.[13] The strength of the boy's sublimated feelings as they are de-sublimated (and more often than not quickly re-sublimated again) comes as a shock to the boy-child who has been denied such feelings for so long.

To his credit Hornby seems unafraid to make direct comparisons in adult life between his attachment to male players and girlfriends. Talking about the transfer of an admired player, Liam Brady, from Hornby's adopted team of Arsenal, and a girlfriend who finished with him, he muses that 'in some strange way I think she and Liam got muddled up in my mind. The two of them, Brady and the lost girl haunted me for a long time, five or six years, maybe...'.[14]

Elsewhere he talks candidly about the pathetic conversational gambits he and other fans try on their 'heroes' when they come across them: 'And what are these clumsy, embarrassing, fumbling encounters if they are not passes, beery gropes in the dark?' But these admissions are carefully steered away from any explicitly homosexual taint. A few paragraphs earlier, when talking about the antics of groupies and comparing them to those of football fans, Hornby makes the 'confession': 'If I were a nubile twenty-year-old, I'd probably be down at the training ground throwing my panties at David Rocastle, although this kind of confession from a man, however New he is, is regrettably still not acceptable.'

For all his New Man candour, even a directly sexual expression of interest in the footballer still needs to be framed 'heterosexually'; the 'unacceptable confession' is the one that Hornby does *not* make: 'if I was *gay*'. The one he does make is no more unacceptable than the traditional joshing line from one mate to another: 'If you was a girl I'd marry you': the 'impossible' desire of man for man expressed through the impossible is not a desublimation and therefore no confession at all.

But perhaps this is to miss the point. A traditional Freudian might interpret Hornby's statement as an example of an incomplete repression of the boy's (and any boy's, not just Hornby's) 'normal' fantasy of taking the subject position of his mother in order to be loved by his father.[15] Certainly he would find further evidence of this in Hornby's dreams about another adored Arsenal player of his, Charlie George.

> I dream about George quite regularly, perhaps as often as I dream about my father [his first Dad who took him to the football game]. In dreams, as in life, he is hard, driven, determined, indecipherable; usually he is expressing disappointment in me for some perceived lapse, quite often of a sexual nature, and I feel guilty as all hell.[16]

The fan's love for the footballer is the taboo desire for the father, and since it is the desire for the father that is introjected (partly as a result of castration anxiety) and transformed into identification, it is the father who becomes the voice of the super-ego, that which says 'no'. In this way desire for the father *becomes* the prohibition. Hence it is not clear whether it is the footballer George or his father whom Hornby dreams of as 'hard, driven, determined, indecipherable', admonishing him for lapses of 'a sexual nature'; the desire to take a feminine position (desire for George?) and fear of castration (the 'hard, driven, determined' father?) are almost inseparable in the heterosexual male.

In the world of football the inability to resolve this conflict is dramatized in the struggle between the two opposing sides. For the Arsenal fans George is an object of love, representing all that is desirable in a man; 'Charlie George! Superstar! How many goals have you scored so far?'[17] To the opposing side he is a figure of hate, representing all that is to be disavowed: 'Charlie George! Superstar! Walks like a woman and wears a bra!' The ultimate 'sexual lapse', ruthlessly exploited by the other side, is the adoption of a 'feminine' subject position. It is the 'fucker not a fucked' opposition again: football is a game played between two goalposts, one 'home', the other 'away', one 'us', the other 'them', one 'love', the other 'hate': one 'masculine', one 'feminine'. But the desperate attempts to enforce that distinction only highlights the interpenetration of the two; the Pele/Moore image depends upon that of Jones/Gascoigne, but Jones/Gascoigne depends upon Pele/Moore as well. Football is a game which attempts to reassure men that the Binary Cup Final of 'Masculine Utd.' v. 'Feminine City' can be played and won by them, that these two 'teams' can be separated *within their own psyches*, just as they attempt to separate them in the all-male world of players where men like Charlie George take on diametrically opposite meanings to different sides. But while football at one level does appear to achieve this, it is enormously problematic – and perhaps it is this problematic aspect of football which many of its fans find most intriguing.

This is clearest in the failure, as in the psyches of men, to effect a complete distinction between identification and desire in the manner in which they are expected. The erotic relation of the male fans to the stars is the evidence of this; men do not merely wish to *be* the footballers but they also wish to *have* them. This is tacitly acknowledged by Hornby's collection of Soccer Stars stickers but is also present in the adult world of football, as an ad for Newcastle

Brown Ale on the back cover of *Footballer's World* hints. Eleven bottles of beer are shown in an imitation of a team picture, with a grandstand behind. Beneath, the legend: 'Newcastle Brown Ale. There is no substitute.' Surely the ad is not working on the basis that its audience wishes to *be* a bottle of beer? Male footballers are desirable, is the premise of the ad: so desirable that there is 'no substitute'. Contrary to appearances, desire on the football pitch is not tidily refereed by Oedipus.

It is 'the goal' that is the ultimate symbol of this desire. The tremendous displays of physical affection and ecstasy of male for male, on the field and in the terraces, that the placing of an inflated pig-skin in a net can provoke is either absurdly grotesque or a beautiful momentary vision of utopia according to whichever perspective you prefer. Hugging, kissing, jumping on top of one another, delirious with pleasure, young men and old, express for a moment, within the sacred walls of the football ground, a love that is as exuberant and irrepressible as it is inconceivable outside those walls. The imagery that footballers like to employ to describe that moment is well-known as sexualized. In the inimitable words of Paul Gascoigne, 'It's unbelievable, you feel like shooting your bolt.' In fact the pleasure associated by the hetero male with goals can go far beyond that associated with mere sex. For it is in the 'goal-fuck' that the player achieves both his goal of manhood – 'a fucker' – *and* the (semi-)fulfilment of his homoerotic desire – 'a fucked'.

The Sun newspaper runs a fourteen-page pull-out Goals section every Monday. It is commonly composed of a selection of reaction shots, displaying the rapture of the scoring footballer and his team-mates. With titles like MAN OF THE HOUR, HAPPY HUDDLE, WOT A HERO, CENTRE OF ATTENTION, it parades pictures of players being mobbed and embraced by their team-mates. 'Huddles' and 'attention' are the reward for being a hero – all this from other men. The photos tell a 'truth' of football – that goals are valued for what they buy the scorer in terms of masculine adoration: a few moments of being at the centre of the male gaze and on the receiving end of his body. 'WOT A HERO ... Everton's David Watson gets the goal treatment' runs the text beneath a picture of a footballer being hugged and kissed extravagantly by a fellow player. Here is the irony of masculinity in full tabloid colour: the notoriously homophobic *Sun* newspaper captures the essence of the goal moment for its (male) readers to share in – a few seconds in which men (of the scoring team) are allowed a few moments of ecstatic release of homo-desire. A 'gay' pornography for straight men, if you will; the equivalent moment of the 'money' or 'come' shot (but a homosocial rather than a homosexual 'shoot' since homosexuality here is still mostly sublimated, for reasons which will become apparent).

Reflecting on the power of a Championship-clinching goal, Hornby considers the orgasm analogy inappropriate because 'the feelings it [orgasm] engenders are simply not as intense'. He describes the 'suddenness' and the 'powerlessness' of his feeling that night and the 'communal ecstasy' of it. For the male fan, the spectator, his team scoring a goal is not just a realization of phallic ambition but a *passive* enjoyment of 'sex' and male intimacy that is unthinkable in the orthodox heterosexual bedroom.

But all this 'joy' is predicated on 'pain'; the team scored against and their fans are a study in dejection and humiliation, eyes cast down, spitting, cursing, disgusted with their team and themselves. They have all become, in a symbolic sense at least, merely 'a fucked', the shame of which isolates them as much as scoring a goal unites: the terrible private secret of the *anus*, the vulnerability of the male to penetration, has been made public. The goal mouths of each team are the acceptable representation of the male orifices that must remain hidden and guarded, admitting no entry. 'Whereas the phallus is essentially social, the anus is essentially private'.[18] This is the script of masculinity acted out by football, where goals are publicly celebrated as phallic victories and defeats as private shames.

> *They suffered from not having enough penetration and being too vulnerable at the rear.*
> ● *BBC TV football commentator*

It is the sublimated eroticism of the anus that makes men social: 'the entire Oedipus complex is anal,' writes Freud.[19] When children are forced to abandon the erotic pleasure afforded them by bowel movements and 'shit to order', they encounter the first interference with their auto-erotic libido and learn to differentiate between themselves and the world: 'Defecation affords the first occasion on which the child must decide between a narcissistic and an object-loving attitude'.[20] The child must 'sacrifice' his treasured faeces (until this point regarded as part of himself) to his love (for his mother). Potty-training requires that the child learns to dismiss the often intense eroticism associated with shitting by dismissing the anus and its products and disavowing it as a sexual organ, avowing it instead only as a shitting organ. Mel Gibson told the Spanish newspaper *El Pais* in 1992 that he was afraid his fans might think he is gay because he is an actor. 'Do I look like a homosexual? Do I talk like them? Do I move like them?' He then stood up, pointed to his arse, and said 'This is only for taking a shit.' Thus the constitution of the boy-child as a social individual, his transformation from narcissism to object-choice libido and onto the genital stage – and thus his success in the world as a man – depends on the sublimation of anality, that is *the privatization of the anus*. With so much at stake, and given Freud's contention that anality is not sublimated completely, it is perhaps to be expected that one of the most characteristic features of heterosexual men is *obsessive, paranoid concern about their own arses*.

The performance of masculinity in all its various rites, from football to war, has more to do with the anxiety a man has about the 'hole' hidden between his legs than his phallus, the possession of which he is forever advertising. If, as Quentin Crisp has suggested, homosexuality is 'the fatal flaw' in masculinity, then the anus is the fatal flaw in *men*, a physical flaw that admits the psychical one, one that they must constantly repudiate because their anus, much as they might like to pretend otherwise, is always with them. Unsurprisingly the anus itself comes to represent homosexuality, that is, homosexuality in its passive form, which is the primary meaning of homosexuality in the masculine sexual economy. The 'fatal flaw' in the masculine body that men carry around with them at all times, even when they are at their most active, only a few inches from their penis, is the access point for the fatal flaw in masculinity – homosexuality: the restoration of the desiring use of the anus.[21] Homosexuality represents not just a desublimation of homoeroticism, making scandalously visible the invisible bond that binds men together, but also a desublimation of anality, a publication of that which must be kept private about the male body, and thus a dissolution of the whole masculine sense of self – predicated as it is upon secrecy and paranoia.

> *The first thing a soldier learns is to keep his asshole shut before going into battle.*
> ● *Attributed to Norman Mailer*

The violence often associated with football is used to suggest that football is, in effect, some form of surrogate war: 'We do it because we haven't had a good war for a while,' surmised a young hooligan in a recent TV documentary. But football does not substitute for war; rather, both boy's games dramatize the paranoid anal anxieties of men and offer some kind of resolution, one more bloody than the other, in which the 'honour' of the nation and the team is really the maintenance of the masculine hymen.

Shedding some light on this phenomenon is Hornby's experience on the terraces during the Gulf War:

> The North Bank chanted 'Saddam Hussein is a homosexual' and 'Saddam runs from Arsenal.' The first message is scarcely in need of decoding; in the second, 'Arsenal' refers to the fans rather than the players. Which makes the chant self-aggrandising, rather than ridiculing, and which paradoxically reveals a respect for the Iraqi leader absent in the speculation about his sexual preference. A consistent ideology is probably too much to ask for.[22]

It goes without saying that the anecdote illustrates that the worst possible insult to man's virility is still the accusation of homosexuality. But as Hornby notes, the second chant relies on a certain respect for Hussein, which appears to contradict the first chant. But Hornby's puzzlement over this 'inconsistent' ideology stems from his belief that 'Saddam Hussein is a homosexual' needs no decoding.

In fact the homosexual represents not just something despicable and ridiculous; he is not just the man who allows himself to be fucked. He also has a secondary status in which he represents a terrible *threat* to the heterosexual male because he, for all his 'castration', still has a penis and the heterosexual male still has an anus, tingling with forbidden anality. So the fear of the heterosexual man's own anality and his own homosexuality is projected into the homosexual who becomes the anal rapist, the invader. Saddam Hussein as a 'homosexual' is a term of simple abuse: he is despicable. But Saddam also 'runs from Arsenal': the powerful dictator threatens British manhood, to 'fuck' and unman them. But they project their fear into him and 'fuck' him instead (or 'Saddamize' him as one US T-Shirt had it at the time).[23] Any victim of queer-bashing will describe how the bashers came in a group and were all armed with baseball bats or knives – straight men have *enormous* respect for the homosexual male.

But the real enemy is man's own body and his forbidden erotic relation to it. Norman Mailer is right when he says 'Being a man is the continuing battle of one's life'.[24] Man is locked in a battle against himself that has no final resolution except in death. A man can 'hardly ever assume he has *become* a man';[25] being a man is a state of constant negation, there being nothing to avow that is as significant as the disavowal. The penis can be taken away but the anus cannot – it can only be *used*. In football the anus 'pushes' men more than the phallus 'pulls' them.

This is shown in the sacrament of the free-kick line-up. The defending players stand in front of their goal, their hands over their balls, while the other side take a 'free kick'. The boys have misbehaved (i.e. committed a foul) and the referee father figure/super-ego intervenes and 'penalizes' the offenders with the threat of castration/a goal scored against them. They stand protecting their 'manhood' with their hands as if in penitent prayer while the enemy does his best to penetrate their goal; the hands that cover their testicles are also covering the entrance to that secret dark place of which the goal is the acceptable signification.

Which brings us back to the image of Jones/Gascoigne. Jones's hand is on Gascoigne's balls, but on one level – that of the anxieties of the hetero male – it might almost be up his rectum. The startled, painful expression that Gascoigne wears could easily be a caricature of anal rape; his mouth is stretched open wider than even this mouthy Geordie has ever managed before. The rape symbolism is enhanced when we hear from his coach that after the match: 'He just sat in the dressing-room staring into space, his eyes all red from rubbing away the tears. He was crying out of shock and frustration. ... He was genuinely in a deep state of shock. Anything anybody said to him to try to buck him up wouldn't sink in. That's what made us realise just how bad the experience had been, and how much it had upset him.'[26] Of course this is not anal penetration as any gay man who has experienced it knows it – this is pain, horror, humiliation: to be 'a fucked' is here equivalent to the threat of castration.

The man responsible for this display eagerly casts himself in the role of the Oedipal father who must wield the shears for the sake of his son's 'proper' development: 'I tell you. He was still a baby then and that experience helped him. Alright he got a bit upset et cetera, but he's a much stronger lad for it. He grew up within six months after I done that to 'im. I mean, I dunno, I don't know why he keeps whingeing. I think that game opened his eyes up a lot.'

It is the Oedipal plot-line of the Jones/Gascoigne image (the latter saved from blindness by his hard father's intervention) which helped to bring Gascoigne so close to the hearts of the footballing public. Thanks to the telephoto lens his transformation from boy to man was a drama they shared in, adding this image to the footballing iconography. Gascoigne's 'castration' and 'rape' could be enjoyed because they were merely symbolic threats and resolved themselves Oedipally into Gascoigne's arrival at manhood: the appearance of 'castration' on the football field can thus be harnessed to its disavowal.

The footballer's body offers the spectator another way of disavowing the possibility of rape/castration. All that running around produces a *physical* reassurance against the possibility of penetration: the famous footballer's arse. The swollen gluteus maximus and quadriceps are the strong, sturdy, vigilant 'goalkeepers' of his rectum. But as ever, the disavowal contains within it the seeds of its failure: the overdeveloped legs and arses of footballers have the effect of drawing the spectator's eye to them, so that the male rectum, his 'ass', which is after all at the centre of the physical performance of football, a fulcrum around which all the sprinting and 'ball skills' revolve, becomes the unacknowledged centre of attention. This is why the Football Association will never allow footballers to wear lycra shorts as other athletes now do – replacing the baggy shorts with sheer elasticated material would expose the footballer's rump to far too much inspection. (It is interesting to note that footballers have begun to wear these pants under their shorts. Is this because of the 'sexiness' of them – all that *clinging* – or is it because of their 'added protection'? Both, at the same time, is probably the answer.)

But for the most part the male body in its very 'maleness', both in appearance and performance, is a method of disavowal and one of the greatest 'goals' in football. The biggest insult is to be accused of looking like a 'big woman' or a 'big poof'; the greatest accolade is to 'look like a man'. 'He was built like a man,' observes the *Guardian* (6 February 1993), eulogizing the Manchester United player Duncan Edwards on the 35th anniversary of his death. A team-mate is quoted as saying 'he was not tall; but his torso and his legs, bloody hell. He was something else.' Bobby Charlton continues in the same virile theme: 'He was as near-perfect as you could get, he was like a man playing with boys.'

But the famous footballer whose body is phallicized by virtue of its solid shape is perhaps the exception: the 'beauty' of the game is precisely the way in which a player is able, by dint of stamina and 'ball skills', to appropriate to himself and his body phallic attributes that would otherwise never be his. George Best is perhaps the greatest example of this; with his slender frame and delicate looks he resembled the kind of boy bigger boys might bully just for the hell of it. But through football he became one of the most admired men in British history, one whose 'feminine' appearance became a virtue rather than a weakness, something fans from that era can remember fondly: 'Apart from the lithe grace of his body,' writes Hugh McIlvanney in *The Observer Magazine* (18 October 1992), 'his attractiveness had much to do with colouring, with the vivid blue eyes set wide in a dark, mischievous face framed by luxuriant black hair.'

Hair, that famous feature that hovers between accessory and body part, has had a particularly revealing relationship to football, showing how 'the feminine' can be accommodated and even celebrated in players by virtue of their skill. In an article on football haircuts in *Footballer's World* (No. 1, 1993) Adam Leyland sings the praises of long hair: 'Flair went out of the game when players started to have short haircuts,' he complains. Long hair is equated not with femininity but with masculine strength: 'For a flair player, his hair is his inspiration, his strength. Like "Samson and Delilah", really.' Long hair and the implied 'feminine' association become wholly appropriated by the footballer into masculine confidence; an *affectation* becomes 'flair'. 'Chrissie Waddle? Long flowing locks, like something from a Timotei advert, and with silky skills to match.' 'Chrissie' Waddle is compared to a female model in a shampoo ad but it's OK – he has 'silky skills to match'. But as ever, there turns out to be a threshold beyond which even this hair enthusiast will not step, a point of masculine no return. What might this be? Perms. 'The appalling, the embarrassing perm, which made nerds of the most fantastic players (Kevin Keegan, Charlie George) and "girlie" pansies of the toughest (Bryan Robson, Graeme Souness).' Apparently, even the most 'fantastic' and 'toughest' players cannot dribble their way out of the affront to masculine sensibilities that a perm on a footballer represents.

For all the paranoia of the football world and its zealous enforcement of a highly restrictive code of manhood, much of its appeal is bound up with what Alan Sinfield might call its fault-lines,[27] its opportunities for dissident readings: interpretations which do not reinforce the coherence of the dominant order but rather show up its contradictions and perhaps offer some escape from its diktat. This perhaps can be seen in the fascination of the fans with the 'feminine' grace and beauty of the game and its players (and their hair). The Gascoigne myth, for all his public Oedipalization discussed above, also offers an alternative reading in which his enormous popularity with tabloid readers is more than just a result of his laddishness and compulsive gurning. It has much to do with his *babyishness* – you never quite know what he will do next, burst into tears, touch his nose with his tongue or just pull out his dick and start playing with himself absent-mindedly like an infant who knows no better.

Gascoigne the footballer embodies 'unmanly' contradictions that go beyond the usual 'boys-together' prankstering that make him such a curious phenomenon: the boorishness and the sensitivity, the burping and the crying. There is an awkwardness and a hint of ambiguity about his slightly pubescent Geordie body – circumscribed, of course, by a phallic certainty (the results of his amazing 'ball skills'). Thus he is 'a highly charged spectacle on the field of play; fierce and comic, formidable and vulnerable, urchin-like and waif-like, a strong head and torso with comparatively frail looking breakable legs' but finally, 'tense and upright, a priapic monolith ...' observes Karl Miller in the *London Review of Books* (30 June 1990). Gascoigne's ambiguities are only attractive, indeed only permitted, on the basis of his phallicism; but perhaps this is to miss the point that his phallicism is only so attractive when taken in contrast with his ambiguities. This phallic-but-frail appeal of Gascoigne is something that appears to obsess journalists. Gordon Burn, writing in *Esquire* (November 1992) spends the first two paragraphs of his interview with Gascoigne ruminating on the 'fifteen-inch purple giblet' that is the scar tissue on his knee: 'The fact is that there is something unquestionably tumescent about the colour and texture and fat violent engorgement of Gazza's war-wound ...' So the very thing that symbolizes Gazza's vulnerability, the reckless and self-inflicted knee-wound that removed him from the field of play and reduced him to a tearful, prostrate blubbering mass, is itself phallicized and becomes that ultimate masculine accolade: a 'war-wound'.

Of course, there is a 'weakness' that cannot be redeemed, a 'frailty' that does not complement phallicism, a dissidence that cannot be reconciled to virility.

> *But Love has pitched its mansion in the place of excrement.*
> ● W. B. Yeats

Such is the prime importance of the footballer's body to himself and his fans that it should not be so surprising that AIDS sends them (and basketball players – cf. Magic Johnson's forced retirement) running for the showers: it is actually because they are 'big boys' that they are scared. A fatal disease, commonly believed to be caught by gay men who allow themselves to be penetrated, AIDS is the paternal law made avenging virus. A man who allows himself to be fucked, who gives in to homosexual desire and adopts a 'feminine' position, surrenders his phallic power and 'unmans' himself, and since, according to Freud, the fear of death is but a shadow of the fear of castration, the incurable and terminal prognosis for those with AIDS is merely the harsh but 'just' verdict of The Fathers.

AIDS is the nightmare that fulfils all the superstitious Oedipal anxieties of the heterosexual male, a grisly penalty for transgressing the anti-homosexual/anal erotic taboo that confirms them in all their private paranoias. Worse, in the mind of the male athlete/footballer, it not only eventually kills/castrates, but also leads to the wasting of the body that they set so much store by, publicly humiliating them.

Gay football referee Norman Redman discovered to his cost just how powerful the symbol of AIDS can be in the football world in 1987 when he refused to hide his HIV-positive status from the press, whose interest had in turn been aroused by his refusal to hide his homosexuality. A whirlwind of condemnation engulfed him and, according to *Gay Times* (January 1993), he had to move from his Sussex home to a secret address because he received 'abusive phone calls and even had excrement pushed through his letter box.'

Redman (who died of AIDS-related illness in 1993) was a gay man with 'Arse Injected Death Sentence' (as schoolboys tagged it at the time) who had the misfortune of acting as a lightning conductor to all the unsuccessfully repressed anality of the soccer world. Sublimation of anality makes shit a private thing; before sublimation the infant is likely to offer turds as gifts. In a twisted version of this, excrement is pushed through his letter-box as if to say 'Here, this shit of mine is really yours', a 'gift' that disavows anality.

Around the same time the FA provided us with another spectacle of masculine paranoia associated with 'the beautiful game' when they took it upon themselves to try to ban kissing between players after goal-scoring, on the grounds that it was 'necessary to prevent the spread of HIV'. Of course there was an element of expediency here – the old duffers at the FA had never been fond of the on-pitch puckering. But their dislike of men kissing and their hysterical fear of AIDS undoubtedly stemmed from the same familiar source: the constant need to guard against any manifestations of homosexuality. In the sad and slightly mad universe of these ghastly men, two boys kissing betokened a taint of homosexuality that might *of itself* spontaneously generate AIDS in their newly desirous anuses.

Naturally their antics had the exact reverse effect to the one they intended. They shouted to the world (which was still denying it at the time) that there were such creatures as gay footballers and drew attention to the paranoia/jealousy of these cigar sucking middle-aged men over the young studs in their charge. Freud identified something he called 'delusional jealousy' in heterosexual men, a jealousy based on the denial of homosexual desire: '*I* do not love him – it is *she* who loves him.' In the world of football, where women have been abolished, this 'jealousy' is probably directed to policing the (delusional) manifestation of homosexual desire in the players themselves, there being nowhere else to project it.

Once understood, the sublimation – threatened desublimation – sublimation pattern of football's treatment of homo-desire (i.e. repressive resublimation) becomes farcical to the point of slapstick. The *Sun* presents a full-page colour picture of 'striker' David Hirst in the classic football 'come-shot' pose, smiling wildly, arms in the air, a team-mate mounted on his back, wrapping his legs and arms around him and (apparently) kissing him. ATKY CALLED ME A POOF FOR HAVING AN EARRING screams the headline. Apparently manager Ron Atkinson disliked his players wearing earrings. 'No player of mine wears those bloody things. Only poofs have earrings,' stormed 'Atky' according to Hirst, in what would appear to be a classic display of delusional jealousy (note especially, 'no player of mine').

Even more illustrative of the pattern is the way the report begins: 'Heaven knows what they would have thought at the pit head. A Barnsley miner's son with a gold ring in his ear?' As a number of them probably wear earrings themselves it is unlikely that they would have thought anything. So the *Sun* ups the stakes and tells us, 'And when it is not an earring, it is a diamond stud.' A diamond stud no less, stone the crows! But do not be alarmed, the *Sun* quickly recoups our beloved footballer's virility by turning it into a sign of a thoroughly modern male individualism and self-assurance: 'But Sheffield Wednesday striker David Hirst is not too concerned about how Yorkshiremen should always come over like Fred Trueman.' In case this does not drive the point home, the following paragraph directs our attention to Hirst's body: 'At 13 stone and as sturdy as one of the pit props that support the Grimethorpe Colliery where his old man Eric worked at the face, you do not tend to argue the point either.'

Of course the *Sun* knows very well that this is a fake piece of 'scandal': men wearing earrings ceased to be a cause for comment in Britain more than ten years ago. This is precisely why it uses this story-line. First it offers the image of 'sturdy' Hirst in ecstasy, his chum climbing on his back, an image that relies upon the reader's sublimation of homoeroticism in order not to appear preposterous. The threat of desublimation implicit in the picture is then almost realized in the headline 'Atky called me a poof ...'. But phew, the threat turns out to be something silly about an earring. Nevertheless, the readership needs even more reassurance, so the phoney conflict between Hirst and his father is set up in the first paragraph only to be resolved by turning him into a phallic pit prop at the coal face where his father worked. The bitterest irony of the repressive resublimation game played out here is that we are reassured about Hirst's virility, his 'non-queer' status, by invoking the phallic appeal of his body (the comparison with Fred Trueman is also designed to emphasize Hirst's sexy narcissism compared to the dour pipe-smoking Yorkshireman of a pre-male glamour era). It is Hocquenghem's circle again: that which is queer is non-virile, and therefore not desirable to other men: that which is virile is not queer and therefore desirable.

> *Football is all very well as a game for rough girls, but it is hardly suitable for delicate boys.*
> ● Oscar Wilde

Football and other team sports do not appeal to many gay men. It might be argued that with their homosexuality completely (or mostly) desublimated they have no need for them; for gay men team sports are experienced not as sexualized aggression, just aggression. The rough and tumble of the sport is just that: there is no sublimated thrill to be achieved. Nevertheless there are of course many gay and bisexual men who enjoy watching and playing football. And some of them are playing it professionally, as has always been the case, though they are almost all fiercely closeted. But if the football pitch is a stage on which the only performance permitted is 'acting like a man', it seems that the casting has recently been amended to include actors who were automatically shown the red card before: 'out' homosexuals.

After an initially turbulent period in which players muttered darkly about refusing to share showers, black footballer Justin Fashanu, who came out to the *Sun* newspaper several years ago, seems to have been accepted by the sport. Homophobia 'almost never raises its head', he told the *Independent* (18 March 1992).

But what about the threat of homo-desire and anality? The fear of desublimation of the male bond? The threat of 'castration' by the 'feminising' penetration of another man which, as in Freud's case history 'Schreber', is both desired and feared at the same time? Has all this disappeared in a puff of liberal smoke? Has Fashanu by his example single-handedly changed the meaning of football? Has the phallocentric economy been disrupted?

The answer is almost certainly 'no'. The 'gay footballer' has forced a renegotiation but probably not a serious change. Male opinion, confronted with the increasing visibility of homosexuals on the sporting field, has been 'educated' to differentiate between the homosexual and Homosexuality, preserving the sexual symbolism of the sport and of masculinity itself. An 'exceptional' homosexual may be a footballer, from time to time, but Homosexuality itself is kept at bay. Alongside this, a distinction is also made between the homosexual and the Homosexual, since ironically it is the apparently 'passive' Homosexual upon whom the straight man projects his fear and fascination with his own anality/homosexuality and by whom he fears 'penetration'.

This differentiation is one that many gay men have employed themselves for years. 'I get respect,' Fashanu tells us. 'I'm not a 5′2″ effeminate stereotype. People say football is a macho business, but I think I'm very macho.'

The Fashanu phenomenon seems to have shown that the active homosexual (and it matters not one jot what Fashanu in fact *does* in his bedroom – something about which the public knows nothing – compared to how he *acts* on the field) who takes part in active sports, apparently disavowing 'the feminine' and penetration as much as if not more than his straight pals, can now gain an honorary, if uneasy, membership of the male club.[28]

> Boys or girls, up the pussy or the arse, whichever you prefer, but you've got to remember there's a cock between your legs and you're a man.

Rather than take the advice of Colin MacInnes' fictional father, the man intent on breaking away from the Oedipal triangle, the binarisms of love and hate, phallus and castration, masculine and feminine, identification and desire, active and passive, should perhaps listen instead to Leo Bersani, who in his article 'Is the rectum a grave?'[29] recommends a 'radical disintegration and humiliation of the self' similar to Hocquenghem's endorsement of homosexual anality. Bersani accepts that being penetrated renders the penetrated powerless and the penetrator powerful, but suggests that this 'castration' should be welcomed as one in which the male body can be feminized and the masculine 'moi' can be 'shattered'. This leads him to endorse the most feared and loathed image society has of the homosexual male: the 'seductive' and 'intolerable image of a grown man, legs high in the air, unable to refuse the suicidal ecstasy of being a woman'.

This strategy, it has to be admitted, is unlikely to win any football matches.

Notes

1. From an unpublished novel, quoted in Tony Gould, *Inside Outsider: The Life and Times of Colin MacInnes* (London: Chatto and Windus, 1983), p. 89.

2. Quoted in *New Statesman and Society*, 19 March 1993.

3. Simon Barnes, 'The harder they come', *Esquire*, November 1992.

4. Nick Hornby, *Fever Pitch: A Fan's Life* (London: Victor Gollancz, 1992), p. 11.

5. *Ibid.*, p. 11.

6. Eve Kosofsky Sedgewick, *Between Men: English Literature and Male Homosexual Desire* (New York: Columbia University Press, 1985) (quoted in Lynne Segal's *Slow Motion*, p. 143).

7. Guy Hocquenghem, *Homosexual Desire* (London: Allison and Busby, 1978), p. 106.

8. Hornby, p. 28.

9. 5 January 1993.

10. Hornby, p. 16.

11. *Ibid.*, p. 27.

12. Derek Hatton, *Inside Left* (London: Bloomsbury, 1988), quoted in Lynne Segal's *Slow Motion* (London: Virago, 1990), p. 127.

13. *Ibid.*, p. 15.

14. *Ibid.*, p. 123.

15. Freud, *The Ego and the Id*.

16. Hornby, p. 169.

17. *Ibid.*, p. 58.

18. Guy Hocquenghem, *Homosexual Desire*, p. 82.

19. Freud, 'On Narcissism: An Introduction'.

20. Freud, 'On Transformations of Instinct as Exemplified by Anal Eroticism'.

21. Hocquenghem, *Homosexual Desire*, p. 84.

22. Hornby, p. 239.

23. Even the name, Arse-nal (as it is chanted), conjures up this aggressive denial of anality. It is the perfect football club name since it conjures up that which is at the centre of the sport – the male anus – and then turns it into an aggressive phallic thing (an Arsenal, a place where weapons are kept), i.e. sublimates it (the symbol of the team is a cannon and their nickname is 'the Gunners').

24. Norman Mailer, *Advertisements for Myself* (New York: Putnam, 1959), p. 222.

25. Norman Mailer, *Prisoner of Sex* (Boston: Little, Brown and Co., 1985), p. 168.

26. 'Gazza: the interview', *Esquire*, November 1992.

27. Alan Sinfield, *Faultlines: Cultural Materialism and the Politics of Dissident Reading* (Oxford: Clarendon Press, 1992).

28. Fashanu's blackness is, of course, a matter of importance as well, perhaps fitting him into a racist white fantasy of 'exotic' otherness. Also, his statements about bisexuality perhaps help to frame him, in the public's mind, as a 'fucker': i.e. 'boys or girls, up the pussy or the arse'.

29. Leo Bersani, 'Is the rectum a grave?', *October*, 1987, No. 43.

Chapter five

Narcissus Goes Shopping
Homoeroticism and Narcissism in Men's Advertising

'The other boys check you out, when you're a boy.'
● David Bowie

'Why, just the thought of boffing some hairy boy makes me sick all over.'

'Not all boys are hairy as you,' I said gaily, recklessly. Mary-Ann looked surprised while Rusty looked uneasy at this reminder of our old intimate encounter. I turned to Mary-Ann. 'It's positively coquettish the way his top two buttons are always missing.'

She was relieved. 'Men are so vain,' she said, looking at him fondly.

'But in America only women are supposed to worry about their appearance. The real man never looks into a mirror. That's effeminate. . . .' I teased them.

'Well, that's *changing*, I guess.' Mary-Ann brought Rusty's hand to her lips. 'And I'm just as glad. I think men are beautiful.'

'So does Rusty,' I could not help but observe.

95: Narcissus Goes Shopping

'Oh, shit, Miss Myra,' was the boyish response. Soon.
Soon. Soon.

● *Gore Vidal, Myra Breckinridge*[1]

NINETIES man, it almost goes without saying, exhibits no bashfulness about gazing at his own reflection – ask any girl who has been locked out of the bathroom by her preening brother. Nor is this self-regarding something that he keeps private. He is to be seen parading in front of mirrors in High Street clothes shops and examining his new haircut in the salon mirror with the kind of absorbed concentration that his fathers might have reserved for the football results. In fitness studios and gymnasia, meanwhile, he pets, pampers and provokes his reflection in full-length wall-mirrors into a shape he finds more appealing.

When not in front of the mirror you will find him at the chemist, stocking up on goods designed to prolong and heighten the ecstasy of his union with his reflection in the bathroom mirror. Shaving equipment (electric, cut-throat and disposable) and access-ories (foams, gels, cremes, pre- and post-shave balms, aftershaves and colognes); hair products (shampoos, conditioners, sealants, hot oils, gels, mousse, pomade); soaps (medicated, hypoallergenic, vitamin-E added) and cleansers, astringents, moisturisers, anti-wrinkle creme, eye-gel, deodorant (perfumed and unperfumed, aerosol, stick, gel and ball), toothpaste, teeth whitener, dental floss, and even make-up. All clearly and proudly labelled 'for men' or 'pour homme', just in case someone should be so old-fashioned as to mistake these for *feminine* products.

But the marital aids the modern male buys do not manage to disguise his dissatisfaction with his love life. For all his apparent bliss, the modern male's narcissistic love-affair is a sham. Deep down he knows that his heart does not belong to the dowdy, all-too human face that peers blearily at him in the bathroom mirror every morning. Instead his real affections are reserved for the idealized, immortal image of himself that is reflected back at him in the million brilliant mirrors of magazines, newspapers, advertising hoardings, TV, cinema and video. And of course, the idealized reflection, with its flashing teeth, silky hair, tanned flawless skin and sculpted body, is promoting the very products – shaving accessories, shampoos, soaps, etc. – that remind our mortal man of his imperfection by bringing him back to his own humdrum reflection and thus feeding his longing for the idealized form.

This is the secret behind the growth of male narcissism in Western society. Nineties man's love affair with his own image, which is itself a misrecognition (to love one's image is not to love oneself), is but a faint echo of his love for what he takes to be his idealized form reflected from the billboards and cinema screens. The products and accessories offer a link that appears to marry the three kinds of 'self' together that modern media separates: the idealized form (the model using the product), the reflected images (looking in the mirror while using the product), and the actual body (wearing the product or applying it to skin, hair, teeth etc.). Ideal, image and body thus come together in a consummation of a love that only money can buy. Of course, this is not a consummation at all: all three types of self are kept distinct, and the imperfection of image and body next to ideal ensures that desire is never satisfied and that the consumer never loses his appetite.

According to Greek myth Narcissus was told by the blind seer Teiresias when he was a child that he should live to a great age if he never knew himself. Narcissus grew up to be a beautiful young man but proud and haughty. An embittered youth, unrequited in his love for Narcissus, cursed him to love that which could not be obtained. One day on Mount Helicon Narcissus caught sight of his own reflection 'endowed with all the beauty that man could desire and unawares he began to love the image of himself which, although itself perfect beauty, could not return his love.'[2] Narcissus, worn out by the futility of his love, turned into the yellow-centred flower with white petals named after him.

The myth tells us something about the relation of modern man to his own image. Narcissus is not seduced by his reflection in any common pool – he glimpses and falls in love with his reflection on Mount Helicon, the sacred mountain where Apollo, Artemis and the Muses danced: the symbolic centre of the *arts*. His reflection is not one of nature but an idealized image refracted through man's art. Thus his image is 'endowed with all the beauty that man could desire' and he falls in love with it. And like nineties Western man, Narcissus finds that it is a love that 'could not be obtained'.

But this doom of Narcissus could also be read as a punishment for a *failure* of identification. Having spurned the desire of one young man, Narcissus finds himself desiring 'unawares' that which he should identify with – his own image. In a sense, the use of the name Narcissus to describe self-love is inaccurate: Narcissus consciously loved not himself, nor even his image. Teiresias' prophecy, as is so often the case in Greek myth, was less than helpful. He told Narcissus that he should live to a great age if he never knew himself. In fact, it was Narcissus' ignorance of himself that ended his life: 'unawares he began to love the image of himself'.

Above all, the story of Narcissus, instead of illustrating what is meant by self-love, points up rather the confusion and slippage between homo-desire and self-love. His inability to return the love of the young man led, through the bitterness of the young man at the realization that he could not possess Narcissus' beauty sexually, to his entrapment in a homoerotic attachment to an image he failed to realize was his own. Both young men's disappointment is the result of (homo)sexual frustration.

Mount Helicon today is the modern media. It offers men idealized reflections of the masculine form 'endowed with all the beauty that man could desire' which, in an inversion of Narcissus' story, they are expected to misrecognize as their own: identification is supposed to supplant desire. But like Narcissus, their melancholy stems from the same confusion of desire and identification and the frustration of homo-desire.

The invert's striptease

In 1985 Nick Kamen washed everything but his birthday suit in front of the British viewing public and announced to the world that the male body had been discovered/uncovered and was literally up for grabs.

The new campaign for Levis in the UK, launched with *Launderette*, increased sales by 800 per cent in the first five months.[3] A powerful new force had clearly been tapped by the advertising agency responsible, Bartle Bogle. In addition to its astonishing success, the boldness of the campaign and the massive media response it created made it appear as if the revolution in the representation of the male body had been invented by them.

It had not, of course. Like the nostalgia their ads exploited, their treatment of the male body took its reference points from the 1950s, from films like *A Streetcar Named Desire*.

> Quite astonishingly, the gum-chewing pop-corn consuming hordes of the remotest hinterlands have accepted a new archetype of love (projected ideally by Anna Magnani and Marlon Brando) in which an aging slovenly, aggressive woman in a black slip – vainly assaults the innocence of a clean, incorruptible young man without a shirt. In ten thousand movie houses the moment in which that infinitely desirable youth strips to the waist has come to represent the expected climax of the more arty film. His invert's strip-tease takes place, of course, in a decaying clapboard house, outside of which the Spanish moss hangs ghost-like in the Southern night.[4]

It was the 1950s that put the naked young male stud in front of the camera for the first time. It was the 1950s that invented another way to sell close-ups of young men: rock and roll. It was the 1950s that invented the mass consumerism that turned 'feminizing' men into big business. And it was the 1950s that invented that ultimately desirable product (and consumer): the 'teenager'.

Bartle Bogle and the host of other advertisers who followed in their wake took the nostalgia for the 'innocence' that era came to represent in the 1980s but used it to present the flip side of the 1950s myth – *awakened desire*.

The product itself embodied this. Jeans in the 1950s were a signifier of the desirable young man, 'the rebel' (the first shot of Kamen in *Launderette* is of his jean-clad crotch). Issued to GI's in the Second World War and the Korean War, they became popular with the men and were worn, so the story goes, by those who went on to attend college on the GI Bill. Jeans thus became associated with the young man who had 'seen the world' and lost his innocence and his dependence on his family – a self-assured *individual* intent on pleasing himself. A male with the privileges of manhood and the freedom/ambiguity of boyhood: a male symbolizing awakening desire, untrammelled and outside of family regulation. Thus the young American male in jeans became a symbol of rebellion – rebellion against the de-sexing of the masculine image that had gone before, a public statement of the desirability of the male body.

Not surprisingly the 1950s was also the birthplace of modern gay male culture, itself intimately linked to the development of mass consumerism. Hence gay men had kept the flame for the 1950s long after their fashionability waned. Leather jackets from *The Wild Ones*, jeans from *Giant* and T-shirts from *Streetcar* had remained constant features of the gay scene on both sides of the Atlantic. This iconography also fed into the 'clone' look of the late 1970s and early 1980s: motorcycle boots, white T-shirts, hair cropped to look like a Korean War draftee, and well-worn and possibly ripped Levis 501 jeans. It was no coincidence that this image (bar the moustache but including the earring) became a mainstream male fashion in the 1980s or that the Levis campaign that was in the vanguard of this 'homosexualization' of young men (tender young men between 16 and 24 at that)[5] was spearheaded by the 'invert's striptease'.

Of course, gay men, like blacks, as an 'extravagant' minority on the margins of society, had long provided a rich supply of fashions for capitalism to appropriate and bring into the mainstream. But in the 1980s straight men were no longer being sold just cologne or disco: instead the whole package was being promoted – the queer *lifestyle*, the individual young man indulging his desires outside the heterosexual family.

Narcissistic, sexy, single young men happy to throw their clothes off for the camera became the advertising ideal. Nick Kamen, as well as stripping for us, is *doing his own washing*. Where is his mother or girlfriend, the 'little woman' who in ad-land takes care of this kind of chore for her man? He is single, unafraid, flouting respectability and passively inviting our gaze: he is 'queer' – his sexuality is outside regulation. In *Bath*, another Levis ad released at the same time, the dangerous singleness of the male subject is made explicit: a half-naked man wakes up alone, except for our voyeuristic gaze, in his single man's flat.

Of course, these men/boys are not completely beyond control, they are not *that* queer. Their 'promotion of homosexuality' is framed in such a way as to blur desire into identification, to reassure the boys buying homoeroticism that they are making a heterosexual identification. In *Launderette* Nick Kamen is given an audience of giggling girls, marking him as heterosexual, mediating his image, and giving the male viewer an opportunity to enjoy the 'invert's striptease' from a heterosexual perspective, imagining he is viewing the male body through the girl's eyes. In *Bath* a similar technique is employed: the model gazes wistfully at a framed photo of a girl on his desk.[6]

But even the heterosexual framing of these ads is at best ambiguous, given its context. In *Launderette* a young boy sitting reading a comic next to the door is the first spectator we see. When Kamen enters, his crotch is at the boy's head level; the boy turns to look up at him, then he and his twin brother follow Kamen to the washing machine, watching him intently (although they are scooted away by a harassed mother who gives Kamen a *filthy* look conveying, perhaps, in its mixture of envy, desire and disdain, the look heterosexual society gives the queer). In *Bath* the male viewer's voyeurism of the male body is not excused by the presence of any women spectators. A Peeping Tom, he watches unobserved as an attractive young man wakes up, strolls around his room showing off his stunning torso, performs some chin-ups, demonstrating his strength and showing off his biceps and back to best effect. The ad ends with the camera looking down on him relaxing, stretched out in a bath, still wearing his jeans.

The ad is an extraordinary prick- (and cunt-) tease from beginning to end. The window to his 1950s apartment (probably in Manhattan) is open (inviting); this and his semi-nudity combine with the 'atmosphere' of the ad to suggest oppressive sticky heat. His chin-ups, given the heat, are deliciously perverse, but not nearly so delicious as the *release* represented by the bath, which appears to be filled with cold water. If the heat is a sensuous narrative, the bath is its climax: the model lies back in the bath, his head falling back over the edge in abandoned ecstasy. The bath image also tantalizes by suggesting total nudity/his prick but failing to produce it. The image itself has 'transgressive' connotations: he is taking a bath in his jeans. The 'naughtiness' of this is amplified by the audience's identification with the illicit infantile sensation of letting water soak through their pants. A police siren even wails in the distance to underline the forbiddenness of this *frisson*.

The sound-track plays Sam Cooke's 'Wonderful World', in which he croons of an unrequited love and how 'if you loved me too/What a wonderful world this would be'. The male viewer's desire for the model is given resonance by the lyrics as well as reminding us that this desire, like Narcissus' for his reflection, is an impossible love that can never be reciprocated ('*if* you loved me too'). The impossibility of that love is further stressed by the shot of him looking at the photo of the girl. But this tiny photo, given the extraordinary queerness already elaborated, is a pathetic attempt to stabilize the ad in terms of heterosexuality. Where is she? Why is she not there to protect him from the queer gaze of all these men (and women)? Is she even his girlfriend? Is she perhaps a sister or merely the 'Good Girl' fiancée whose 'tragic death' gay bachelors in the 1950s used to explain their single status? All we can say with any certainty is that the poor boy is *lonely*, a passive condition inviting attention. Thus the very device which is supposed to serve as a stabilizing effect actually introduces more instabilities.

Later Levis ads have been much more careful in their framing. *Swimmer* (1992) offers the same enjoyment of the male body as in *Launderette* and *Bath*; this time another hard-muscled attractive young man coolly dives into a series of private swimming pools wearing only his pair of 501s. While exploiting the same visual sensuality as in *Bath*, in the form of wet jeans, *Swimmer* makes sure that, as in *Launderette*, admiring women look on. But the ad goes much further than *Launderette* in its attempt to bleach out any homosex stain. The sound-track, 'Mad About the Boy', is sung by a female; 'Grapevine' and 'Wonderful World' are both sung by men. The admiring women also have husbands who witness his appearance with jealousy/anger; the swimmer is to be enjoyed from the heterosexual subject position of the women but with the added guarantee of the *disapproval* of the heterosexual men. One man *is* allowed to enjoy the spectacle of the swimmer, but as an undesirable faintly ridiculous old queen his presence is tolerated merely to emphasize the otherness of the queer. His otherness to the hetero male audience and the swimmer is ironically used to point up the desirability of the swimmer.

Nicely wrapping up this narrative, the model dives from a high board, magically joined by a young female swimmer (whom we do not see clearly). The final shot is a determinedly heterosexual disavowal of any queer enjoyment of earlier close-ups showing water cascading down the swimmer's body, as the man and woman dive into the water together in cold, graceful slow motion (compare the cool chasteness of this use of water with the queer heat of *Bath*).

The signification of heterosexuality in ads like *Swimmer* is not simply employed to disperse any queer implications; rather it is used to draw a veil over the queer reading while exploiting it at the same time. Quite often the signification of heterosexuality is used fairly cynically to confirm the masculinity and hence the desirability of the male model to the audience.

A campaign for Calvin Klein men's underwear (1992–93) includes black and white billboard posters of white rap star Marky Mark wearing only a pair of Calvin Klein Y-fronts, grinning and laughing at the camera, mouth open, in an inviting way. But ironically this is arguably not the most homoerotic ad in which he features. This accolade goes to another b/w ad in the Calvin Klein campaign, featured in the men's magazine *GQ* (US edition, November 1992). This time Marky is wearing Calvin Klein jeans, beltless and lowered just enough to show off the top third of his Calvin Klein briefs, and, of course, the logo. He is naked from the designer waistband up, and is lit craftily from above to emphasize his upper musculature, outlining his deltoids, biceps and triceps.

But this time he is joined by a woman, British 'supermodel' Kate Moss. Like him she is topless and stands alongside him, apparently leaning on him. While her presence might help to defuse surface anxieties about the homoerotic quality of the exploitation of Marky Mark's body, on another level she actually increases the homoerotic charge by contrasting the fragility of her frame with the massiveness of his. Even next to her his overdeveloped body is still not swollen enough, so she is positioned sideways-on to the camera, thinning out her image even more. Her head is perched on his shoulder, looking over her own towards the camera, half profile, with an almost frightened expression, her mouth half-open: Marky Mark gazes manfully straight at the camera, eyes half-closed, lips fully closed, with his lower jaw jutting arrogantly forward. Moss is just a flattering contrast, positioned by photographer Herb Ritts to throw Marky's awesome body, his awesome *virility*, into sharper, more desirable relief.

Compare Marky's pose and expression accompanied by a woman to his solo shots: alone he laughs at the camera, mouth open, eyes smiling, body relaxed; with Moss he frowns, lids his eyes, stiffens his body and puffs it out as far as it will go. When framed alone for our voyeuristic enjoyment his appeal depends on his easy boyishness which can be 'taken' any way you like it; with the female model his image rigidifies into an almost hysterical statement of sexual difference in which his appeal is based squarely on the visual evidence that he is not female: look how much more attractive, how much more *substantial* boys are compared to girls, the picture seems to be saying.

It is also interesting to note that in his solo pictures Marky Mark contravenes the codes of male pin-ups suggested by Richard Dyer.[7] According to Dyer, male pin-ups 'more often than not do not look at the viewer. ... When they do, what is crucial is the kind of look it is, something very often determined by the set of the mouth that accompanies it. When the female pin-up returns the viewer's gaze, it is usually some kind of smile, inviting. The male pin-up , even at his most benign, still stares at the viewer ... seems to reach beyond and through and establish himself.'

The code Dyer describes is adopted only in the picture of Marky Mark with Kate Moss. Taken with the solo photo that appears to breach the code – he is smiling, inviting and his eyes appeal very directly *to* the viewer – the sudden return to the code in the presence of a woman turns the code into an ironic statement that undermines rather than asserts his active male heterosexuality.

Strangely enough, the contrast between the two models, designed to establish his masculine hetero status *vis-à-vis* the feminine body of Moss, focuses upon the breasts. Moss's half-turn away from the camera has the effect of putting her breasts in profile and shadow, diminishing their size and significance, as well as blurring her left nipple, the only one we can see. Marky Mark's chest is offered to us full-frontal, the light bouncing off its air-brushed skin, occupying the centre of our vision, the shadows under his pecs outlining their massiveness, acting as sight-lines drawing in the gaze to those ripe, firm (apparently) erect nipples which are so much more 'substantial' than the female model's.

It is worth recalling that not so long ago the male breast was officially erotically neutral, as sexually redundant as the nipples on them, while the female breast had achieved the status of universal (at least in Western countries) signifier of sex. Female 'tits and bums' were fetishized to the point of pathology in the media – especially tits. The merest visual reference to cleavage was expected to produce excitement in males just as surely as the presence of a milky nipple would produce salivation in a baby. The first modern men's magazine *Playboy* was launched in 1953 with Marilyn Monroe's famous pneumatic breasts splashed across the front cover. Forty years later the men's magazine *Penthouse* devotes its cover to Marky Mark's pumped pectorals (with another topless female model). What a transformation!

But the male breast now hangs in a kind of limbo where it is acknowledged both as erotic and yet not erotic, an ambiguous state which facilitates its appeal beyond women and gay men to *heterosexual* men. On the cover of *Penthouse* magazine Marky's breasts are presumably there to be looked at pleasurably by heterosexual men and yet this would not be possible were it not also the case that for them the eroticism of his breasts can be disavowed: 'Those are a man's breasts and therefore they are erotically neutral to me as a heterosexual man and I may gaze at them without anxiety.'

The contrast between the modern representations of male and female breasts is demonstrated further by Britain's *Esquire* men's magazine (November 1992). It features a topless male, with a chest as overdeveloped as any Jayne Mansfield, advertising aftershave; his body, and in particular his chest, occupies most of the page: clearly it is not considered a neutral image. Overleaf a female model advertises another brand, and while the image is stereotypically sexualized (wearing a blue jacket and apparently naked underneath, she is in a traditional 'orgasmic' soft porn pose, hand between parted legs, head thrown back, lips apart), in contrast to the explicit presentation of the man's chest in which no detail is hidden, all we can do is glimpse her cleavage darkly through her jacket. The curious double erotic/non-erotic official status of the male breast actually allows it to be more exploited/enjoyed than the female variety.

Torso trouble

The use of topless male models in adverts promoting products targeted at men has become astonishingly popular in the

1990s. In addition to Levis 501 and Calvin Klein underwear, Italian jeans label Energie ran a campaign showing a topless male torso clad only in a pair of beltless jeans, apparently dancing or in some state of physical excitement representing 'joy' or 'vigour'. As if apologizing for the fact that the model had to wear anything at all, the top two buttons of his fly are undone and let us in on the secret that this boy is wearing no underwear. In fact the only thing he appears to have on under those jeans is a hint of a tattoo, tantalisingly glimpsed over the top of his jeans. Beneath the legend: 'Energie, Jeans and Transgression'.

What is the transgression invoked here? Could this be the transgression of the 'queer' male again, the young man outside of society, taking his pleasures where he pleases? And more specifically could this be, like the tattoo, a hint at something just hidden, something forbidden? The unspoken and unspeakable premise that all these torso ads depend upon is the model's phallus and the homoerotic/narcissistic desire it symbolizes for the male viewer.

In his 'Sexual Theories of Children' Freud suggests that boy children believe that all humans have penises. This appendage seems such a vital piece of equipment to a boy (who has already discovered some of the joy that it can bring him, both in looking and touching) that when he discovers that his mother is without one he disavows this, refusing to accept that she could be so 'lacking' since the very possibility arouses anxieties about losing his own. One strategy employed by the little boy is fetishism, where some other item, such as fur or his mother's foot, stands in for lack.

Some feminists, following Lacan, have pointed out the way in which (male) Hollywood denies anxiety about the female's lack by 'accessorizing' her.[8] Women's accessories, in other words, become fetishized. (Just as do parts of her body such as 'tits and bums' – the accessorization of the female proceeds from an accessorization of her body.)

But the male has the phallus: how could clothes/accessories come to substitute for the phallus in an advert like Energie's, which features the male body? The answer is in the way nudity of the male body promises the phallus but never actually produces it. Instead we are offered the product, the accessory which compensates for the 'lack' that the image presents. Gay men have long understood the way in which the male body can be fetishized through accessories which perhaps in their youth came to stand in for the penis that was hidden from view (as Christian modesty dictates): personal columns often feature men looking for 'heavy boot sex', or 'swimming trunks enthusiasts'.

The 'castration' of the torso ads is more than hinted at. In a style which appears mandatory for almost all topless male ads not featuring a celebrity such as Marky Mark, the top of the page slices off the model's head just below the chin. It is a *faceless* body: a body, a torso, a *butchered* man. Givenchy's Xeryus *eau de toilette* (*Esquire*, November 1992), Chanel's Antaeus *pour homme* (poster campaign, December 1992), and Calvin Klein's Obsession, 'For men. For the body' (*GQ*, US edition, November 1992) all feature faceless slabs of masculine meat. But the aftershave torso ads are not merely topless, but *bottomless* as well – the model is clearly completely naked (unlike the Energie ad), but his penis is not there; just like the model's head, it has been cut off by the edge of the page. Without the accessorizing of the product and the phallicizing of the torso these might be rather unpleasant images for men to look at.[9]

The truncating is contradictory in its visual effect: it 'castrates' the male body and yet helps to phallicize it. With the head and legs and arms gone, the hard phallic muscularity of the body is an even starker, sharper, more powerful image. In the Energie ad it seems to be literally rising out of the jeans, the missing raised arms implying some kind of flight (again a phallic image).

The dismemberment of these bodies, while deploying the desire of the male viewer towards the product in the fashion described, also helps to disavow its queerness. The absence of the phallus helps to maintain the pretence that this is not what is desired, while the absence of a head allows the male viewer to imagine his own in its place, thus forging desire into identification.

But the body's mutilation has other effects. It has no face, so desire for it is nameless. It has no head, so it is an object, and the male viewer's desire does not place him in a passive position in relation to it. The absence of a mouth is another disavowal – contrast this with the Ungaro ad of the woman: she has legs, arms and a mouth, open and inviting. The male model is not allowed an orifice, for this would provoke too much anxiety about penetration. This is also part of the phallicization of the body: it is so hard and powerful that it has no openings, no points of access.

The active/passive, straight/queer conundrum thrown up by these images of men has no easy resolution; the effect is complex, often contradictory. For example the headless torso might 'murder' the projected queer desire of the male viewer at the very moment of facilitating the enjoyment of it: the headless man has no eyes, so the man gazing at him is not observed (sustained looking between men has an aggressive challenge attached to it in straight male society); nor are his fantasies about what he might like to do to this naked male flesh witnessed.

Most ironic of all is the possibility that the decapitation/depersonalization of the model allows the male viewer to substitute any face and fantasy he desires (including his own: marrying narcissism and homoeroticism) to make a perfect vision of a queer Eros. In much the same way as women have tended to be photographed for male consumption as 'Woman', *the* object of desire, *the* perfect female body, rather than *a* woman,[10] these men are the 'essence' of masculinity: *the* desired male body. In fact this technique has long been understood by advertisers in the gay press who have often employed photos and drawings of headless idealized male bodies, allowing the punters to complete the fantasy themselves. In effect, advertisers of gay saunas in the gay press and expensive men's aftershave in *GQ* both exploit the power and attractions of *anonymous gay sex*: nameless, faceless, endless desiring.

Hidden appeal

The taboo nature of homoeroticism is not merely an issue of custom or ignorance. It isn't just advertising aimed at men that requires queer desire to remain unspoken. In fact the whole category of masculinity depends upon queer desire remaining *secret*: homoeroticism is intimately connected to the whole apparatus of masculine power, both in terms of images and operation. As Freud pointed out, not only is its sublimation vital to the functioning of male society and the development of the super-ego, but its remaining unspoken and hidden is necessary to its own operation. Explicit homoeroticism defeats itself as, according to heterosexuality, that which is masculine is not queer. This is something inherent in the nature of power itself. As Foucault put it, 'the success of power is proportional to its ability to hide its own mechanisms ... for its secrecy is not in the nature of an abuse; it is indispensable to its operation.'[11]

So a feature in *The Independent on Sunday* (December 1992), illustrated by the Antaeus torso, examining the recent trend of using 'boys with the bodies of prizefighters and the career-structure of starlets' in ads targeting men, takes as *a priori* that none of the men seeing these ads could respond to them sexually: not only are there no queers in the world presented in this article – there is no queer desire either. Instead, women magically intervene between men and their viewing of images of naked male bodies (which feature no women) in order to heterosexualize the looking: 'I suppose women are getting choosier these days', one man is quoted as saying.

Men's style magazines, whose *raison d'être* is to provide images of attractive men to be looked at by other men, are acutely aware of the imperative to disavow homosexuality, and endeavour to protect their readers from any disclosure of the *existence* of homoeroticism, let alone the possibility that it could be implicated in their enjoyment of the magazine.

As an example, picked out more or less at random, *For Him* magazine (February 1993) sports a fashion spread of a type common to these magazines. Ten pages of glossy large-format photos entitled 'New York Story' sell us a *fin de siècle* Italian immigrant look (without, needless to say, the immigrant price tag – a suede overshirt costs £500). The spread features two suitably classic Latin-looking young male models. The blurb tells us, 'Giuseppe and Tony walk the streets of New York City – homeboys looking for the good times in this land of opportunity.' The following pages show our 'homeboys' walking the streets arranged in a variety of *faux* proletarian/peasant designer workwear, the New York skyline beckoning behind them. But never in the same picture. These poor lonely Italian boys who are so obviously made for each other (they apparently even shop at the same tailor) never actually get to meet. The 'New York Story' is a tragedy. The 'good times' these boys seek in the Big City, like millions of other single, well-dressed boys before them, are always just out of their grasp: the realization of homoeroticism must remain always just out of reach. The final image is appropriately bitter-sweet: Tony stands alone and expectantly in his best suit and straw boater, clutching a bunch of flowers. Will Giuseppe finally turn up? We will never know.

Frustrated by all this coyness? Turn to page 81 in the same issue and read 'Night Moves' by Tony Warden, a 'no holds barred' enquiry into sex introduced by the tag line, 'In an ideal world sex would be propelled by such an intense passion that simply *everything* would not only be acceptable but also enjoyable.' Great! *Now* you're talking! Except he isn't. Not about male homosexuality. Not once. The 'frank' discussion turns out to be resolutely directed at an equally resolute (mostly imaginary) straight male reader. When discussing threesomes the piece goes out of its way to stress the preferability of finding 'two willing women' rather than another man and a woman (naturally, three men is inconceivable). You are advised to 'sniff out' your 'girlfriend's' past for 'any vague lesbian leanings' (notice the double safety of 'vague' and 'leanings'), while it is taken for granted that any threesome scenario involving the male reader and another man and woman would not even involve the vaguest gay 'leanings'.

This is why the torso ads are so remarkable. The nudity of the aftershave models, for all its built in fail-safes and disavowals, is *clearly* sexual, available to be desired in a way that is undifferentiated. Unlike ads for jeans or underwear, these ads have no requirement for any clothes whatsoever, so there are none. What the Energie jeans ad can only hint at through a couple of undone buttons, the aftershave ad can state freely and provocatively. And this is the way it should be. Scent has always been the commodity closest to sex: an insubstantial but overpowering quality; a signifier of receptive skin and desirable flesh; a promise of the body. Perhaps the reason for the recent extraordinary popularity of the male torso with aftershave advertisers is the exquisite lean economy of the image: a 'body' which is undressed; a myth made flesh; ethereal and corporeal, overpowering and yet available, cool and *arousing*. And like scent itself, something that registers in the consciousness of men *and* women, hetero *and* homo.

The myth has a history as well, carefully encoded. It is Hellenic. The torsos are lit and photographed in such a way as to portray them as living marble, breathing statues of Apollo and Hercules. And just as the mythology is Greek, so is the Eros. They

are artefacts of the male body, made by male hands, for the enjoyment of other males. Like the women in Ancient Greece the women
in the world of these ads are elsewhere. The names themselves
speak in pagan accents: Xeryus, Minotaure, Antaeus. They represent a masculinity that is narcissistic in both aesthetics and psychology: Antaeus was a giant who wrestled with any stranger that
passed his way, invulnerable *so long as he remained in contact with
his mother* Gaia, the earth (Hercules choked him to death by holding him off the ground). Antaeus' strength (and his weakness), in
other words, flowed from his narcissistic relationship with his
mother.

And, true to Greek standards of masculine beauty, these
aftershave bodies offer us cool, white, boyish *smoothness*. Rusty's
dislike for hirsuteness was shared by the ancients: the thought of
'boffing some hairy boy' would probably have made them 'sick all
over' too.

The best a man can get

Shaving is perhaps the last non-religious masculine initiation
ceremony in the Western world. Certainly it is the only one intimately involving fathers (excepting, of course, fathers who model
themselves on Hemingway novels and procure their son's first
woman). From an early age boys are fascinated by the ritual their
father enacts before the bathroom mirror every morning, and the
paraphernalia associated with it. Many play-shave long before their
cheeks begin to bristle, sensing that there is something almost magical about this manly preparation for the day and the world, without
which their fathers cannot leave the house, and look forward to the
time when this sacred daily rite of masculinity will be part of their
own lives.

Long before they learn the secrets of sex, boys learn to
regard shaving as the signifier of manhood, marking the boundary
between boys and men. And in a sense they are right: whiskers and
the rituals associated with them are the socially acceptable
reminder of a man's 'balls'; a constant reminder on a man's *face* of
his *body*; a secondary sexual characteristic that is irrefutable evidence of the presence of that vital manly essence, testosterone.

Traditionally, when the time finally arrives for the adolescent male's first shave, it is the father who teaches him this holy craft. While a father may be unable or unwilling to involve himself in his son's awakening sexuality, he can teach his son how to shave, how to control the visible indicator of that maturing sexuality. And as with much other father-son/male-male activity, an expression of physical tenderness is presented as a 'doing' thing, something practical and necessary. It is also a tenderness balanced by a shadowy terror. The tutorial has certain primal resonances. In effect, the father is instructing his son how to wield a blade/knife (less evident now that cut-throat razors have been all but replaced by safety razors) with all that may involve of visions of the hunt, the kill and perhaps a residual Oedipal castration anxiety.

The very expression 'clean cut' connotes a ritual wounding such as circumcision (itself a symbolic castration, a sign of the Law of the Father). The idea of civilization itself is suggested by shaving: not just the initiation into the culture of manhood but also the triumph of order over chaos, artifice over nature. The razor is the most masculine of tools: cunning, sharp, true, ruthless; cutting back the primitive, bestial, bristles. This latter idea includes the contradiction culture represents for men: it is something to be both proud of as evidence of man's prowess – his victory over nature – and resented as enervating and feminine – his exile from nature. This is also the contradiction of mass consumerism for men: it must appeal to their sense of manhood, their desire for masculine attributes, but only in order to persuade them to adopt ever more luxurious commodities that bind them passively to a 'soft' civilization.

An ad from the 1940s for shaving soap solicits men to 'Try "Jif" for a Real Man's Shave'. Shaving is immediately associated with 'authentic' masculinity. But the contradiction of shaving is brought out in the copy below: 'Try Pears "Jif" and you will find that you've never used a shaving stick that lathered so quickly, softened the beard so thoroughly and gave such a smooth and comfortable shave.' 'Softened', 'smooth' and 'comfortable': all words suggesting 'feminine' qualities. So while shaving may be the proof of a 'real man' it is also about softness, smoothness and comfort. With the passing of time manufacturers have come to emphasize these 'civilized' qualities more and more, while the names and designs of the razors themselves exhibit 'hard' hi-tech qualities. The 'softness' of consumerism is often resolved by marketing commodities aimed at men as 'technology' – 'things that go', phallic 'tools'.

Razor giant Gillette produces two extremely popular razors, with techno-sexy names, Contour and Sensor, which emphasize their comfort and smooth shave with impressive mechanical features such as swivel heads, lubricating strips and spring-mounted blades. The copy on a brochure for Gillette Sensor manages to convey the sense of luxury and sensitivity offered by the product in masculine techno jargon:

> Gillette Sensor: the shave personalized to every man. It starts with twin blades, individually and independently mounted on highly responsive springs. So they continually sense and automatically adjust to the individual curves and unique needs of your face.

The name itself, 'Sensor', literally a device designed by men to feel for them, separates the act of feeling from the shaver: sensitivity is projected into the product. The design of the razor pictured above the copy, looking like an electronic instrument that might be used in advanced aerospace engineering, helps to convey the sense of being cocooned by technology: 'Innovation is everywhere,' the text assures us. 'You can feel it in the textured ridges and the balance of the Sensor razor. You can appreciate it in the easy loading system and the convenient shaving organiser.' Surrender to 'passivity' is acceptable and even commendable if it comes in the form of man-made technology (as opposed to the 'woman-made' womb – that which technology is trying to emulate/replace). The passive position of the Sensor-ized man is summed up in the last passage:

> All these Sensor technologies combine to give your individual face a personalized shave – the closest, smoothest, safest, most comfortable.
>
> The best shave a man can get.

The phrase 'The best a man can get', adopted by Gillette in all their current campaigns, is the modern equivalent of Jif shaving stick's 'a real man's shave', linking the product with manliness. Unlike the 1940s slogan, Gillette's usage 'The best shave a man can get' also succeeds in combining the idea of *authentic* manliness ('best' and 'man') with the *cosmetic* commodity that they are trying to sell ('shave').

The TV ad for Sensor illustrates this tactic even better, linking visually the techno appeal of the product with the idea of *masculine* tenderness. In an extraordinary soft-focus male-bonding love-fest we are shown sons, fathers and grandfathers smiling, laughing and hugging while the sound-track plays the Gillette anthem (a quasi Michael Bolton soul/rock number performed with the kind of emotion usually reserved for classic heterosexual love songs), 'Father to son/It's what we've always done.' The final frames show a young boy (pre-Oedipal) being picked up and hugged by a proud father while the song reaches its climax, aided by what sounds like a Gospel chorus: 'Gillette! – the best a man can get!' The alienated affections of father for son, son for father, man for man can be recaptured safely in the product. The final frame shows us 'Gillette' and the slogan 'The best a man can get' being *cut* into the screen by a blinding laser beam, while the anthem reaches its final climax, reiterating in the most economic visual form the idea of masculine techno love.

The 'best a man can get', the ad seems to acknowledge, is male to male tenderness, but the idealized world of men loving men that it presents can only serve to remind the viewer of the loveless-ness of his own masculine world, encouraging him to displace his unrequited affections for other men onto the razor, the totemic symbol of masculine membership and belonging.

Shaving sequences tend to be composed of three types of shots. The first, the Spectator, is positioned over the shoulder of the model (always naked in wet shave ads), focused on his reflection in the mirror. We occupy the subject position of either a father proud-ly watching his son shave, or a son watching his father shave (or a lover watching his/her partner).

The second, the Shave, involves extreme close-ups of the model's lathered, invariably tanned face, playing up the contrast between pink/brown skin and white foam, as the camera follows the razor moving effortlessly and carelessly across the model's face with astounding speed – no spots or razor nicks or bumps for him. This creates the impression of an effortless ease and a fearless mastery over the masculine world and its dangers. Multiple and quick editing combined with continuous camera motion are often employed during the Shave to encourage a sense of excitement and thrill involved in the ritual of shaving. At the same time the extreme close-up intimacy of these shots creates a rush of motion, with rapid cuts to different parts of the face – ears, lips, eyes, chins, flashing skin – which would normally be associated with sexual imagery.

The third, the Mirror, is shot in close-up as if from behind the bathroom mirror. In fact the camera is the mirror. While this shot is often used in the course of the shave itself, it is almost invariably used at the end of the Shave, after the baptism of the rinse, (usually in slow motion), when the model splashes his face with water and then buries his face in a towel, looks us straight in the eye, runs his manicured fingers across his chin and detonates an expensive smile, whiter and purer than the shaving foam itself.

The touch to the face and the devastating smile tell us that the shave is smooth as a baby's bottom. But they also tell us something else: the experience has been *pleasurable*, admitting – insisting – that a shave is much more than just a shave. Not only has the shave been a faintly sexual encounter, as evidenced by the extreme close-ups etc., but the mirror perspective of the camera has the effect of identifying us with the model, imagining him as our idealized reflection, and so *it was good for us too*. The mirror perspective allows us to desire the model narcissistically in such a way that it is also our hand that strokes his face, just as much as it is our face that is stroked. The grin is a cheeky acknowledgement of his willingness to entertain our desire for him and our desire for ourselves. Advertising offers man a reflection in Narcissus' pool that hints at a love that might be returned. Buy our shaving products, their love note reads, and you might possess this image 'endowed with all the beauty men could desire' ('The best a man can get') in your own bathroom mirror.

Shaving ads of this kind, like the headless torso ads, blur the supposedly discrete categories of desire and identification to the point where distinguishing them is almost worthless. In a sense these shaving ads are bolder than the torso ads in their shy facelessness. The mirror and the manly and necessary activity of shaving make the *personal* sexual address possible. The world behind the looking-glass of shaving advertisements gets queerer and queerer.

Nor does the shaving ad's traditional focus on the face have to be at the cost of the body. In one memorable mid-1980s ad for Gillette, a young, square-chinned man (square chins and strong jaw-lines are a *sine qua non* of shaving ads: *manliness* has to shout from every feature of the face), furiously works out in what appears to be his own private gym; managing to combine in one image the two 1980s obsessions: success and *hard* bodies. One shot shows him hanging upside down from a bar wearing 'gravity boots' (boots with hooks attached), working his abdomen by bending himself double. The spectacle offers ruthless ambition – this is a man who is going to succeed even if it kills him – and yet also voyeurism with the accent on sadism (his body has something of the look of a side of beef hanging in a butcher's shop). The camera lingers on the sweat of his honest exertions and tracks along his body, picking out the ribbed effect of his abdominal muscles struggling to persuade the upper half (now lower) of his body to defy gravity. All this is justified by the frenetic activity of the model.[12]

After the work-out comes the Shave. As the camera follows the razor cutting its swathe through the lather, the extreme close-up of the razor sliding over the model's muscular jaw, leaving wet exposed skin behind, echoes the movement of the camera across his body earlier; the contours of his wet face blend into those of his sweaty body as the razor sweeps away the sweat/lather, leaving our boy clean cut and fresh. In effect the shaving sequence offers a repetition of the enjoyment of the work-out, for both him and us, with a similar justification – this time the activity of shaving. The shaving sequence ends with the customary mirror shot, face stroke and dazzling smile: we enjoyed that didn't we? Then, as if suddenly self-conscious of the queerness of it all (there is no 'little woman' in the ad to heterosexualize the images), the model socks a punch-ball conveniently positioned next to the sink – pow! What a guy! Nothing queer about him/us! What could be more natural, more vigorous, than a regular guy who feels good and ready for the world punching something. This man is a *winner*.

The growing unfashionability of 1980s individualism (and perhaps also the growing visibility of lesbians and gays) seems to have made the portrayal of single men like the man in *Work Out* more problematic. The new generation Gillette 'Best a man can get' ads have been careful to blend individualism with a sense of belonging and identity that places men firmly in the locus of the heterosexual family. As shown by the Sensor TV ad discussed above, this is achieved by emphasizing the initiation into manhood – the father-son bonding – that the shaving myth represents. This is even clearer in a brilliant 'pop-promo' sixty-second type ad for Contour (dating from 1989), consisting of very quick cuts and the Gillette rock anthem. It offers all the homoerotic and narcissistic enjoyment of *Work Out* and a similar exploitation of the masculine body, but in a much more circumspect fashion, emphasizing 'love' (man-woman, but also father-son) over 'lust' – all these desires explicitly bracketed within the institution of marriage.

(The following analyses of the Gillette Contour and Phillishave advertisements are taken from my own transcripts.)

Gillette Contour, TV, 'The Best a Man Can Get' (1989)

Shot action/Soundtrack

1 *'You're lookin' sharp'*

Three laughing young men in white shirt, black tie, with white carnations; probably at wedding; one embraces the other.

2 *'You're lookin' good'*

Reflection of man in mirror in white shirt and tie; woman behind smiling and adjusting his tie.

3 *'You've come so far'*

Wall Street young man in white shirtsleeves gripping phone is patted on the shoulder by hand of man off-camera (father figure?). Young man pleased: clenches fists and looks heavenwards.

4 Hunky sweaty runner.

5 Product shot.

6 *'We know how to make'*

Man shaving in front of mirror, son (about 4 years old)

next to him; takes white foam from face on end of finger
and puts it on son's face.

7 *'The most of who you are'*
Newly-weds rushing towards limo, groom stopped by older
man; look into one another's faces, 'father' about to cry –
embrace.

8 Sportsman kisses trophy and crowd cheers.

9 *'Father to son'*
Tiny toddler boy lifts little dumb-bell with dad's arms
around him ready to catch the dumb-bell.

10 Reflected image of another father and very young son couple
combing their hair in mirror.

11 *'It's what we've always done'*
Dad tosses teenage son keys to first car.

12 Smiling dad cuddling just-bathed naked baby.

13 *'Gillette! the best a man can get!'*
Close-up of razor head.

14 Man surfing.

15 Woman running towards man.

16 Man embracing woman.

17 Extra close-up of packaged product.

18 *'On so many faces'*
Greek-American wedding. Men in white shirts smiling and
dancing with arms around one another (fathers and sons).

19 Extra close-up of handsome man in profile touching his chin
(gloved hand = manual labour/weightlifting), turning
towards the camera, smiling sexily.

20 Close-up on bodybuilders in gym holding dumb-bell and
looking to camera.

21 Another profile shot of man touching chin, turns towards the
camera and smiles, hand falling away.

22 '*It's plain to see*'
   Young men in white T-shirts (military?) running through water (*Chariots of Fire*).

23 Extra close-up, profile, man's head tilted up, razor moving along neck and off end of chin.

24 Man kissed by girl on cheek.

25 Close-up of young male runner's face (from #22).

26 Close-up of girl kissing man.

27 '*We give you all we have ...*'
   Boy on moped chatting up girl walking down street (hand on heart).

28 '*... to give.*'
   Extra close-up, hand grabbing Contour.

29 Extra close-up Mirror Shot, half shot of lathered tanned young face, green-blue eyes (colour of gel in #38); razor 'clean cut' through foam from sideburn to middle of cheek.

30 Triumphant boxer hugged by coach.

31 Racing cyclists taking fast bend on mountain-side.

32 '*For all a man can be*'
   Astronauts (The Right Stuff) walking towards camera (floor shot making them look like gods).

33 Wall St. sign.

34 Man at desk in white shirt on phone with computer screens behind him.

35 More young businessmen/brokers in white shirts.

36 Extra close-up of screens and buttons, camera sliding across them to the right ...

37 ... extra close-up of razor cartridge connecting to razor (motion continued).

38 '*When the race is won*'
   Extra-extra close-up of Gillette gel on hand.

39 More men in white shirts and braces.

40 Extra close-up of man rinsing (slow-motion and back-lit – water catches *white* light as it sprays everywhere).

41 Young broker punches the air.

42 *'You're the champion'*
    Black runner hurdling.

43 Shot putter spinning in slow-motion.

44 *'Gillette! ...'*
    Razor sweeping under water.

45 *'The best ...'*
    Footballers celebrating goal; one jumps into another's arms, rest jump on top of them.

46 *' ... a man can get.'*

47 Product shot.

48 *'Gillette!'*
    Extra close-up of razor being rinsed.

49 *'The best a man can get'*
    Newly-weds in radiant white stroll towards camera, strewn with confetti.

50 Logo sequence (name cut into screen by laser).

The ad exploits narcissism/homoeroticism with mirror shots (#19–#31) and the use of the male face to connote the male body in a manner similar to *Work Out*, but this is carefully framed by heterosexuality every time. Shot #18 introduces the 'mirror' section with the line 'On so many faces'; we then see three different men (#19, #20, #21) gaze into the camera in classic mirror-shot style (although there is no evidence of a mirror present); all of them are touching their chins, reminding us that faces are *corporeal*. Further reminding us of the way shaving of the male face signifies the male body, the second man is working out in a gymnasium and the first is wearing a glove that signifies manual labour – 'It's plain to see'. But shot #18 that begins this 'mirror sequence' is a Greek-

American *wedding* and the close-ups of the male face (#23, #25) are immediately followed by shots of men's faces being kissed by girls (#24, #26). (Interestingly, shot #29, which is the *formal* mirror shot of lathered face being shaved, is immediately followed not by a girl kissing his cheek but by a boxing scene, as in *Work Out*.)

Marital bliss seals the ad hermetically from beginning to end. The opening and penultimate shots are wedding scenes. The homosocial/homoerotic flavour of shot #1 (three white young men laughing together, two of them hugging) is also immediately stabilized by the heterosexuality of shot #2 (man in front of mirror with woman adjusting his tie over his shoulder), while the lyrics accent this by telling us in shot #1 'You're lookin' sharp' (clean, wholesome, competitive) and in shot #2 'You're lookin' good' (pure, healthy, conformist).

This clawback is set up as a theme that runs through the whole ad, represented most vividly by the use of white. The white boys are wearing white shirts, white carnations and white smiles. Whiteness of skin, of shirts, of foam, of light, of water is *the* visual theme of the ad. Whiteness here represents purity: purity of the male-male (buddy) love ('lookin' sharp') and the male-female (married) love ('lookin' good') and the purity of the product, which is portrayed as cleansing, *clean* technology (the shaving gel [#38] is liquid soap/technology). The whiteness of the shirts on the men's backs and the lather on their faces combines the two ideas: successful manhood (as represented by winning in the man's world of business and sport and winning the 'trophy' of the bride [#8]) is about 'lookin' sharp' and 'lookin' good'. The white carnations and the white wedding show that whiteness is also a metaphor for the purest institution of all – heterosexual marriage. The theme of success which is constantly invoked ('the best', 'when the race is won', 'you're the champion') is about succeeding as a man: successfully performing masculinity; and in that performance/competition marriage represents some kind of finishing line. But what is clear from the ad is that the homoerotic/narcissistic shots vastly outnumber the heterosexual shots; this is underlined by the fact that all of the 'fathering' scenes involve sons – there appear to be no daughters in Gillette World. What the ad seems to say is that manly love is 'the best a man can get' and yet it must be sublimated into business and sporting success and ultimately into marriage which will provide you with sons to carry on the sublimated homoerotic attachment (until they grow up and cars have to substitute for tenderness: cf #9–11).

This homoerotic attachment is also narcissistic. Freud points out in 'On Narcissism: An Introduction' how the joys of parenthood are essentially narcissistic. This is more than suggested in shot #10 of the reflected image of a father and son combing their hair in the same mirror. The types of narcissism outlined by Freud involve not just a love for what the subject is now, but also for what he would like to be and what he once was: the Gillette ad exploits all these, but especially what the subject would like to be ('for all a man can be', 'the best a man can get') and what the subject once was ('from father to son').

But 'When the race is won' has another resonance. If white = clean = good = success, then white also = WASP. Given this, the appearance of a black man (#42) is especially jarring and tokenistic. His representation as a hurdler is the ultimate visual cliché: the black man is 'the body' again; 'success' is available to him only through sporting prowess.

An ad for Phillishave electric razors (Christmas 1992), *True Strength*, seems to owe a great deal to Gillette's *The Best*, not only in style (soft-focus quick frames in slow-motion), but also in its uneasy relationship to the individual and the male body – exploiting the appeal of both but trying to portray a 1990s aura as well.

Phillishave 'True Strength' B/W TV (Christmas 1992)

1 Extra close-up (mirror shot) of young man's face (left side).

2 Close-up of naked male torso and arms with boxing gloves punching ball, slow-motion showing arms sweaty and muscles shaking.

3 White screen, black lettering: '*True strength is not a measure of the body ...*'

4 Young father holding 3 to 4-year-old boy on knee in café, smiling proudly.

5 'It is a measure of the soul'

6 Head shot of young man holding snooker cue and young woman laughing.

7 *'Shaving is about personal grooming'*

8 'Peeping Tom' shot (from child's height) through door of bathroom of back of boxer shaving without shirt. Two mirrors carefully positioned to show us left profile and right-hand view of his raised square chin (and mouth) with shaver underneath.

9 *'Phillishave is about personal choice'*

10 Right-hand over-shoulder shot of boxer's reflection in mirror, shaver on cheek, other hand touching his neck.

11 Extra close-up of shaver head (shiny and pure).

12 Extra-extra close-up of whirling blades.

13 Demonstration of cutting action (nasty black whiskers dispatched by gleaming technology).

14 Shaver shot (matt-black, leatherette look – something from the interior of a sports car, like an automatic gear-shift lever).

15 Boxer framed by white light of window, shirtless, looking towards camera; punches punchball.

16 White screen superimposed over shaver heads.

17 White screen:
   PHILLISHAVE [blue lettering]
   FOR THE MAN INSIDE [black].

The ad begins with a classic 'mirror shot' extreme close-up on the left side of a classically attractive young man's face. The body is immediately connected to the face by the following shot (#2) which is a close-up of a sweaty naked male torso with arms and boxing gloves flailing at a punch-ball in slow-motion, well-defined muscles and tendons vibrating under the skin. Having made this connection as strongly as possible (#3) the next screen then appears to break it, showing us the legend 'True strength is not a measure of the body ...' followed by (#4) a smiling ordinary-looking young father holding a young boy on his knee; then the legend, 'It is a measure of the soul' followed by a head shot of an attractive young man holding a snooker cue and an equally attractive young woman laughing.

Individualism, the idea of the man outside the family, and undifferentiated desire are used to attract the viewer's attention with the close-up of the apparently single boxer's face and body, only to be quickly resolved into the family and heterosexuality: 'the soul'. Once this resolution of 'flesh' into 'spirit' is established the ad does not feel the need to return to the father/son, boy/girlfriend images and concentrates instead on offering us the enjoyment of the male body introduced in the first couple of frames. It is not the ordinary-looking dad we see reflected in our TV 'mirrors' in the shaving sequences but the half-naked hunky boxer (#8, #10): 'true strength' in men's advertising is *very much* 'a measure of the body'. The final 'person' image is of the boxer exhausted and shirtless, framed by the white light of a window behind him, looking towards the camera in a final mirror address (without a mirror). Suddenly, like the man in Gillette's 1980s *Work Out*, the model hits the punch-ball in front of him.

The popularity of the boxing motif in shaving ads (see also Henry Cooper and Brut in the 1970s) goes beyond the ready-made 'toughness' of the boxer as an antidote to any 'feminine' anxieties; boxing is an acceptable way for a man to touch another man's face: a social convention that extends well beyond the ring. A man might demonstrate affection for his 'mate' by play-boxing him on the chin, while a father might encourage mock fisticuff matches with his growing son when overt displays of affection become uncomfortable. The 'punch' used at the end of both *Work Out* and *True Strength* is the model making contact with the male viewer's face, strengthening the 'mirror' narcissistic/homoerotic effect but in an acceptably masculine way: that of aggressive tenderness (it also echoes the way in which shaving might provide father and son a pretext to touch each other's faces).

In the end *True Strength* is less scrupulous in its heterosexual framing than *The Best*. Its messages about 'true strength' and 'the soul', combined with a usage of whiteness as a symbol for the purity of the product and its consumers, and the victory of love over lust, are very much borrowed from *The Best* (note the nasty black whisker in #13, removed by the gleaming pristine 'white' technology), but this ad is sexually much more ambiguous. Even the 'clean' style in which it is filmed fails to extirpate 'filthiness' completely; the grainy black and white images are the trademark of Bruce Weber and his vernacular of frantically homoerotic male body photos (Weber also seems to have a thing about boxers).

The mark of a paranoid

Perhaps what is most significant is that despite the new anxieties about the male body and homoeroticism that have emerged in these ads since the 1980s there seems to be no suggestion of a return to the kind of maniacal heterosexuality that was compulsory in the 1970s. Even the paean to marital bliss in *The Best* is a screaming gay parade next to the macho hetero classic *Surfer*, an Old Spice ad first released in the mid-1970s and used occasionally until the end of the 1980s. *Surfer*, which has been pastiched and parodied many times, features, as the name might suggest, a man in a long shot riding a vast roller off some exotic beach, inter-cut and superimposed with a ghostly shot of a woman's head, her hair billowing around her in corny imitation of the waves. The sound-track plays the climactic finale to Carl Orff's *Carmina Burana*.

The message of the ad is deliberately naive: the Old Spice man is rugged, outdoors and able to tame nature (in the form of the sea/woman) by sheer force of his manliness. But the ad is not without subtlety in communicating this message. The chorus sings of 'Oh Fortuna, Imperatrix Mundi' (Oh Fortune, *Empress* of the World), a passive attitude to life which the surfer manfully refuses to accept. He makes his *own* fortune, defying feminine Fate and riding his own destiny on the waves that even Canute could not humble.

Reminding us that Old Spice is an old-fashioned product about an idealized *masculinity* rather than the physical *embodiment* of it, the camera stays a respectful distance from the surfer; no facial or bodily features are distinguishable. He is *activity*: he exists only in the performance of surfing and disavows the passive position that the gaze threatens him with. The viewer is invited to admire and desire that performance of masculinity; the connection of that desire with the product is made at the end when a bottle shot is superimposed (on the left of the screen) over a freeze-framed image of the surfer (on the right), who, almost as a silhouette, runs the ideas of essences together: essences of manliness and essences to splash on a manly face. Re-emphasizing the ludicrous machismo of the ad that threatens to tip over into comedy, the bass, throaty voice-over tells us that Old Spice is 'The mark of a *man*'.

Even the bottle is determinedly butch. It is designed to look like an apothecary's bottle, suggesting that the product is as traditional and tested as the masculinity on display, allaying men's fears about succumbing to luxury or fashion. Its design carefully eliminates any 'feminine' curves in the bottle's outline, presenting us instead with honest straight edges and forthright sharp angles. The bottle also carries an image of an 'olden days' sailing vessel, perhaps the *Cutty Sark*, racing to deliver spices and teas from the Empire back to Liverpool or the East End. This again reassures the male consumer of cosmetics that *Old* Spice is 'timeless' and 'traditional' and about 'adventure'. The image of the surfer freeze-framed on the right of the bottle brings the sense of adventure up to date: he and his board are pointing in the same direction as the ship.

From beginning to end this classic ad, which appears so terribly tough, is in fact a lesson in the *delicacy* of masculinity, its tendency towards paranoia: its terror of any feminine/queer contamination. The ad tries (successfully) to persuade men that buying something traditionally 'feminine' – a cologne – is in fact the very summit of masculinity: as functional and as virile as a surf along a 20-foot wave. This contradiction is contained in the very notion of 'aftershave'. Men are told that the astringent alcohol in aftershave is a vital component in their shaving regime, closing the pores of their skin. (Of course a few splashes of cold water would have the same effect for less outlay, but water has no perfume and cosmetic companies do not make it.) It was the success of the similarly hypermasculine Brut/Brute ad of the 1970s in which boxer Henry Cooper exhorted other men to 'splash eet on all oh-vah' (no sissy, economic, sprinkling here) that finally legitimized the idea of cologne for the masculine masses.[13]

Although this Brut campaign was briefly revived in Christmas 1992, with folk hero footballer Paul Gascoigne replacing Henry Cooper, the advertiser of men's shaving products no longer has to be so careful in exorcising the fear of the feminine. Many men today actually appear to wish to flirt, however, shyly, with femininity rather than throttle it the moment it shows its face. Evidence of how far we have come is shown in a startling new Old Spice ad broadcast in late 1992 that employs homoeroticism and narcissism and a semblance of femininity in a way which would make *Surfer* fall off his board.

The mark of a boy

The ad opens with a soft-focus close-up on a gorgeous young blond Adonis' head on a white pillow. He is fast asleep but we can see that it is morning as the sunlight streams onto his white sheets pulled half way up his naked brown back and glints in his golden hair. He is lying on his stomach, head turned towards us, hand clutching the pillow, dreaming his easy, handsome dreams. Thus the very first shot of this ad places the male in the most vulnerable and passive position conceivable (without recourse to positions that would have the ad banned); unlike the surfer, who is furiously taming the sea, we can do anything we like to this sleeping boy.

Cut to a pretty girl's head above his (she is approximately the same age), blowing in his ear. The sudden appearance of the girl and the impeccable innocence of what she does to him compared to what we might have thought about doing ourselves helps to clawback the dangerous implications of the previous image. Cut to close-up of his opal blue eyes blinking open. Cut to him raising himself halfway out of bed, resentful at being roused but not so resentful that he does not turn over and afford us a good look at his finely muscled *hairless* chest, the healthy eggshell tan of his flawless skin contrasting succulently with the brilliant white of the sheets.

Cut to him looking into the camera, sleepy-eyed and child-like. Cut to him hauling himself out of bed and walking uncertainly towards the camera (the girl has magically vanished – was she a dream that woke him?). His procession towards the camera affords us a full-length opportunity to check out his smooth Apollonian body clad only in his light-coloured boxer shorts. He is still groggy and adorable.

Cut to him bent over his sink looking in the mirror/camera like a tired puppy. Ahhhh. Cut to him splashing Old Spice on his face and – he 'wakes up'. Until this moment the sound-track has been silent, now it roars into life with a US Middle of the Road rock cover of James Brown's 'I Got You (I Feel Good!)' Our boy breaks into a grin and jigs around the room; he is now no longer a passive but an active subject. Cut to him driving off in a chunky jeep, with the miraculously reappeared girl by his side, to meet the day.

The most immediately striking thing about this ad is the multiple identifications it exploits. To begin with, our enjoyment of the boy asleep is not structured and we are free to make whatever sexual interpretation we like of the image. When this is stabilized in the form of the girl, the camera then seems to occupy her position so we enjoy the image of the boy from a 'feminine' subject position and thus a heterosexual one, one that is sustained until he reaches the mirror. Now the mirror position of the camera invites us to identify with him and desire him narcissistically as our own idealized reflection.

The sleepiness of the boy also queers the picture, because it allows us to gaze at him actively while he remains passive; later, when he is in front of the mirror, we are then allowed to identify with the passive male subject which we desired actively: we love him loving ourselves loving him. Splashing Old Spice on his face restores him to the position of an active, phallic subject as he 'wakes up' and regains his power, driving off with the girl, who sits in the *passenger* seat. In this way the product is successfully associated with a strong homoerotic and narcissistic desire *as well as the heterosexual victory over it*. The flirtation with femininity/passivity and homosex remains just that – a flirtation.

One other detail in this fascinating ad is intriguing. The boy does not actually shave. There is no suggestion of a razor and in fact his face is so boyish and his body so smooth as to deny the possibility that he might ever need one. While the absence of a razor undoubtedly has much to do with a wish on the part of the manufacturers to suggest that, like Brut, Old Spice can be used for its own sake rather than only after a shave, the hairlessness of this aftershave ad is visually indicative of something else. The boy's pre-pubescence is part of the infantilization of him that precedes his 'waking up'. His baby-face looks and the idyllic innocence of his sleepiness underline the fact that he is *not* a man: he is a boy-man. Shaving would disturb this image of him; the point of his use of 'after-shave' is that it is no longer a signifier of shaving and the initiation into manhood which that represents. Instead, Old Spice offers him phallic power (the significance of the 'wake up' sequence after the application), while still retaining his boyhood, with all the flux of desire: the 'feminine', the passive, the homoerotic. So we have an ad promoting an aftershave as something which *substitutes for* the initiation into manhood rather than betokens it. Fun, jeeps and girls are all available without the now *undesirable* responsibility of actually becoming a man.

This Peter Pan condition has an effect on the way that the male audience might desire him. Put into the context of his infantilization the girl blowing in his ear might easy be his mother, and thus the subject position of those watching the ad might be that of his mother. According to Freud, in his 'Three Essays on Homosexuality', homosexuals take themselves as their sexual object and 'proceeding from a basis of narcissism they look for a young man who resembles themselves and whom they may love as their mother loved them'. In *Wake Up*, it could be argued, the male viewer is invited to 'proceed from a basis of narcissism' and misrecognize the good-looking model as his ideal image and love him *as his mother loved him*. Once again we can literally see that narcissism and desire, far from being separate and distinct, are in fact intimately linked.

But even the flirtatiousness of *Wake Up* pales beside the staggeringly confident queer address of Davidoff's *Cool Water* ad (Christmas 1992), which must be as significant a landmark in men's advertising as Nick Kamen's 1985 strip. It was as if one of the torso posters had come to life, and, limbs, arms and head restored with all the art of a Michelangelo, had gone swimming.

Filtered, sepia tint shots of a Latin bodybuilder with smouldering good looks show him wandering around a Mediterranean town *sans* shirt; edits flash different sections of his torso at us and greedily offer as many different perspectives as possible from which to view him. The camera particula:ly enjoys taking a submissive position: with the camera-man apparently at the model's feet we are offered a perspective of his powerful chin between his stunning breasts. As with *Bath*, heat is implicit in every frame, 'explaining' the model's nakedness and signifying the sexual tension: in case we have missed this a voice-over informs us 'The air is heavy with heat' at the moment the model peels off his damp T-shirt, revealing his bodybuilder physique (raising the temperature still further).

We see him, apparently in his mind's eye, *sans everything*, splashing and gambolling in the sea and presenting us with what must be a first in any British TV ad – a naked male arse (albeit in shadow). Two perfectly formed smooth moons of flesh are glimpsed tantalizingly for a second and then are gone. Before the viewer can recover from this outrage a cunning edit fools him/her into thinking that he might have caught sight of the swimmer's penis (alas, frame by frame analysis proves disappointing).

Finally we see our man buy a block of ice with a blue bottle (the product) frozen inside. He holds it up to the sun, allowing the light to shine through the ice onto his face which he presses against it, turning so that his sultry profile is framed next to the bottle. A voice-over pleads, 'Soothe me!' Davidoff is 'relief' in the same way that wet Levis were in *Bath*.

Women trying to decide what to buy the men in their lives for Christmas were undoubtedly part of the target audience, but this serves to underline how changes in the way men look at themselves have been brought about by the way that women look at men as well as the way that queers look at them. 'Soothe me!' implores the man in the ad, a passive plea and an open one, without specifying, beyond the product, who or how.

In the water the 'mild image' of David/Davidoff (David the smooth boy slew Goliath the hairy giant) is reflected for our mournful gaze. For 'relief' from this 'love that cannot be returned' men can only purchase a bottle of 'Cool Water' for themselves, splash the aftershave on their freshly denuded faces and watch in the mirror as the 'Cool Water' curls around those marble buns 'endowed with all the beauty that man could desire'.

And one is reminded of the alternative ending to the Narcissus myth: instead of turning into a flower, another version holds, he fell into the pool and drowned.

Notes

1. Gore Vidal, *Myra Breckinridge* (London: Grafton Books, 1989), p. 123.

2. Sabine G. Oswalt, *Collins Concise Encyclopedia of Greek and Roman Mythology* (Glasgow: William Collins and Son, 1965), p. 196.

3. *The Observer Magazine*, 'Unzipping the jeans war', 28 February 1993.

4. Leslie Fiedler, *Love and Death in the American Novel* (New York: Stein and Day, 1975), p. 368.

5. 'Bartle Bogle plans record Levis push', *Campaign*, 18 October 1985.

6. Nor is it merely in the homoerotic content of these ads that their queerness is felt: it is also present in the idea of women viewers actively desiring male sex objects who have no girlfriends for them to identify with passively. So the introduction of the token women in these ads serves to heterosexualize not only the male audience's pleasure, but also the female's.

7. 'Don't look now', *Screen*, No. 23 (1982), pp. 3–4.

8. Mary Ann Doane, 'Women's stake: filming the female body', *October*, No. 17 (1981), pp. 29–30. Quoted in E. Ann Kaplan, *Rock Around the Clock* (London: Routledge, 1989), p. 93.

9. An ad for Paco Rabanne's Excess *eau de toilette pour homme* (*The Face*, October 1993) is so explicit in its substitution of the product for the phallus that it almost renders analysis superfluous. A b/w close-up of a reclining man's smooth, muscular torso (sans head, sans legs) shows him clutching a bottle of Excess in his left hand, just above his jeans' chunky belt-buckle, spraying his chest. In its (gay) pornographic style the ad makes an explicit link between autoeroticism and homoeroticism in men's advertising.

10. E. Easthope, *What a Man's Gotta Do* (Winchester, MA: Unwin Hyman, 1990), p. 144.

11. Michel Foucault, *The History of Sexuality: An Introduction* (London: Penguin, 1990), p. 86.

12. Linda Williams, 'Film body: an implantation of perversions', *Cinetracts*, 3(4) (1981), pp. 19–35 (cited in R. Dyer's *Only Entertainment* (London: Routledge, 1992)), p. 110.

13. It could be argued that the success of this campaign was based on the strange desire of men to smell like Henry Cooper. Nothing in the ad suggests that Brut will attract women; the appeal of Brut rests entirely with the idea that Henry Cooper uses it. The man who buys Brut inspired by this ad (and thousands did) is, in *essence*, buying Henry Cooper's body.

Chapter six

A World of Penises
Gay Videoporn

You like that don'tcha!

He's got the boyish face, perfect body and long fat,
incredibly juicy cock that won't quit coming ...
● *The Year in Sex (American gay porn review)*

'I am whatever you want me to be,' the world's first male
porn superstar recently told viewers of the British youth TV magazine programme *The Word*. He was answering, or rather evading,
the interviewer's question, 'are you gay, straight, bisexual or what?'
'I consider my sexuality universal,' he added.

Jeff Stryker is the star of countless gay, straight and 'bi' (as
they are always called) porn flicks. Featured in magazines such as
Interview and apparently about to 'penetrate' Hollywood itself,
this man has a 'life-like', 'skin-toned' latex dildo ('with moving
balls') cast from his gargantuan penis and named after him, and he
seems set for the kind of media exposure once unimaginable for a
male porn star.

But the most interesting feature of Jeff's career in the sex
industry is where it began: very much on the queer side of the
tracks. He was groomed for his current 'star of porn stars' status by
two of his gay lovers who also happened to be veteran gay porn
producers: John Travis and Matt Sterling. Whereas the history of
porn cinema is full of 'straight' male models who also featured in
gay films, this is probably the first example of an already estab-

lished star in the gay industry crossing over into straight porn on this scale.

A fag playing a straight stud? How can he manage to carry off both roles successfully? In fact Stryker only plays *one* role in both gay and straight films: that of the 'total stud', a rutting machine that 'fucks anything'. But nothing and no one fucks *him*. Stryker's success in both industries points up how much gay and straight male porn have in common: in both, the prick takes centre stage; the bigger it is the bigger the stage. The key difference between the two genres is the presence of women in straight porn. As Anne McClintock has observed, 'Women are there to guarantee heterosexuality in a world populated by penises.'[1]

In fact the 'heterosexuality' that is guaranteed in straight porn of this kind is really *virility*; in other words, the women are there to guarantee the power and appeal of the penises which are on display. In this medium, pricks are only phallic so long as they are framed 'heterosexually', i.e. mediated through women.

Gay porn is also a 'world of penises', but of course, without women. In gay porn men offer their penises to one another without mediation; they contravene the taboo on direct homosexuality and so, classically, their penises lose their power and virility. The problem that gay porn is faced with is how to represent a 'world of penises' that is virile – i.e. attractive – despite the absence of women. In other words, how to depict the men who are attached to them as masculine at the very moment that they are being faggots for one another.

Gay porn has typically responded to this challenge by not trying at all and submitting instead to the logic of straight masculinity and disavowing anything faggoty, i.e. anything 'gay' (apart from the sex itself, of course). The 'gay porn video', then, depicts not gay men having gay sex but 'straight' men having gay sex – or rather men having sex with other men where the absence of women is generally treated as accidental or circumstantial. 'Straight' men just blunder casually into sex with other men, find out that they enjoy it and carry on doing it: so called 'situational' homosexuality is the order of the day, and not just in terms of the military/penal context: hot work-outs, straight porn (a favourite), swimming, horse-riding, cycling, beer-drinking, bus journeys, camp fires, dope, hot weather, cold weather, and even sleeping, all produce pesky erections that just have to be taken care of – by your buddy (after all, there are no 'chicks' around). The 'straightness' of these characters is so assumed and yet carefully signalled that often it is not even necessary to suggest that they actually chase 'chicks'; their straightness is defined by their location and the fantasy. Almost never is the scenario a recognisably gay one: men are hardly ever picked up in gay bars or bath-houses.

In this narrative of 'conversion', the straight man is not converted to a gay identity (this would defeat the object of using a 'straight' character in the first place) but to 'gay' sex. But without a gay identity it is difficult to argue that there can be such a thing as 'gay' sex. Thus what gay porn does is to represent a world in which men have sex with men *where there is no such thing as 'gay'*. (This is why condoms are so rarely seen: they remind the viewer not just of AIDS – 'the gay plague' – but also safer sex, something invented by *gay* men and now something of a credo, a sign of belonging, in the gay community.) The fantasy of gay sex in gay porn starts with idealism, the desire to validate gay sex in an anti-gay world, to show the irresistibility of gay sex compared to straight, to excite an appetite for that which is labelled disgusting, but ends up with a *negation* of gayness, or at best an evasion of it.

This is evident in the drawings of Tom of Finland, whose early work set up virtually all the styles and conceits that are used in gay porn today. 'I started drawing fantasies of free and happy gay men,' he wrote. 'Soon I began to exaggerate their maleness on purpose to point out that all gays don't necessarily need to be "just those damn queers", that they could be as handsome and strong and masculine as any other men.' And so his drawings depicted a guilt-free (and gay free) world of spontaneous public sex between willing, youthful square-jawed cops and grinning, tattooed sailors, all with pendulous penises swinging between their perfectly flared thighs; in Tom Land, homosex is discovered to be the most natural, most *masculine* thing in the world. Here is the narrative of the lonely hitchhiker, lorry driver, mechanic, delivery boy who is converted, not to gayness, but to a joyous brotherhood of the male body.

The utopianism of these kinds of images (some might argue that they are in fact *dys*topian) has a quasi-religious, redemptive quality which gives the pictures an iconographic appearance.

Indeed the heroic masculine features and god-like attributes of Tom's men give an other-worldly feel to them; they appear as inhabitants of Valhalla, an all-male heaven, open only to the strongest and bravest specimens of manhood.[2]

Virtually all of this has been carried over into gay videoporn which, with its models' exaggerated (boyishly) masculine characteristics and appendages, resembles nothing so much as a kind of animated version of Tom's drawings.[3]

And so we are left with a quandary: what should be the most obviously, unapologetically, *explicitly* gay images – that of men offering their penises to each other – becomes something not very gay at all, something that instead goes out of its way to distinguish its men from 'those damn queers': a position rather similar to straight male porn.

Film theory offers no way out of this impasse. Rather it confirms this unpleasant conjunction of gay and straight porn. In his essay 'Coming to terms: gay pornography', Richard Dyer points out the way in which the filmic narrative of gay porn matches that of straight male porn: 'The basis of the gay porn film is a narrative sexuality, a construction of male sexuality as the desire to achieve the goal of a visual climax.' In both gay and straight porn the 'come-shot' is the sign of virility that is sought. Even the portrayal of the ultimate 'hard core' act of gay male sexuality – anal sex – does not of itself disrupt this narrative: '... although the pleasure of anal sex (that is, of being anally fucked) is represented, the narrative is never organised around the desire to be fucked, but around the desire to ejaculate (whether or not following on from anal intercourse).'[4]

In fact, since Dyer made this observation in 1985, the portrayal of anal sex seems to have become even more constructed as the 'desire to achieve the goal of a visual climax' – the desire, that is, of the fucker, who in the person of Jeff Stryker (and several other imitations: e.g. Ryan Idol, tipped to steal his tiara) is one who never experiences the pleasure of anal sex in any other position except that of the fucker. In other words, Stryker's screen persona in gay videoporn seems to deny his own anality and just endorses the pleasure a 'stud' can get in plugging any hole. Unlike the Tom of Finland drawings, the stud is never studded, but is a mythic penetrator who never gets penetrated. As porn producer Jerry Douglas has observed, 'He's the ultimate example of who gay men love to hate.'[5]

Stryker is a comically phallic phenomenon. His body, with its smooth, clean homogenous skin and perfect muscular development, makes the ideal vehicle for his stocky prick, which of course it both resembles and serves to direct attention towards; Stryker's featureless face and hygienic, flawless bodylines draw the eyes always downwards to his dolphin-sized dick. His small stature, carefully concealed on screen (without much difficulty, since the other models are usually either bent double or on their knees), helps to swell the perceived size of his cock, making it look even more preposterous than it is. Visually, Jeff Stryker resembles nothing so much as an illustration of the human nervous system in a medical textbook where the size of each region and appendage represented is related to the number of nerve endings. Thus Jeff on screen is remembered by the eye as a huge face, a vast pair of hands (all the better to grab and slap ass with) and grotesquely outsized genitalia.

Not only does his name connote thrusting violence (one of his most famous films is called *Stryker Force*), but his penis is celebrated for its ability to inflict pain; it is slapped across faces, rammed down throats (accompanied by the sweet nothing line, 'Choke on dat fat cock'), and jammed up rectums without so much as a 'please' or 'thank you'. His name is synonymous with a certain sadism towards his 'partners' (who never approach the equality this word suggests); they are always total 'bottoms' to his total 'top'. The reality of the topsy-turvy versatility of gay male relations is denied; in porn, it would seem, gay men demand that the fucker and the fucked remain distinct categories in a way that they often fail to in 'real' life.

Thus gay men want from their porn star a portrayal of a kind of 'straightness' that even straight men do not possess (gay men know only too well the annoying tendency of straight male 'conquests' to 'bottom out'). Stryker is a gay man's idea of what a straight man should be: he is clean filth, threat without violence, a stud without anality, a prick without an arse, a top man *who does not have a bottom of his own*.

The creation of the mythic penetrator in the person of Jeff Stryker is not just a function of power, it is also a function of the medium's (hopeless) attempt to 'show sex'. Ironically, for all the emphasis in porn on seeing ejaculation, the supreme phallic arousal, the fucked shows more of himself on screen than the fucker. Not only is the fucked a body while the fucker is only a penis, but the fucked is, by implication of the pleasure shown on his face when the fucker's penis is inside him, in a very real sense *turned inside out*. His private anal pleasure, his innermost masculine secret, the repression of which masculine identity is supposed to be predicated upon, becomes *obscenely* public. This is what the porn camera records far more effectively than the act of fucking itself which always seems to elude it.

For all its attempts with special lenses and lights, angles conceivable and inconceivable, probings and zoomings, the camera tries in vain to *show* intercourse – all we can see is the penis disappearing and reappearing. The porn video's inherent commitment to 'showing' actually results in the portrayal of 'sex' as a kind of temporary castration which tells us that the disappearance of the penis is the only representation it can make of 'sex'. In fact, 'sex' is shown more on the faces of those who are being fucked. Their expression of joy is the guarantee of the penis' presence; without those looks of agony/pleasure that the director is careful to capture we would not know that the penis did not in fact literally disappear when it ceased to be visible.

The fucked, then, has the responsibility of showing everything, and in that display cannot help but show too much. He becomes disposable, his image is 'worn out', used up, redundant: everything has been seen, time to turn the page; this is why 'bottoms' in gay videoporn are so often swept away with each scene change. In a medium that cries out for total revelation and then, in its measureless fickleness, discards whatever is revealed, the mythical fucker, on the other hand, can go on to the next scene, and indeed on to the next video, because he has kept something hidden, something in reserve, something *private*. His anus remains off-camera, except to be licked by 'bottoms', not as a sign of his anality so much as *theirs*. The porn star 'top' is bottomless – his co-stars 'plug that gap': his anality is projected into them (hence the famous 'rapping' lines, 'You like that big cock up your ass, don'tcha!'). Thus his audience, which hungers for everything to be shown so that it can be consumed and negated, which wants to see Stryker's face reflect the pain/pleasure of another man's penis up his arse, which wants to see him 'turned inside out', finally *naked*, is left wanting more from him, ironically precisely because the porn star does *not* 'show sex'.

There are, however, signs of a move away from this type of erotic economy in gay porn films, away from the 'straight' scenarios and from the top man star; towards, in fact, a 'gay' porn that is gay.

Jerry Douglas' *More of a Man* (1990), winner of the Las Vegas Adult Video Award and named Best Feature video of 1990 by *Advocate Men*, is a step in this direction. This remarkable video appears to offer a narrative in which the star not only gets fucked but learns that to be fucked is not shameful but rather a sign of 'strength' – hence the title. This narrative is bound up with a political statement about coming out, which previous porn films have avoided as the ultimate turn-off. In *More of a Man* conversion to the joys of same-sexing becomes a conversion to the joys of a gay *identity*.

Rather than simply appropriate 'straight' masculinity, 'More of a Man' self-consciously attempts to present a gay masculinity. The script lines up the 'showing' of gay politics, i.e. coming out, the importance of visibility, of 'showing yourself', with the showing of anality – specifically the showing of the central character's acceptance/enjoyment of being fucked which leads to his embrace by the gay community, rather than his disposal by the top man and the gay viewers, as with the classical type of gay porn.

The male lead, Vito (Joey Stefano) is a Catholic construction worker; that is to say, precisely the kind of 'straight' fantasy man that gay porn videos have traditionally featured. He is also closeted and a public sex-seeker; the film's first sex scene shows him on his knees by a glory hole. This comes immediately after the opening scene in which we see him also on his knees, this time in church begging to be released from his 'impure thoughts', promising prophetically, 'You name it, I'll do it.'

He fellates enthusiastically (if guiltily at first) a penis jutting through the hole in the wall and then manoeuvres his arsehole against it, allowing himself to be fucked royally through the wall. Once he has come he is covered in shame and makes to leave, but is stopped by the man who has just fucked him: face to face, i.e.

visible, Vito rejects his advances and reacts violently to his suggestion that he 'really likes to get fucked'. But during the course of the
video Vito learns to accept his sexuality and a gay identity, symbolized by being fucked on a table in a free-for-all orgy in a gay bar. In
this ritual initiation/confirmation the private shame of the cottage is
contrasted (somewhat naively) with the public joy of anality in the
gay community.

In this way the sign of ultimate masculine 'surrender', the act
that exiles man from the community of men, turning him from a
fucker into a fucked, is transformed into a victory, a manly victory
for Vito over his guilt, his religion, his 'hang-ups' – his 'cowardice'.
This gay videoporn does not reject the redemptive overtones of gay
porn but rather turns this theology on its head (ditto with its
attitudes towards Catholicism). Instead of the dream of a queer
Valhalla we are presented with a vision of the ecstatic embrace of a
gay community of brave and noble men here and now.

As a sign of his new gay identity Vito now has a boyfriend,
Duffy, who is a Dodgers fan and an activist in ACT-UP. These
characteristics take on a kind of masculine equivalence: a visible
gay identity and supporting gay rights are as *definitively* masculine
as supporting the Dodgers (this is what Tom of Finland is avowing
about homosex in his drawings of 'manly' men): an out gay identity
becomes, so the video hopes, as easily virile as a Dodgers sweat-
shirt.

Meanwhile the unabashedly redemptive theme is taken even
further, almost to the point of parody in the final scene set inside a
float on the Los Angeles Gay Pride parade. To the joyous sounds of
the cheering parade crowds (congregation?), Vito and Duffy fuck,
but the geometry of this is carefully drawn: Vito is the fucker but
Duffy is on top. Duffy wants to use a condom, but Vito protests,
'It's against my religion.' 'Well, it's not against mine,' Duffy replies.
Mandy Merck has shrewdly observed that the eerie blue light of the
interior of the float could almost be the interior of a condom as the
prophylactic usage in this scene seems to betoken Vito's final introduction into the gay community (thus exploiting the 'gayness' of
safer sex that other 'gay' videoporn abjures).[5] But it could also be
the interior of a *cloud*; after all, Vito is joining the ranks of the
'heavenly' brotherhood.

More of a Man sets out not just to politicize gay porn but to

eroticize gay politics; within the quasi-religious iconography of
conversion in gay porn this eroticization of gay politics comes to
mean sanctification as well. Vito looks up to Duffy as more masculine than him, 'more of a man': and thus becomes, within the
economy of worship of masculinity that is the gay porn film, *holier*.
Vito even imitates Duffy by having a tattoo like his (needless to say,
the tattooist, the dispenser of the signification of the manly body,
turns out to be gay as well and Vito hungrily sucks him off under
the table). Activism, in the shape of Duffy, is shown to be manly,
and therefore erotic, bridging the gap that has until now separated
gay porn from a gay identity. As Merck has noted:

> In the crewcut figure of Duffy the Dodgers' fan, activism is
> assigned the youth and muscularity of contemporary
> videoporn, with added details of class and ethnicity –
> touches which both enhance the masculinity of the
> character and elaborate it in realist terms. These traits
> enable Duffy to offer Vito – gay politics to offer gay
> pornography – the virile identification which its multiple
> eroticisation of the male body (penile *and* anal, active *and*
> passive) both troubles and requires. Thus 'More of a Man'
> ... has its phallus and eats it too.[7]

In having its phallus and eating it too, the film manages to overcome the problem of how to portray a world of penises without
women and still retain the power/attraction of the phallus, without
disavowing its gayness, or the intervention of a Stryker-type caricature. In a very real sense the film suggests that gay men have created
their own version of masculinity: this is the religion into which Vito
is initiated.

And yet the gay masculinity it offers, for all its careful
balancing of anality with virility and political courage, still shares a
very basic assumption of straight male porn: the denial of lack. An
androgynous type of masculinity is perhaps too much to ask for
from a porn film but this is exactly what *More of a Man* pretends to
in the form of Belle Zahringen, a drag queen, who watches over the
proceedings 'like the plastic virgin on Vito's dashboard.'[8] 'She'
mouths the political line of the film and 'she' sings the title song at

her stage debut in the gay bar, just before Vito's anal debut into the gay community/scene.

> ... And folks, you can take it from me,
> This incredible creature you see
> Has the best of both worlds,
> Yes siree.
> I'm more of a woman
> Than you'll ever have
> And more of a man
> Than you'll ever be.

The 'gender fuck' of Belle and the film's anthem slyly try to pass off the masculinity on offer as some kind of radical and romantic androgyny. In fact androgyny is exactly what is *not* on offer here. It is not the 'best of both worlds' that is portrayed: this is very much a world of penises, literally 'more of the *same*'. As Merck points out, 'women are still what men "have" – the phallic complement that enables them to "be",' and Belle offers the 'phallic femininity of sexuality without lack.'[9] The 'other world' is disavowed here as much as in any other porn film aimed at men: the 'other world' of 'lack'.

What Vito embraces, in the end, is a world which is 'more of men'. This is clearly signalled by the course of his coming out: when he complains to an older woman about harassment from 'fags' she turns out to be Belle, i.e. a man; later he is having sex with a prostitute but we see instead a fantasy scene of him with Duffy.

Most revealing of all is Belle's enforced state of virtue throughout the film: she is the only main character who does not have any kind of sex – not even during the orgy scene when everyone is at it hammer and tongs, and it was supposed to be *her* evening. The idea of Belle getting involved is so inconceivable that it is not even explained. Even the superficial androgyny of a drag queen is far too distasteful to be countenanced 'in action'. A *really* radical androgyny would have had Belle, on stage, skirts hitched up around her midriff, wig skew-whiff, *fucking Vito*.

For all its considerable achievements *More of a Man* does not reinvent gender.

·   ·   ·

Vito's prayer-promise 'You name it, I'll do it' made at the beginning of his sexual odyssey is strangely echoed by Stryker's 'I am anything you want me to be.' But while Vito's promise is then ironically fulfilled in the following 'impure' scenes, where he literally *does* do it, Stryker is always required by his audience just to *be* a mythic penetrator. But if the character of Vito is a slave to his own desires, then perhaps Stryker is always slave to the desires of others – his audience.

Stryker's audience wants him as a top man so that he can 'be' a *thing* for them ('a rutting machine'). His gay audience does not wish to identify with him (as a straight male audience might in his straight porn features). Seeing him get fucked would create a point of identification. In allowing his audience to witness his face reflecting the pleasure of anality he would not only cease to keep a part of himself hidden, he would cease to be Other, he would cease to be objectified, he would cease, in other words, to occupy the traditional position of female porn stars. Jeff Stryker, the total top, the serious studman, the stallion rampant, is just a sex slave utterly in the thrall of an audience of pushy controlling bottoms.

Finally, in the curious shape of Jeff Stryker we might find the evidence that an attempt to eroticize a new type of masculinity in gay videoporn is redundant, there being no 'real' masculinity left to deviate from, kick against or even submit to. Jeff Stryker, the gay porn star who plays at being straight, the sex actor who embodies a fantasy of straightness for gay men, has crossed over into straight porn itself. The self-sufficient 'stud' is now 'anything you want me to be': an admission of passivity which characterizes him as, in effect, a thing to be handled and fantasized about – *used* – in the same manner as the dildo named after him. Phallic? Certainly. *But in whose hands?*

Stryker's confession of passivity – at the very moment of emphasizing his appeal to straight audiences as well as gay ones – suggests that in the world of simulated sex the distinction between active and passive, 'top' and 'bottom' has been effaced, or at least has lost any intelligible meaning.

This approach has enormous ramifications. Stryker's 'rapping' style is now a familiar feature of gay bedrooms on both sides of the Atlantic: porn simulates sex, while sex simulates porn. Thus the world of simulated sex is no longer just 'porn' but 'the world' as well. Edward Albee has already formulated this: 'As children we use porn to substitute for sex; as adults we use sex to substitute for porn' (*The Zoo Game*). And just as the distinction between the active and passive production/consumption of porn breaks down, so does the active and passive polarity itself, and with it the hetero – homo distinction, since there is no longer any reality of 'sex' itself to be compared with. Stryker's sexuality is 'universal' because it is a simulacrum, and the very distinction that his 'universal' persona is built upon – between 'top' and 'bottom' – is blurred away into nothing. As Jean Baudrillard writes:

> Everywhere in whatever political, biological, psychological, media domain, where the distinction between poles can no longer be maintained, one enters into simulation, and hence into absolute manipulation – not passivity but the *non-distinction of active and passive*.[10]

The punter, gay or straight, male or female, sitting in front of the flickering TV screen, eyes glued to the latest Stryker epic, latex 'life-like', 'skin-toned', 'with moving balls' dildo in one hand and remote control in the other, may soon come to the conclusion that there is no original for the copy they hold; that what they have in their hand, *is* Jeff Stryker's dick, and, in a very hyper-real sense, *is* Jeff Stryker.

Electric dreams

'Fully aroused male sex organs? Penetrative sex? Oral sex? Actual sex acts rather than simulated sex? Gay scenes?' According to a somewhat flustered Det. Supt Michael Hames, head of the Obscene Publications Squad, as reported in the *Sun* (2 October 1992), if any of these images appeal then the recent explosion of educational sex videos will be right up your proclivity. With names like *Better Sex*, *The Lovers Guide*, *Supervirility* and the *Gay Man's Guide to Safer Sex*, videos depicting explicit sex scenes can now be bought over the counter in Britain instead of having to be smuggled past customs in a *Sound of Music* jacket. Hames baulks at the idea that they should have been passed by the British Board of Film

Classification on the grounds that they are educational: 'Turn the volume off and just watch the action – as I'm sure most people do – and what have you got? Pure porn.'

But despite this very *ancien* outrage there does seem to have been something of a revolution in British attitudes towards sexual explicitness in the last few years: for all Hames' blustering he is unable to touch these new videos.

AIDS has been the paradoxical agent of all this. While encouraging an anti-gay, anti-sex backlash it has also prompted more public discussion about sex, in all its manifestations, than at any time in British history. The details and hydraulics of safer sex (and unsafe sex) fill our newspapers and TV screens in a way that would have been inconceivable just ten years ago. The taboo on anal sex, for example, was broken in the 1980s by a government spokesman no less, when it was openly discussed on TV by the recently retired Chief Medical Officer, Donald Acheson. Even the historian Michel Foucault might be astonished by how much modern life is bearing out his assertion that we now regard sex as 'a causal principle, an omnipresent meaning, a secret to be discovered everywhere ...' (*The History of Sexuality: An Introduction*).

The discourse of AIDS taken together with the proliferation of adult cable channels, the spread of satellite broadcasting (e.g. *Red Hot and Dutch*), and the growth of the European Single Market has begun to open up the frontiers of uptight Britain to pornography, by no means the only but certainly the frankest medium for telling the 'secret' of sex.

But the most significant departure from the past is the argument deployed to help bring this about: the explicit description and portrayal of sex acts is now justified in terms of its ability to affect behaviour.

For years the defenders of porn have tried to refute the same argument coming from a censorious State, an argument which maintained that porn 'depraves and corrupts', the definition of obscenity contained in the Obscene Publications Act (1959). Certain feminists, meanwhile, argued that porn was 'the theory and rape the practice'. This unholy alliance for censorship was met by an equally strange combination of liberal arguments against it: porn was 'just fantasy', a *private* matter which had no effect on behaviour, *and* an issue of free speech, (the sacrosanctness of representation was at stake), and therefore a *public* matter; and in both cases neither the State nor feminists had any business in its regulation.

The AIDS crisis seems to have turned the 'harmless' liberal argument irrevocably on its head. Explicit images are now valued precisely for their power to influence behaviour. The *Gay Man's Guide to Safer Sex*, chief sinner in the eyes of Hames (and ironically the most seriously educational of this whole genre), is passed, in the words of the BBFC, because 'to stress the fact that safer sex can be enjoyable it is obviously necessary to show it being so'. Well, absolutely, and congratulations to the BBFC for having the conviction to say so. But a venerable British institution whose job it is to protect public morals from corruption talking of the need to portray (safer) sex as 'enjoyable'? Clearly Britain is not the country it was.

Britannia's reputation as the prudish old maid of Europe is well deserved. It is no coincidence that we have some of the most stringent censorship laws and the harshest anti-gay laws in Europe. Both pornography and homosexuality represent sex: pornography in terms of images and homosexuality in terms of the concept itself. The idea of homosexuality is one of naked 'sex'; sex-for-pleasure, sex for, in and of itself, sex unmediated and unprivatized by the family or reproduction, as an undifferentiated public Eros: homosexuality is, thus, by its very nature 'obscene'.

But Britain's historic prudery is not, as some would have it, the result of a horror of the body or sex, but rather *an all-pervading fascination with it*. It is a commonplace of British life that the fiercest of moralists are the filthiest people you could ever have the misfortune to meet. But riding alongside this common-sense impression is the contradictory idea that such people are 'anti-sex'. In fact they are nothing of the sort, rather they value sex far more highly than those who claim to be 'pro-sex', according it a divine status. It is precisely because sex is divine that it must be accorded the greatest respect and obeisance. That Mary Whitehouse is scoffed at when she denies the charge that she is frigid, which is often implicit in attacks on her, is a sign of the ignorance of her critics, who in their liberal attitudes towards sex reveal not a 'pro' sex position but rather a kind of indifference, an agnosticism. For the Whitehouses of this world sex is the most sacred, powerful, *real* thing in the world: sex for the moralist is quite literally God.

The liberal is right to point to the British experience of the Reformation and puritanism to explain Britain's censoriousness, but they are usually mistaken in their reasoning. It is the flame of *iconoclasm* rather than a horror of the body which burns in the heart of modern-day moralists, an iconoclasm based not on anger at the corruption of the 'divine idea' that images represent but rather fear of their all-too-sharp focusing of an unpleasant truth. In Baudrillard's words:

> Their [the Puritans'] rage to destroy images rose precisely because they sensed this omnipotence of simulacra, this facility they have of effacing God from the consciousness of men, and the overwhelming, destructive truth which they suggest: that ultimately there has never been any God, that only the simulacra exists ... their metaphysical despair came from the idea that the images concealed nothing at all, and that in fact they were not images, such as the original model would have made them, but actually perfect simulacra forever radiant with their own fascination.[11]

The latter-day iconoclast's devotion to sex, his/her faith in its 'truth', requires that it remains private, a secret that is never told, a name that is never invoked, *because in the telling of it we might learn of its death*. The moralist's urge to smash the graven images of sex is not because he/she considers that they sin against sex by offering an imperfect copy of it, but rather because they know well enough that these images represent all too truly 'sex' and thus threaten to reveal that there is no such thing. The Victorians draped their table legs in heavy velvet not so much to ward off impure thoughts as to keep the divine idea of the phallus free of the impurities of doubt.

That the videos which Det. Supt Hames of the Metropolitan Police Iconoclasm Squad bemoans are 'educational' is no defence; rather it compounds their crime in the eyes of the man who fears and loathes graven images. Pornography which is 'educational' is pornography which is explicit in its admission that it no longer pretends to simply represent. Instead it boasts of its ability to *affect* sex: 'to stress the fact that safer sex can be enjoyable it is obviously necessary to show it being so.' It is not just 'sex' which is offered by these ideas but *better* sex, *better* 'loving'; nor is it just better than sex; it is also *safer*. How could the mere representation of sex live up to the promise of 'making sex even better' (sub-title to *The Lovers Guide II*), unless sex as a divine idea has disappeared?

The iconoclast knows in his or her bones that in the telling, the 'secret of sex' ceases to be an 'omnipresent meaning', and instead breaks down into unintelligibility and meaninglessness. The very concepts of 'better sex' and 'safer sex' interrogate 'sex' and encourage endless chat-show confessionals and colour supplement enquiries about 'what sex means to you', turning the universal into the parochial at the very moment of its supposed universality. As Hames and Whitehouse are both painfully aware, 'this death of the divine referential has to be exorcised at all costs'.[12]

The feminist censor, like her right-wing bedfellows, has long known that the graven images of sex are simulacra, 'radiant with their own fascination', that the division between sex and its representation is specious. But the formulation that appears to acknowledge this, 'porn is the theory, rape is the practice', is itself specious since it pretends to a distinction that it blurs. Rather the slogan should be: 'Sex is the theory, porn is the practice.' As with Whitehouse, the criticism that the followers of Andrea Dworkin are anti-sex is erroneous. As iconoclasts they are devout and fervent in their belief in sex (although it needs to be reinvented, i.e. it is too good for this world); their support for censorship is an attempt to withhold the news of the demise of sex.

Those feminists who are opposed to censorship are the iconolaters: in a world where sex has replaced God as the divine referential they worship icons knowing that 'underneath the idea of the apparition of God in the mirror of images, they [have already] enacted his death and his disappearance in the epiphany of his representations'. Instead of a refusal of the news of sex's abdication they recommend the reverse: a celebration of the simulacra of porn, precisely in the knowledge that it is a copy for which no original exists. For them it is not porn but the monopoly of it by heterosexual men that is degrading since, in a world without the 'real thing', to monopolize the images of sex is to monopolize sex and to monopolize sex is to monopolize *bodies*; 'Behind the baroque of images hides the grey eminence of politics.'[13]

Women have begun to engage with porn, with its power, extending its surfaces rather than simply trying to say 'no' to it or allowing *it* to extend over *them*. Thus women sex workers like Candida Royalle, a former New York porn queen, have begun to assert themselves in the industry. 'I didn't feel that porn films were addressing women's sexuality,' she has said (*Time Out*, 27 May 1993). Women are also beginning to consume porn, creating a market for this simulacra which creates its *own* demands. And the power of the new market is already phenomenal. In the United States women account for 40 per cent of all X-rated video rentals, and in France and Germany two out of three women watch porn regularly.[14] But in Britain this advance still encounters stiff resistance. According to Royalle, 'We've just started selling in the British market and there has been great interest. My only regret is that we have to conform to the insidious censorship that exists in the UK. Eventually they will have to get better. I mean, what do they think, that adults can't handle looking at penises?'

And there is the nub of British censorship law: it is designed to restrict pornography to the sexist depiction of women, to keep the phallus sacrosanct – after all, it is the ultimate symbol of the 'secret of sex' for the male establishment. The irony is that women can be shown precisely because their bodies do *not* represent 'sex' to these men, merely its *invocation*. They do not tell its 'secret'; they keep it enclosed in their bodies since it is through their possession by men that the phallus is represented. So technicolour tits, bums and digital masturbation in a wide-angle lens are acceptable material for the newsagent's top shelf but anything approaching an erection, even in the quarantine of a sex shop, is deemed worthy of the personal attention of Det. Supt Michael Hames and his pocket protractor (anything above 30° is the informal definition of an erection at the OPS). Images of women's bodies are considered natural commodities but the hard cock is still sacrosanct; the phallus must keep its mystery.

So we can understand and sympathize with the special fury and bile poor Mr Hames reserves for the *Gay Man's Guide*. Here the idolatry of pornography *and* homosexuality come together in a simulacra which 'unmasks' the phallus, showing that there is nothing behind it at all: 'fully aroused male sex organs' are offered on screen to other 'fully aroused male sex organs' (note how this phrase is far more inflated and impressive in its conception than ever a man's penis could be in action or representation).

Gay porn and the emerging homo- and heterosexual female porn demand a world that Hames can only blanche at: commodified cocks, dethroned from their phallic position, women behind the camera not just in front of it, and lesbians celebrating sex for the benefit of other lesbians rather than in some 'Swedish Lesbian Lust' fantasy entertainment for straight men.

This shift of consumer power coincides with technological changes which are pushing porn into the realm of a polymorphously perverse media. Cyberporn (computer networking porn), dildonics (software-based porn), interactive video, telephone sex and virtual sex will soon bring home the dictum: the more realistic the image the more apparent the non-existence of the thing it is meant to represent. More than this, it becomes apparent that pornography will not just be a copy of something for which there is no original (i.e. sex): soon it will bear no relation to any appearances, any reality whatever.

Already it can be seen that even and especially in fuddy-duddy old Britain the distinction between public and private, on-scene and ob-scene, erotica and porn, porn and sex is redundant. In Baudrillard's 'ecstasy of communication', all modern culture has become obscene, 'no longer the traditional obscenity of the visible, [but] of the all-too-visible ... of what no longer has any secret, of what dissolves completely in information and communication.'[15]

So it is entirely apt that as not only Hames and Whitehouse but British cabinet ministers and royalty as well learn the meaning of these last rites for the demarcation between public and private, the debate about the good/bad meaning of explicit images dissolves into a tabloid circus of 'Disgraceful – Those Shocking Videos in Full'.

Notes

1. Anne McClintock, 'Gonad the Barbarian and the Venus Flytrap', quoted in *Sex Exposed*, ed. Lynne Segal and Mary McIntosh (London: Virago, 1992), p. 111.

2. In the late 1980s the sexo-religious quality of these pictures was realized in

their projection onto the walls of some of the more chic gay night-spots; the icons of a guiltless (and 'gay-less') masculine heaven towered above the clubland worshippers.

3. Due to Britain's antiquated censorship laws US porn videos cannot be imported legally. This, combined with incompatibilities between the American TV system (SECAM) and the European system (PAL), results in most of the available US porn consisting of second-, third- and even fourth-generation copies. However, the resulting loss of definition has an interesting effect: the models' features and flaws are bleached out and their skin takes on a luminous, blemishless quality; they themselves become an ageless but youthful, anonymous but recognisably masculine face on a muscular, over-endowed, frame. In other words they end up resembling in their almost cartoon form Tom's idealized men.

4. Richard Dyer, 'Coming to terms: gay pornography', in *Only Entertainment* (London: Routledge, 1992), pp. 128–9.

5. *The Best of the Superstars 1993: The Year in Sex*, ed. John Patrick (Sarasota, FL: STARbooks Press, 1992), p. 203.

6. Mandy Merck, 'More of a man: gay porn cruises gay politics', in *Perversions: Deviant Readings* (London: Virago, 1993), pp. 217–35.

7. *Ibid.*, p. 232.

8. *Ibid.*, p. 233.

9. *Ibid.*, p. 233.

10. Jean Baudrillard, *Simulations* (New York: Semiotexte, 1983), pp. 57–8.

11. Jean Baudrillard, *Simulations*, p. 8.

12. *Ibid.*, p. 9.

13. *Ibid.*, p. 10.

14. Anne McClintock, in *Sex Exposed*, ed. Lynne Segal and Mary McIntosh, p. 130.

15. Jean Baudrillard, 'The ecstasy of communication', in Hal Foster's *Postmodern Culture* (London: Pluto Press, 1987), p. 131.

Chapter seven

Marky Mark and the Hunky Bunch
The Hustler Syndrome

Missing the Mark

HERE'S white rapper Marky Mark, on stage, stripped to his Calvin Kleins (he's contractually bound to wear them), gripping the mike in one hand and his packet in the other. And here's Madonna in her *Express Yourself* video also grabbing her crotch. Superficially similar – but what a difference in symbolic meaning! Maddy's stylized crotch-grabbing, dressed in a parody of a man's suit, pulses with power while Marky Mark's groin-gripping pulses with pathos. No matter how many times that boy grabs himself, he still only possesses a mere cock, whereas Maddy wields a *phallus* which grows bigger with every press launch.

Marky Mark's tragedy is that for all his desperate rap-ismo and genitalia display he cannot break out of the trend to portray young male pop stars as passive, fluffy playthings for teen girls. Worse, the more he resorts to his body as proof of his virility the more he 'unmans' himself, in effect admitting that his only asset, artistically and politically, is his body – the traditional position of *female* stars.

Girls at a Marky Mark or Take That! concert are just as much in control of the young male sexuality cavorting on stage as their mothers are at a Chippendale show. While their mothers delight in the spectacle of brawny men jiggling their most prided private parts for their delectation (just the reverse of their experience of men in the bedroom), their daughters throw, not knickers, but soft toys at Take That!, puncturing any delusions the boys might have about their sexuality being threatening. 'Take that!' challenge the boys, legs akimbo, hands on hips, and the girls just throw them Flopsy the Bunny.

Of course the pedigree of cutesy, butter-wouldn't-melt, harmless teen idols is a long one. In the 1960s there were Cliff Richard, Billy Fury and the early Beatles ('mop-head' even sounds like a brand of cuddly toy). In the 1970s there were David Cassidy, The Osmonds and the Bay City Rollers. By the 1980s what was left of pop music after Dance was dominated by the spending power of teen girls, bringing us acts like New Kids on the Block, Brother Beyond, Bros and – the doyen of harmless pop – Jason Donovan. All of them were mummy's boys with clean-cut looks (difficult, in fact, to imagine them shaving at all, so testosterone-free were they). And all of them were less likely to make unpleasant demands on a girl than her pyjama-case.

Rumours of homosexuality became *de rigueur* for those boy-men. You might be forgiven for thinking that the association of sex and deviance with these Mr Cleans would spell hit-parade oblivion. Not a bit of it. Instead it only served to enhance their appeal among young girls looking for a 'nice' boy they could pin on their bedroom walls. Jimmy Somerville, one of the first 'out' teen idols, was astonishingly popular with the *Smash Hits* and *Just Seventeen* set in the 1980s. What could be more desirable than a boy-man pop star who is successful and a *sister*? Young girls happily chased Somerville whenever they sighted him, safe in the knowledge that the hunted would not suddenly turn hunter.

Even crop-headed teen-pop Geminis Matt and Luke of Bros, who toyed with 'raunchy' imagery dressing up in leather and denim, had girlish faces and vocal-chords untroubled by puberty which made you wonder what they would look like in drag.

In the 1990s boy-men in various states of undress fill our screens and our airwaves. Although shows like *The Partridge Family* helped to blur the boundaries between pop and telly stars in the 1970s, it was the 1980s with soaps like *Neighbours* (launch-pad for Jason and Kylie) which saw them dissolved. It now goes without saying that top-rated US shows like *Beverly Hills 90210* and *Melrose Place* rely for their success on how many cute laddies like Luke

Perry and Jason Priestley they have mooning around. On the big screen stars like the late River Phoenix, Brad Pitt, Johnny Depp and Keanu Reeves bring us downy-faced easy prettiness, replacing the surly brat-packers of the early 1980s like Matt Dillon and Sean Penn, who seemed slightly self-conscious about the exploitation of their bodies.

And of course, they were right: the more of their bodies we see, the less powerful they are. Could you imagine Elvis performing 'Good Rockin' Tonite' in his underwear in the 1950s? His body, when we saw it in his nadir in 1960s films like *Blue Hawaii*, was bound to be a disappointment. His mystique depended on keeping his trousers on.

It's a long way from Memphis to *Melrose Place*. A flick from Elvis' hips once produced an earthquake that was felt around the globe. Now Marky Mark's crotch-grabbing provokes some giggles and an underwear promotion deal.

Poor Marky Mark. With a man's body and a boy's head he literally embodies the condition of male idols today: muscular, vigorous, even lewd, but just a *boy* nevertheless. Tits out for the girls!

And like a boy, Marky cannot quite cope with manhood when it slaps him in the face. According to New York magazine *QW* (25 October 1992), the boy whose trousers just won't stay up was recently confronted with an enthusiastic young male flasher at a nightclub. 'Get the fuck away!' he shouted at his imitator, 'You have no fucking class, get out of here!' Now Madonna, she would have snapped a photo for her next book.

(Originally published in *The Guardian*, 16 December 1992)

And hitting it

When did this become okay? He's got hold of himself! I guess I'm the dumbest guy alive. ... Is it okay to do that? When I was a kid you could get arrested for doing that anywhere near a bus.

● *David Letterman on* Late Night *after seeing a six-panel Marky/Klein ad on the side of a bus*[1]

For all his teen-girl pleasing fluffiness, Marky Mark is a phenomenon that deserves to be taken seriously. Young Mark R. Wahlberg has achieved, albeit unwittingly, something rather extraordinary, something rather peculiar, something rather outrageous: something, it might be said, rather *queer*.

Between him and Calvin Klein, America has been subjected to a multimedia 'homosexualization' bigger than Madonna's *Sex*. There is no aluminium foil wrapped around this boy's breasts, no cover price on his nakedness – he is offered gratis to the American public, as much a part of everyday American life as Sesame Street or Dunkin Donuts. Exhibitionism? Autoeroticism? Homoeroticism? Pick your perversion, they are all available now on the sides of buses that take America to work and to worship. American capitalism now sees fit to use billboards fifty feet high to present a young stud in his prime and in his underwear, alarmingly aroused by himself and our attention, teasing us with the hefty contents of his briefs. The cliché cover of the gay porn video, the come-on to what were once private and policed pleasures, has become in the Marky myth a public advert for a new way of treating men, their bodies and their cocks.

The Marky myth has made possible the final realization of the process begun with the explosion of post-war consumer culture and accelerated in the mid-1980s by the rediscovery of the male body: the commodification of men's cocks. While Marky Mark's c.v. may read 'rap star', he has more in common with the profession of male porn star: Marky Mark and Jeff Stryker are brothers under the Panstick. While Jeff offers his famous penis to the public through the 'private' medium of porn and personally cast dildos bought in sex shops and wrapped in plain paper, Marky gives away his appendage wrapped in white cotton on Main Street.

Of course, we may never actually *see* his penis, not merely because this would be 'indecent', but because it would defeat the object: if desire/curiosity is satisfied then why buy the product? Unlike Jeff it is not Marky's penis *itself* which is being sold but the confusion of it with the underwear. His 'packet' literally becomes the packet. His body becomes as fetishized as the product. Instead of lurid close-ups of his penis (à la Stryker) we are given endless photos of his phallicized body. This is the meaning of Marky's declaration that Lynne Goldsmith's collection of erotic photos of his flesh *Marky Mark* is 'dedicated to my dick'. He knows what the punters are really after, but it is also what *he* is after: Marky Mark himself is 'dedicated to his dick'. His bodybuilding is a daily auto-erotic prayer to his penis.

'You have to be totally dedicated. I eat all the right things. ... And I sweat my butt off in the gym. One and a half hours a day. Five circuits, five to ten sets of weights. Two different muscles a day. I really go for it, man!'

The 'revolution' in attitudes towards male autoeroticism represented by the Marky myth reaches right back into the belly of the American Family itself. 'When Marky Mark was about three he would get in front of anything where he could see his reflection,' his mother confides in *Marky Mark*. 'It could be the toaster or the oven and he would climb up on top of the counter and sit in front of us and *pose*, you know, trying to flex his muscles, when all there was was little bones.' In the Marky myth even the traditional narrative of mother as guardian of her son's morals and sexual purity is transformed into the narrative of proud spectator of her son's self-pleasuring.

Not so long ago autoeroticism was the cause of terrible enervation of manhood: lethargy, blindness and bodily wasting were the fruits of this perversion. No longer. Marky's 'little bones' cannot be seen for muscles – tangible evidence of the healthiness of modern self-love. Gone also is the social failure that such self-pleasuring represented for boys; in its place is undreamt social success: *Interview*, *Rolling Stone*, *Vanity Fair* and even *Penthouse* have all obliged in the realization of this little narcissist's dream, providing him with something rather better than a toaster in which to admire his reflection.

> *There's something about him. Believe me, we girls can tell that kind of thing.*
> ● Teen girl quoted in *Sky Magazine*

How does the little horror get away with it? Like Maddy he is the 'low other': immigrant (Irish), Catholic, body-centred, white trash and 'street'.[2] And yet he is Pepsi sweet. His freckles and orthodonti-cally correct smile are reassuringly wholesome and American, framing his 'low' status in an acceptable way. He is very much a *boy*, an adolescent head on a man's body, a laughing impish smile atop a massive torso belying its threat; he is *Marky* Mark, an affectionate diminutive of himself. Pumped up and flexed for us in front of the camera, dick pushing against pants or grabbed through the cloth, he is a *filthy* urchin, a satyr prancing and leering in front of us, stroking himself, crying 'Look at this! Isn't it great? Aren't I lucky to have one! Bet you'd like to touch!'

But he is a *smooth* satyr, shorn of his hair and his strength to shock – tamed; his body is photographed by Weber and Ritts in their grainy, creamy black and white 'art' photography (keeping the image distinct from the lurid technicolour of porn) presenting his body as ice-cream: an advert for Boyflavour Haagen Daaz.

The sobriquet 'The Madonna of Rap' pays tribute to his sexploitation of himself, his own commodification of his body. But where Maddy is admired for her ironic masquerades, Marky is valued for his *authenticity*: what you see, his public fondly imagines, is what you get (the myth of 'rap' itself: a vaudeville of violence verging on operetta sold as 'street-real'). This is the prerequisite of his blatant sexuality which would otherwise appear self-conscious and therefore unmasculine. Hence the emphasis on a background as blue-collar as Budweiser beer: how his dad drove a pick-up truck and his mother worked as a nurse, how eleven Irish Wahlbergs crammed into a three-bedroomed house with grandma stowed in the basement, how his 'little bones' grew on food stamps. Struggle and simplicity, the essential ingredients of American Dream masculinity, are the moral of Marky's story: the triumph of spunk over sophistication, vigour over class, 'rootiness' over respectability, America over Europe.

And in America the boy must also be a rebel. America is doomed, as Leslie Fiedler puts it, to love boys 'precisely because they play hooky, cuss, steal in a mild sort of way, and dream of violence'.[3] So we learn that after his parents divorced, Marky 'smoked, drank, played hooky from school and shoplifted'.[4] His PR machine is quick to grasp the marketability of this period and calls it his 'collision with law and order'. Marky himself asserts 'I don't want to go on about how hard I am, but I know about life on the street. I've been there.'[5] You can take the boy out of the street but you can't take the street out of the boy; not if you want to sell a rap star. The distance between him and the street is important: it is a part of his past that remains past, a rebel phase he moved through, lending credibility and strength to the reformed and redeemed Marky we see today, but moved through and left behind nevertheless. 'My music has helped me escape from stealing stereos or selling bombs, getting drunk and beating people up' (*The Face*, December 1992), he tells us, thus distinguishing himself from those rap artists who glamorize crime. Our Marky is not the Bad Boy rap star; he is rather the Good Bad Boy, 'America's vision of itself, crude and unruly in its beginnings, but endowed by its creator with an instinctive sense of what is right.'6

Marky's masculinity is as real and as robust, as rough and ready as his body, and like his muscles it provokes as much tenderness as respect on the part of the audience; a compassion, a *pity* for his deprived past and his present-day over-achievement. This is the lovable tearaway, the boy kicking against the pricks, the boy in a hurry to be a man: the Marky Man Child. Asked about his habit of grabbing himself he explains, 'When I was younger I used to wear my older brother's trousers and they were always too big so I had to hold them on.' Even his most vulgar, most obscene attributes are really just a measure of his endearing *boyishness*.

But how can a male supermodel, clothes-horse for Gap and Calvin Klein, be a regular guy? Easy – if he is 'not a model'. 'I almost blew the deal,' Marky confides. 'I told them I'm not a model, you can take a picture of my normal look but you gotta do it my way.'7 Marky disavows the passive position that modelling threatens the male with – 'I'm not a model' – by portraying himself in control: 'you gotta do it my way'. He is a 'normal guy' with a 'normal look', there can be nothing suspect about his posing and pouting for the camera because he does not pose or pout, the camera merely records the 'honest', 'straight up', fleshy phenomenon that is Marky Mark: and at *his* behest. There is no dissimulation and his 'raw' masculinity is not compromised. When Klein, the fashion *designer*, suggests that he wear tight jeans Marky the *un*-designed boy-man stands his ground and protects his masculinity (choosing an expletive metaphor that aptly conveys the real sexual threat at the root of it all): 'I said, "Yo, man! This is me! I don't want to fuck up my rap career!"'

Of course there is nothing natural or normal about Marky

Mark's look. What could be more contrived than a *white* rap star? What could be more cultivated than a *bodybuilder*? Unlike that employed for female supermodels, this is a dissembling masquerade, a dissembling that the fashion industry is only too happy to conspire with. His job description 'rap artist' is the epitome of this: apart from lending gritty authenticity to his image, it also provides the alibi for the total commodification of his body while preserving the very thing that was being consumed: his virility – he's not a model, he's a rap star. By a process of double-bluff Marky is a male supermodel who does not model: masculinity cannot be exposed as a masquerade if it is to keep its power. Having your beefcake and eating it is the only way you *can* eat it and keep its flavour. Our 'rap star's' second album *You've Gotta Believe* was a hook on which the glossies could hang his body for the drooling inspection of their readers. With some of the most enviable publicity in pop music history, and probably the best for any rap star, Marky's album flopped. Marky's old fans were no doubt put off by the fashion world's interest, while his new fans who enjoyed him and his body in the 'rap star' fantasy were not willing to carry the pretence the whole way and actually buy his records.

While Marky might like us to think that he cannot spell 'irony', his image encompasses it as a boy's head on a man's body. More, he is a *white* boy's head on a *black* man's body. Through his bodybuilding and rap-ismo he appropriates the sexual stereotyping of black men as bodies – bodies implying fabulous phallic endowment. One of his favourite poses is to face the camera manfully head-on, body braced and tensed with his lower lip thrust out emulating an arrogant facial stereotype of black 'gangsta' rap stars. And yet on Marky's face it appears more that of a sulky child seeking our attention than a white cop's nemesis. His white skin and boyish facial features reassure us that this 'blackness' is just a semblance, the sexiness without the threat; we know that in a moment he will grin and stand on his head. This is the secret of his kosher 'low other' status, a 'blackness' in white packaging; Marky is a latter-day minstrel. He has done with the male body what Elvis did with the blues. Hence the gossip about the size of his penis is the acceptable white expression of unacceptable white racist fantasies.

No wonder gay men took the homeboy to their hearts. In Britain the admiration took the form of *Capital Gay* newspaper voting him Hunky Hunk of '92 but in America the appreciation took a more substantial form. It was David Geffen, recently 'out' gay media mogul, who suggested to Calvin Klein, whose label has long benefited from the spending power of gay men, that he use Marky Mark to promote his men's underwear line.[8]

It was a marriage made in heaven. Calvin Klein got *devoted* brand loyalty from the pink dollar (gay men became less likely to be caught wearing non-Calvin Klein underwear than Marky Mark), and priceless advertising as the campaign became the most talked about in years. Marky meanwhile got a fat fee (rumoured to be anywhere between $100,000 and $7,000,000) and the chance to see his features reflected across America.

It is only apt that it was gay men's devotion to Marky Mark, their response to his 'queer' signals, which launched him into the media stratosphere, turning him from a novelty act aimed at teen girls into a worldwide phenomenon; making his torso the most famous since Michelangelo's David (and a whole lot ruder).[9]

So successful was the campaign that posters of the Boy Wonder sporting nothing but Klein's handiwork and that blinding grin fuelled a mini black-market boom as kids in the cities temporarily abandoned drug-dealing for the more lucrative business of crow-barring Marky Mark posters from bus-shelter hoardings. Gay men eagerly parted with $50 to have their favourite 'rapper' in their bedroom. As one gay American columnist reported:

> At a well-appointed flat in the Castro this Christmas, the tree was fab, the guests handsome and erudite, but the buzz was over the huge Marky/Calvin bus-shelter poster, freshly bought from a kid on the street for $50. Guests were admitted into the room one at a time, and were cautioned not to touch. 'I kicked myself in the head after I only bought one,' said the host.[10]

But for all his display of the pumped male body and his commodification of his cock, all his 'queer' resonances, Marky is loved by gays precisely because of his official heterosexuality. Despite hopes to the contrary, they *want* to believe in Marky's authenticity, his American wholesomeness, his 'uncontrived' masculinity – his *straightness*. The success of his boyish I'll-drop-my-pants-for-you performance is utterly predicated on his heterosexuality. The boy whose image is hysterically macho, a form of 'homovestism', of exaggerated masculine posing and dressing (and here the muscles are a form of drag as much as the rap gear, jive and gestures) that is almost *camp*, is loved by gay men for his lack of irony, his spontaneous masculinity. 'New Kids? Who cares? 90210? Poseurs. Marky Mark is *real*. He's got that twinkle in his eye, that dopey grin, and oh yes, the body.'[11] To gay men Marky Mark is 'genuine' masculinity, uncontaminated by effete professions like acting: no suspension of disbelief is required to enjoy his performance, because his performance is just him. His hypermasculine masquerade is taken as the real thing by gay men, something 'irony free', in a way that they could never from a gay man.

In short, the secret of Marky Mark's gay success is that he is a *hustler*. He is a straight boy who 'plays the queers', queers who have invested even more in his heterosexuality than he. But Marky is a postmodernist hustler, no longer to be found standing on the sidewalks of Times Square waiting for punters to light his cigarette. Instead he is to be found looking down on the old-fashioned trade going on fifty feet below him, reified and transfigured to godlike proportions. Modern media techniques offer his body to millions of punters simultaneously, turning the strictly small-time private transaction of hustling into a big-time enterprise making millions for 'pimps' like Klein who 'procure' his body for the public.

But for all the sophisticated selling, Marky represents the classic contradiction of the hustler: a straight boy who lives by offering his body to gay men, but takes this as an affirmation of his heterosexuality. Asked about his gay fans Marky replies, 'Yo! If you're gay you're in the house!'[12] Well yes, gays are 'in the house' – after all, they are paying the mortgage. But even this 'strictly business' relationship is almost too much for the poor lamb and is quickly followed by more heterosexual male paranoia: 'Just don't try to do that shit around me! Don't try to fuck me!' This is a condition of the hustler: the threat implicit in the (lucrative) attentions of gay men, that of being placed in a passive position, has to be hysterically disavowed.

But it was his final pronouncement on the subject which confirmed categorically his hustler status: 'Bring your sister though, you can watch.' In other words, the homeboy tells the homos, 'I'm not gay, man, no way. But if you fags wanna enjoy my studly heterosexuality – for a price – then go ahead, be my guest.'

Here is the hustler *Weltanschauung* in its 'barest' essentials: the attention of homosexual men (which is secretly needed/desired) threatens to put him in a passive position (act-ually and media-lly) – 'don't fuck me!' – and must be turned round into an assertion of his hetero-fucker status. The old-fashioned kind of hustler would achieve this by playing only the 'insertor', 'top man' role in his transactions with his 'faggot' clientele. But the new-fangled hustler cannot allow even that carefully circumscribed sexual contact and instead offers to 'fuck your sister', inviting you to watch his stirring performance of phallic prowess. His 'straightness' is redeemed in gay dollars even as he leads a 'gay' lifestyle, celebrating/exploiting the male body. This is why the hustler is the very apotheosis of American masculinity: the hustler is the heterosexual male narcissistic libido made flesh, *a way of life*. His is an ego composed of a condensation of alienated homosexual desire. It is this alienated desire which he sells to gays, an alienation which ironically confirms his successful performance of masculinity. The hustler puts himself to the test with every punter, but wins through in the end, symbolized by the exchange of money – a reward not for allowing a homosexual to enjoy his body but rather a prize for managing to remain heterosexual.

The modern gay Marky fan's relationship to the Marky myth, for all his 'gay pride', is clearly mapped out in Proust's text of maudlin 'doomed' homosexuality, *Sodom and Gomorrah*:

> They fall in love with precisely that type of man who has nothing feminine about him, who is not an invert and consequently cannot love them in return; with the result that their desire would be forever insatiable did their money not procure for them real men, and their imagination end by making them take for real men the inverts to whom they had prostituted themselves.[13]

Shortly after making his 'liberal' remarks, Marky betrayed the hustler's contempt for his punters when he appeared on the youth TV programme *The Word* with black reggae star Shabba Ranks. When Shabba declared that gays deserved to be 'crucified', Marky refused to join the host Mark Lamarr in condemning the outburst. Instead he went on to perform a song with Shabba and announced to the angry audience, 'all you who can't deal with it, step the fuck off.'

When news of this débâcle filtered across the Atlantic, American gays began to sense they had been robbed. The Gay and Lesbian Alliance Against Defamation (GLAAD) protested to Calvin Klein at the hypocrisy of his label using a homophobe to sell men's underwear. But worse was to come for Marky. The Committee Against Anti-Asian Violence (CAAV) unveiled another view of the little stripper that he had been strangely bashful about: two convictions, dating from his mid-teens, for harassing Afro-American school-kids and assaulting two Vietnamese men. The white rap star had raps for racist attacks.

What a consummate hustler! Marky thieves the clothes off the backs of blacks and gays and then fucks them up the ass! The Marky myth is finally undressed, the last jockstrap is removed and tossed away, the grand finale unveils Marky as the story of modern America's attitude towards those on the margins. What began as the young white Mark Wahlberg's fear of the Other, blacks and gays, was resolved into their *exploitation*. Rather than hate and fear black men for their 'big dicks' he would steal one for himself and become the rapper Marky Mark. Rather than hate and fear gays for their threat to his heterosexuality he would rob them of their love for the male body and then sell it back to them.

For gay men in particular the revelations about his violent past and allegations of homophobia struck a familiar note. The prickly contradiction of the straight hustler who lives parasitically on gay culture has always threatened to be resolved through violence. The hustler's self image as a 'fucker', the demarcation between him and those he lives on, sometimes has to be hammered home with fists. For this reason the old-time hustler often threatened to turn from fag-pleaser to fag-basher. This is the *Midnight Cowboy* narrative: a penniless virile young Texan (Jon Voigt) beats up his sad old fag pick-up to finance and purify his buddy romance with Ratso (Dustin Hoffman).

But times have changed. Twenty years later the 'sad fag' bashes back: GLAAD and CAAV demonstrate underneath the Klein/Marky poster in Times Square, making the *New York Times*, and our rapping millionaire Midnight Cowboy almost loses his (under)pants. A jittery Calvin Klein is forced to issue a statement condemning homophobia and racism and assuring the public that his model is 'a reformed young man who has grown way beyond his years as a result of a particularly difficult childhood.'

Marky was not at all pleased with what this CAAV/GLAAD 'strip' had revealed. For perhaps the first time in his life he found himself looking at a reflection of himself in the media that he found less than flattering. Realizing just how badly a reputation for homophobia and racism could affect his career hustling gay/black imagery, he issued an apology to the press: 'Asian Pacific Americans, African Americans and all people have the right to live free of violence and harassment. I want to make it clear that I condemn anti-gay hatred and violence.' He also announced that he would work with GLAAD and CAAV in making ads 'to help spread the word that bigotry and violence are wrong.'

While he may have satisfied the protesters and clung on to his Calvin Kleins, Marky Mark may not have salvaged his career. The Marky myth is compromised. Now his 'street' credentials are taken seriously and his 'low other' status overwhelms his wholesomeness: his 'roots' threaten to strangle him. No more Good Bad Boy, he is simply the Bad Bad Boy. His breezy narcissism no longer looks so innocent, his smile no longer so cute and his body no longer so friendly. Like a boy stepping over the line from adolescence into manhood Marky has lost the *sweetness* that appeals to girls and boys alike.

The final irony in the story of the boy in a scampering hurry to be a man may prove to be that precisely at the moment when he achieved his ambition the world lost interest. When the Man Child grows up his audience grows bored.

Notes

1. David Letterman, quoted in *Entertainment*, 15 January 1993.

2. I am indebted to Nick Haeffner for the notion of Madonna's 'low otherness', *Remembering the Present*, unpublished Ph.D. dissertation, University of Sussex, 1993, p. 2.

3. Leslie Fiedler, *Love and Death in the American Novel* (New York: Stein and Day, 1975), p. 270.

4. *Sky*, December 1992.

5. *The Face*, December 1992.

6. Leslie Fiedler, *Love and Death in the American Novel*.

7. *The Face*, December 1992.

8. *Entertainment*, 15 January 1993.

9. The image of David is unerotic: the sexiness has been sublimated. 'He exists for himself and his father' (Anthony Easthope, *What a Man's Gotta Do*, Winchester, MA: Unwin Hyman, 1990, p. 16).

10. Jim Prosenyaro, *Frontiers*, 15 January 1993.

11. *Ibid*.

12. *The Face*, December 1992.

13. Marcel Proust, *Cities of the Plain*, trans. C. Scott-Moncrieff (New York, 1927).

Chapter eight

A Crying Shame
Transvestism and Misogyny
in The Crying Game

Desire is a danger zone.
● *Poster for The Crying Game*

A British-made film made a big splash in Hollywood in
1993. Rave reviews and a shoal of Academy Award nominations
greeted the arrival of Neil Jordan's *The Crying Game* in the United
States. Critics jostled as they rushed to out-hyperbolize each other.
'The first movie in ages whose advance reviews should be restricted
to two words: see it,' panted the *New York Press*. 'Dazzling. Quite
literally amazing. ... A dizzying exploration of sex, loyalty,
betrayal and unexpected love,' gushed the *New York Times*. By the
end of March, provoked by this critic's love-fest, the American
public had parted with over $50,000,000 at the box office to see a
low-budget film about an IRA man's love affair with a transvestite.

The rapturous American response was not matched in
Britain. Many took this as yet another example of the healthy
potential of British cinema frustrated by British apathy. The film's
producer Steve Wooley put the blame for this squarely on the
media, complaining to the *Guardian*: 'No one would write about
The Crying Game here.' He suggested that this was due to the fact
that it dealt with taboo issues like Northern Ireland and transvestism.[1]

In fact the film *was* noticed in Britain, but generally only by
'progressive' types who welcomed what they saw as the film's radi-

cal sexual/political agenda. The gay national weekly, the *Pink Paper*, sang its praises in an editorial and claimed, like Wooley, that it was the victim of British timidity, this time on the part of distributors. Julie Wheelwright, author of *Amazons and Military Maids: Women Who Dressed as Men in Pursuit of Life, Liberty and Happiness* (Pandora), glowingly described Jordan's film in *New Statesman and Society* as one which 'brilliantly fuses anxieties about sexual identity with questions of nationalism'.

On the contrary, *The Crying Game* is neither a 'progressive' nor even a 'British' film. Instead, it is a thoroughly *American* film which women, gays, blacks *and* transexuals should be deeply distrustful of. But most especially women.

Female trouble

At the 'liberal' heart of Jordan's film is a culmination of the Hollywood Good Girl/Bad Girl tale told over and over in the *Fatal Attraction/Hand That Rocks the Cradle/Single White Female* genre of misogyny which Judith Williamson and others have identified as revolving around anxieties about the 'single working woman' (SWW). Potent, independent women – sexually as well as economically – had become *the* threat to be articulated and resolved in Hollywood movies in the 1980s and early 1990s. While the stylistic roots of this genre reach back to film noir, popular in post-war America when the last backlash against independent women was underway, the Good Girl/Bad Girl narrative pursued by Jordan reaches right back to the treatment of women in American literature outlined by Leslie Fiedler:

> Our great novelists shy away from permitting in their fictions any full-fledged, mature women, giving us instead monsters of virtue or bitchery, symbols of the rejection or fear of sexuality.[2]

As the publicity hints, *The Crying Game* does not offer us 'desire' so much as 'fear' – fear of 'woman', in particular her body. This is the 'danger zone' that male heterosexual desire has to negotiate.

This is the real 'terrorism' of the film: male terror of the castration threat represented by 'woman', a castration threat that must be disdained. The 'danger zone' cited in *The Crying Game* is perhaps best envisaged as the *vagina dentata* that Freud suggested some men fear lurks within the female genitals, threatening to unman them at the very moment of the consummation of their manhood.

The film begins with an off-duty black British soldier, Jody (Forest Whitaker), at a fairground in Northern Ireland (one of many unrealistic features which betray the way in which Northern Ireland is merely a plot device – British soldiers in the Province do not leave their barracks except in convoy). We see him enjoying himself amidst the lights and music, drunkenly kissing and fondling Jude (Miranda Richardson), a strikingly attractive young woman, in a scene of carefree 'joy' which is the most luxuriant shot in the whole film, perhaps the only occasion the wide screen is put to good effect, generating a sense of expansiveness and freedom that contrasts with the narrow, mean, 'shorn' shots that follow.

Jude lures him away from the fair to a beach where, instead of sexual gratification, Jody finds himself kidnapped at gunpoint by the IRA. So in the first few minutes of the film Jude's body is introduced as 'the danger zone', the Venus Man-Trap. Underlining Jody's impotence as a result of coming into contact with this horror, his hands are tied behind his back and a hood is placed over his head (loss of sight symbolizes castration: Oedipus is blinded after he sleeps with his mother). Finally the deal the IRA hoped to extort from the British authorities fails to materialize and Jody is sentenced to be shot. Thus Jude, the 'monster of bitchery', the ultimate SWW (her career is the IRA), has employed her seductive siren body to trap and kill/castrate the soldier.

We are offered some relief from the horror that Jude represents. While in captivity, Jody is befriended by one of his captors, Fergus (Stephen Rea). He shows him kindness where the others show contempt or indifference and attempts to shield him from savage assaults by Jude (his removal of Jody's hood is especially symbolic, as is Jude's anger when she discovers this). Jody tells Fergus that Jude was 'not even my type', and shows him a picture of his half-caste girlfriend Dil, saying, '*That's* my type'. Dil is thus introduced as the opposite of Jude, as the Good Girl, or the 'monster of virtue', to Jude's monster of bitchery. Before his death Jody exacts a promise from Fergus that he will find Dil and 'take her for a margarita in the Metro'.

After Jody's death (Fergus allows him to escape but he is killed under the wheels of a British armoured personnel carrier arriving on the scene), Fergus flees to London where he starts a new life outside the body of the IRA. He keeps his word to Jody, meeting Dil and taking her for a margarita. They then begin a relationship in which Dil offers a caricature of 'femininity' which contrasts with the ball-busting threats of Jude that are still fresh in our minds. Such is the doting, cloying, *embarrassing* nature of 'her' submissive 'feminine' attachment to Fergus that even Julie Wheelwright is forced to admit, 'Dil is a fantasy created from outdated gestures of femininity. Dil clings to "her" lover like a houseplant, bringing him a kiss-and-make-up lunch at work, fellating him with enthusiasm and assuring Fergus, "I fix on anyone nice to me." '[3]

If Jude represents the fear of castration, Dil is the rejection of that fear: monsters of virtue and bitchery evading fully-fledged womanhood. This is Fiedler's equation, but it is also the Hollywood convention, documented by feminists such as Mary Ann Doane, that femininity has to be portrayed as a kind of *masquerade*, a fetishistic disavowal of the castration threat. In *The Crying Game* that masquerade is taken to the absolute limit, through the use of actual masquerade instead of metaphor; transvestism as employed by Jordan presents an opportunity for excluding the feminine altogether until nothing is left but a semblance, an empty echo – something that, despite the SWW panics of recent years, is still inconceivable in the portrayal of on-screen *biological* females. Dil can embody a femininity that would be laughed out of the cinema if played by a woman, even by the audience that rooted for the saccharine-sweet Good Girl wife of Michael Douglas in *Fatal Attraction*. But Dil's unconvincing portrayal of femininity is made acceptable, even desirable by the way in which she embodies the fantasy of rejecting that which is most convincing (and therefore terrifying) in 'the feminine' – i.e. 'woman'.

If *The Crying Game* is original it is not in its misogyny but in its *extremity*. This extremity is not in the 'monster of bitchery' – Jude is no more horrific than Glenn Close's deranged character in *Fatal Attraction* – but rather in the monstrosity of the monster of virtue. The shock of this film does not reside in images of paint-stripped cars, boiled bunnies or women hiding in the bath clutching carving knifes. No, in this 'progressive' film the sharp intake of breath, the thrill that the audience seeks, is to be found in the show-stopping discovery that the Good Girl is so 'good' that *she has a penis*.

The monstrosity of this revelation is played for all it is worth when Fergus and the audience are literally presented with Dil's penis at eye-level as he sits on the bed, looking forward to their first act of intercourse (their sexual contact has so far been restricted to fellatio). Where there should be a 'lack' there is an obvious endowment; retching, Fergus rushes into the bathroom. This shock is absolutely essential for the technical success of the film (press notes implored secrecy from reviewers) and it contains within it the evidence, if any were needed, of the real terror of the film. Fergus' nausea and shock are caused not so much by seeing a penis as by a displacement of his own castration anxiety. Being confronted with a penis where he expected to find lack (disavowed by the 'exotic' fetishistic femininity of Dil) only serves to remind him of the *reality* of lack.

According to Freud disavowal is not simple denial; in disavowal one says, 'I know very well but all the same....' Thus two contradictory opinions are held simultaneously: 'All humans have penises', the primal belief and 'Some humans are without penises', based on perception, i.e. vision. The first belief is held under the second and maintained through fetishism. When Fergus *sees* that Dil has a penis it inverts his system of disavowal: 'all humans have penises' is no longer held under the perceptual idea that 'some humans are without penises'. This collapses the disavowal and the fetishism of Dil's 'feminine' body – bringing him face to face with the reality of castration. For a moment. Fergus, of course, quickly realizes 'she' must be a man and he has been 'tricked'. But it is *fear* which arises first, not anger. The importance of 'vision' to disavowal and the assumed epistemological 'superiority' of male genitals (they can be seen) brings a special irony to the New York critic's comment, 'The first film in ages whose advance reviews should be restricted to: see it.'

But for all Dil's 'monstrosity' it is still a monstrosity of virtue. After an initial estrangement, her relationship with Fergus continues without sex, emphasizing the virtuous rejection of (female) sexuality that Dil represents. But all is not well in paradise; the sharp-toothed serpent is still at large. Jude makes a hissing reappearance dressed up to the nines, complete with vicious bob and devastatingly made-up face with red gash for a mouth; a femme fatale figure for Fergus, signposting his doom. Appearing in his bedroom as if by magic, she places her taloned hand on his crotch and threatens him with death if he does not perform an assassination for the IRA; once again the SWW's sexuality is coded as the threat of castration/death. Fortunately for Fergus, before the monster of bitchery can carry out her threat, his monster of virtue intervenes and slays her: the White Witch sees off the Black (reversing the sign of their skin colour).[4]

Like the bath scene in *Fatal Attraction* the showdown comes at the end of *The Crying Game*: the annihilation of the Bad Girl, to cheers from the audience, is both the plot and moral finale of both films. Douglas' wife and Dil empty a revolver at the monster that threatens their man, producing a satisfyingly mutilated corpse. (The dramatic requirements of this genre stipulate that only the White Witch can see off the Black.)

But where *The Crying Game* improves on *Fatal Attraction* is in the finality of the triumph over female sexuality that it offers: here the mutilated body is that of the only biological female in the picture, and the smoking gun is in the hand of a literally – not just symbolically – *faux* woman. The symbolism of the other key moment, the scene where Fergus vomited after being presented with Dil's penis, is recouped: now the phallus triumphs over lack; what previously threatened his sense of identity now preserves it.

The Crying Game, under the guise of an adventurous exploration of desire and terrorism, has succeeded in bringing together two unoriginal and reactionary Hollywood trends, both of them inimical to women: the Good Girl/Bad Girl narrative and the tradition of portraying transvestites as homicidal women haters. In films such as *Psycho*, *Dressed to Kill* and *Silence of the Lambs* innocent women are bumped off by men who turn out to be transvestites. In *The Crying Game the* woman – who is far from innocent – is killed by a woman who turns out to be a man. In the same way as the logistics of the denouement are reversed, the 'moral' of the tale is also reversed: as Dil fires at Jude, having guessed that it was she who seduced Jody to his death, 'she' asks how *she* did it.

'Was it with that cute bum, those hips, or was it those tits?' she asks with bitter sarcasm. Firing off all 'her' bullets into Jude's envied body, 'she' reduces it to a gory tangle of limbs on the floor. The TV's jealousy of the woman's natural endowments is shown triumphant. Her virtue is, in the end, more beautiful and lasting than the bitchery of the biological woman; more than this, the 'real' feminine body of Jude is once again, as at the beginning of the film, connected to man's betrayal and death. Jude's dying words, having realized that Dil is a transvestite, complete the rehabilitation of the transvestite at the cost of the denigration of 'woman': 'You sick bitch,' she rasps.[5]

In the dubiously radical cause of trying to show that *faux* women can be better women than biological women, Neil Jordan has achieved something repugnant to both women and transvestites, but something that has earned him a place in the Hollywood pantheon (and not just for his Oscar for Best Script). By combining the anxieties about the SWW exemplified in films like *Fatal Attraction* with the women-killer male fantasy projected into the cross-dresser in films like *Silence of the Lambs* Jordan has succeeded in making a film in which the transvestite has come to represent sympathetically the fantasy of doing away with woman altogether.

The tranny-fucker

> *If the idea of a woman with a penis becomes 'fixated' in an individual when he is a child, resisting all the influence of later life and making him as a man unable to do without a penis in his sexual object, then, although in other respects he may lead a normal sexual life, he is bound to become a homosexual, and will seek his sexual object among men who, owing to some other mental and physical characteristics, remind him of women.*
> ● *Sigmund Freud*[6]

A gay audience also has good reason to be distressed by what Jordan has done in his film, and not just out of solidarity with women. Homosexual desire is deeply implicated here in the realization of the fantasy of doing away with woman. However, latent homosexuality acts as a kind of subtextual red herring, covering the tracks of the film's heterosexual misogyny – the threat which the female body (the 'danger zone') represents to those men who desire it.

What is presented is the homosexuality of the 'tranny-fucker' type – what might be termed a *male heterosexual* variety of homosexuality: desiring 'women' who have penises.

It is pertinent that the 'homosexual' subtext of the film is, like the transvestite's penis for the transvestite fucker, hidden and yet always on view (in the mind's eye): the film's 'homosexuality' is almost all visual in its signification, a signification that is guarded yet obvious, easily overlooked by those who do not wish to see such things.

Fergus and Jody fall very much in love with one another in a way which is constantly telegraphed to the audience. Fergus displays many acts of tenderness towards Jody, from feeding him to holding his penis for him when pissing, which place Fergus in the position of 'mother' to impotent Jody. Fergus' removal of Jody's hood, causing him to be reprimanded, is not just an act of kindness: it allows Fergus to see Jody's face. The fact that Fergus can see Jody at all is the indirect result of flattery: Jody manages to persuade Fergus to remove the hood by telling him that he had already got a good look at him; asked to prove it, he replies, 'You're the handsome one.' Even when Fergus is forced to replace the hood, he pulls it up over Jody's mouth, keeping the rest of his face hidden; extreme close-ups present this vulnerable, full and fleshy orifice to us, indicating the sensual attraction it holds for Fergus. The sexual tension between them is made glaringly obvious in a scene where Jody wishes to piss and, hands tied behind his back, asks Fergus to take his penis out and hold it for him. Fergus is overly bashful to the point of *preciousness* about this and Jody exclaims, 'It's only a piece of meat.' Fergus' problem appears to be that it is both *more* than just a piece of meat and precisely that it *is* something appetizing for him (perhaps precisely for the reason that he throws up when he sees the 'meat' on Dil). When he finally capitulates he prissily averts his eyes from the 'meat' in his hand.

An awareness of the film's 'homosexuality' has the added effect of dispelling any remaining notions of the film's 'examination of nationalism'. It is evident that the problem in the relationship of these two men, the thing which threatens and brutalizes them, forcing them into their roles as enemies, is more 'Jude' than 'war'. *She*, after all, was the one who seduced Jody in the first place, resulting in Fergus being put in a position where he has to kill the man he loves. *She* is the most violent and the most bloodthirsty of all the terrorists: when Jody defends Fergus from a verbal onslaught from Jude, insisting 'He's a good soldier!', she smashes him across the face with her pistol. After she leaves the room Fergus rolls the hood up over Jody's mouth and we see blood oozing from it – the gash? And, most importantly, it is Jude who complains to the CO that Fergus has removed Jody's hood – she wants him impotent while he wants him potent.

So when Jody exclaims 'She's not my type, anyway' and shows Fergus his picture of Dil (who, it must be said, is an obvious transvestite to anyone who has not lived a sheltered life – pointing up again the heterosexual assumptions of the film), Fergus agrees that she is very attractive. The effect is to express a preference for 'women' with penises, consciously on the part of Jody and unconsciously on the part of Fergus.

The deadline approaches and Fergus realizes that he is going to have to kill Jody. Their lightning courtship reaches its climax when he spends the night before Jody's execution consoling him. When the fatal hour arrives, Fergus cannot bring himself to shoot Jody (he refuses to be the agent of the cycle of castrating events set in motion by Jude) but is saved from having to do so when Jody escapes, only to be run down by a British armoured personnel carrier.

Fergus' break with the IRA and his journey to London to meet Dil become part of his repressed and now unrealizable love-affair with Jody. This perhaps explains why he is so slow to grasp Dil's dissembling and even fails to realize that the Metro is a gay club (although in its utopian blend of old and young, male and female, transvestite and 'straight acting', it is so unrealistic that many gays might not recognize it). The way that Dil stands in for Jody becomes apparent when he is given his first blow-job by 'her': as he climaxes we see his mind's eye image of Jody bowling (he bragged to Fergus that he was a 'demon bowler').

Fergus also exhibits a fascination with Jody's clothes that

Dil keeps littered around the flat as mementos. This fascination develops into a *Vertigo*-like necrophile obsession (after Fergus discovers that Dil has a penis) when in order to disguise 'her' and protect 'her' from Jude he persuades Dil to cut 'her' hair and wear Jody's cricketing clothes. They check into a hotel and sleep fully-clothed in the same bed, Fergus wide awake and rigid with fear, fear of what Jude will do to Dil if she discovers them, and fear of himself. This is the other meaning of his vomiting when he sees Dil's penis for the first time: it is the corollary of the pissing scene with Jody. Fergus' nauseous fear emanates from his own repressed homosexuality, the same fear which made him queasy about touching Jody's penis. Once again, the root of the fear is a kind of castration threat: Fergus' erotic attachment to the penis has to be given up because it represents his homosexuality which in turn represents his 'unmanning', his *own* sexual difference within the phallocentric economy.

The irony here is that for Fergus, on a *conscious* level, Dil was, like any man's 'girl', 'the phallus' for Jody; but through Fergus' subconscious desire Dil has literally come to be Jody's phallus for Fergus; Dil's dark sin and the generous development of 'her' 'manhood' when we see it connote very directly the black Jody's penis we and Fergus never see.

Fetishism is at the root of it all: Fergus fetishizes Dil as the replacement for a phallus which is no longer there (Jody is dead); Dil in turn provides a fetishistic performance of femininity, a masquerade of 'exotic-ness', which has the double effect of denying both woman's and Jody's lack, and yet it is a masquerade designed to *hide* 'her' own penis.

When Dil agrees to dress in Jody's clothes, like Judy in *Vertigo*, 'she' is reluctant but does it to please Fergus (unlike Judy 'she' does not know at this stage that 'she' is standing in for Jody). As in *Vertigo* the film is saying something about the dishonesty of desire and the male gaze: the masquerade which men use to deny lack. As the assistant at the women's dress shop in *Vertigo* observes wryly as Scottie makes his meticulous requirements maniacally clear, 'The gentleman certainly seems to know what he wants.' And just like Judy, Dil seems especially uncomfortable in the role of the deceased paramour, in this case Jody. Both Scottie and Fergus attempt to rewrite their past and their loss through the masquerade of an Other. And both films reduce woman's body to a corpse in the process: in *The Crying Game* Dil is more Midge, the homely Good Girl, than Judy, the Bad Girl (who is of course, Jude – but unlike Judy she has no redemption; she is not shown to be in the end the *Good* Bad Girl).

The 'homosexual' reading of *The Crying Game* works to show that just as the unusual 'monstrosity' of the creature of virtue in this film is still less terrible than the monster of bitchery, the fear of castration embodied in woman is a more serious and immediate threat to Fergus' identity than that represented by the taboo desire for the penis. In the film's resolution the eroticized penis-bearer – Dil – dispatches the castrating bitch and saves the other penis-bearer (Fergus).

But the taboo desire remains taboo: the 'homosexual' plot-line to *The Crying Game* never goes beyond the fantasy of doing away with woman and denying 'lack' altogether. Fergus' desire for Jody's penis, his hunger for his 'piece of meat', as represented in the body of Dil, is never consummated; the evasion of the castration threat from woman is achieved in tandem with the denial of homo-desire. After his discovery of 'her' penis the sex discontinues and never threatens to re-emerge (the oral sex they had engaged in before this revelation is here reminiscent of Freud's ironic observation that some men, fearing the *vagina dentata*, being 'swallowed up' by the woman's genitals during intercourse, choose to put their penises in mouths where there are *real* teeth which can be seen – this is the importance of vision again in disavowal).

After Jude is eradicated we see Dil, dressed up again, hair growing out, happily visiting Fergus in prison. They sit face to face, watched by prison warders and separated by bullet-proof glass. Although Dil embarrasses Fergus by calling him his 'boyfriend', the film's final image leaves the audience with the reassurance that the desublimation of Fergus' homo-desire has been averted for the foreseeable future at least. Fergus is not imprisoned by the British State so much as locked away for his own safety by the taboo on homo-desire, even of the pseudo variety: the bullet-proof glass is first and foremost penis-proof, allowing Fergus to look at but not touch the penis that is always hidden but always on display in the transvestite. Dil's virtue and Fergus' heterosexuality are preserved like butterflies under glass.

It is the surreal quality of this final scene which alerts us to the fact that we have been witnessing a dream. A dream, moreover, which could be one belonging to a patient of Freud's:

> The idea of a woman with a penis returns in later life, in the dreams of adults: the dreamer, in a state of nocturnal sexual excitation, will throw a woman down, strip her and prepare for intercourse – and then, in place of the female genitals, he beholds a well-developed penis and breaks off the dream and the excitation.[7]

In Neil Jordan's *The Crying Game* we are treated to the assimilation of otherness to sameness under the male gaze of the film director. Like the man in the dream described by Freud he engages in a heterosexual male sadistic fantasy ('strip her and prepare for intercourse') of denying difference and yet, when faced with the homosexual reality of what that implies – 'a well-developed penis' – he cannot bring himself to go through with it and 'breaks off the dream and the excitation'. The straight, white, male film director is the *real* masquerader in this film, dressing himself up in a veritable cavalcade of exotic marginalism and difference – blackness, femininity, homosexuality, transvestism – and yet offering nothing but a *(dis)semblance* of difference, a parody of Otherness. Real femininity is exterminated, real homosexuality is kept at bay, blackness is not engaged with but merely appropriated, and transvestism – something that *might* represent an identification with femininity – is used to do away with the feminine altogether.

After employing the usual Hollywood mechanism of coping with difference through creating polarities (Good Girl/Bad Girl), difference is then dealt with by *effacing* it – but only on Jordan's terms, in this bad drag show of liberal humanism. Otherness, itself created by the male gaze, is thus sold back to us as a *simulated sameness*.

'I hate Northern Ireland. It must be the last place where they call you nigger to your face,' Jody tells Fergus. But compared to Jordan's deceptive dream-world of *The Crying Game* Northern Ireland's racism seems almost healthy in its blatant assertion of difference.

Notes

1. Wooley did not actually mention transvestism as he would not have wished to give the film's central 'trick' away; I am inferring that he would have done so if he could.

2. Leslie Fiedler, *Love and Death in the American Novel* (New York: Stein and Day, 1975), p. 24.

3. *New Society and Statesman*, 30 October 1992 ('Opening the borders').

4. Both Dil and Jude are 'glamorous' and their different kinds of glamour represent the ambiguity of glamour in the Hollywood tradition: both as masquerade of the kind outlined by Doane, exhibited in Dil, but also as *threat*, as in the femme fatale figure of Jude.

5. The reference to 'sick' also brings to mind Laura Mulvey's description of the two strategies employed by Hollywood to neutralize anxiety aroused around lack: (a) establish her guilt or illness and (b) fetishization, giving her erotic over-investment. Jude clearly has plenty of guilt (she, not the IRA, is morally responsible for Jody's death); Dil is erotically over-invested. Laura Mulvey, 'Visual pleasure and romantic cinema', *Screen*, Vol. 16, no. 3 (Autumn 1975), p. 11.

6. Freud, 'The Sexual Theories of Children', Penguin Freud Library, Vol. 7, p. 194.

7. Freud, 'The Sexual Theories of Children', p. 194.

Chapter nine

Dragging It Up and Down
The Glamorized Male Body

Glamour in drag

We know, too, to what a degree depreciation of women, horror of women, and a disposition to homosexuality are derived from the final conviction that women have no penis. Ferenczi (1923) has recently, with complete justice, traced back the mythological symbol of horror – Medusa's head – to the impression of the female genitals devoid of a penis.

● *Freud, 'The Sexual Theories of Children'*

Glamour, n, & v.t. 1. n. magic, enchantment (cast a glamour over, enchant). 2. v.t. delusive or alluring or exciting beauty or charm; (esp. feminine) physical attractiveness.

● *The Concise Oxford Dictionary*

IN the fifteenth century the war against heresy, the Inquisition, produced the *Malleus Maleficarum*, a book used as the basis of the persecution of millions of women as 'witches'. A charge frequently made by this text of misogyny against feminine witchcraft is its ability to 'disappear' men's *membrum virile*. A typical example of this fiendish sorcery tells of how 'some glamour was cast over him so that he could see or touch nothing but his smooth body'.[1]

Glamour, then, is woman's 'magical' power over man, her power to enchant and allure; and as ever, woman's power is also a castration threat to men: glamour is both desirability and fearsomeness. But more than this, glamour is both the fear of lack *and the disavowal of it*; it is both fear of woman's power, her affinity with nature, and man's early attempts to explain it away as the result of diabolic *artifice*: a man, Lucifer, is at the root of it all. Glamour is Janus-faced, looking towards both feminine power and masculinist plot.

And so it is with that masculine attempt at glamour – drag: Is it incitement to gender rebellion or misogynist turn? This is the perennial question, and the answer is, of course, both and neither.

The mother of all glamour, and therefore of drag, is Medusa, who with her serpent hair, tusks of swine and golden wings, could turn her audience to stone with a look: freezing fear in a glance – every drag queen's dream. To appropriate glamour and desirability to the masculine body against the cultural grain, a gay man has traditionally had to put on the appearance of femininity, the point of which is not to become a woman (they wish to keep their penis) but to bind the fear and fascination of the feminine to the male body. This produces a dilemma for the gay man: how to reconcile his own fascination with his own fear – or in other words, how to emulate Athena and fix the Medusa's head in the centre of his shield without himself being turned to stone. The ambiguity of glamour itself is his Perseus here: in the wake of Hollywood, glamour is associated with a masquerade of femininity designed by men, a fetishistic defence against the horror of lack which the Medusa's head represents. Glamour in this fetishistic form can be 'put on' by men very easily.

The respectable men of learning who wrote *Malleus Maleficarum*, in an attempt to counter the manifest irrationality of their charges of castration by witchcraft, explained the effect of the witches' 'glamour' as working 'not indeed by actually despoiling the human body of it [the penis], but by concealing it'; in other words, an affect on the poor man's ability to *perceive*. The Medusa's eyes are the centre of her horror: the active female gaze of the Gorgon rebels against the masculine priority accorded by possessing visible genitalia. The victim bewails his loss of manhood while his friends point out, to no avail, that his *membrum* is still very much *virile*. Likewise the man in drag has his manhood concealed but not despoiled: the 'castration' is *visual*. But this effect is in a reverse order to that experienced by the victim of the witches' glamour – his manhood is concealed not from *him* but from his *audience* (albeit only through the suspension of disbelief). The travesty of a man's body that was feared as a result of women's power is disavowed through a travesty of vestments, through *transvestism*; glamour works at man's behest, and his eyes not the gorgon's gaze out at us.

This kind of drag draws attention to the concealment of manhood by its crudeness or its exaggeration to make sure that it is taken as concealment and not despoilment. Much of the entertainment of drag depends upon the improbability and inappropriateness of a man in a frock, wig and 'falsies'. But this in turn depends upon not just the improbability of a man dressed as a woman but the 'improbability' of the female body itself. The man in a frock *looks* preposterous but this is just a shadow of the *essential* preposterousness of the female body itself, that which the frock represents (and hides). Likewise the false tits are funny, not just for their falseness, their obvious failure as breasts, but also because they do in fact represent very well those *innately* inappropriate and therefore humorous accessories. The anxiety that glamour might travesty man's body is thus displaced onto woman's body.

This is the 'misogynist turn' aspect of drag. But true to its ironic heart, drag points glamour in another direction, placing another meaning on travesty, that of carnival. For all its possible denigration of the feminine body, drag has the effect, unwitting or not, of pointing up the foolishness of gender *performance*; by putting a man in a frock, gender itself is *de*frocked and put in the stocks for a day. As Judith Butler puts it in *Gender Trouble*:

> In imitating gender, drag implicitly reveals the imitative
> nature of gender itself – as well as its contingency. Indeed,
> part of the pleasure, the giddiness of the performance is in
> the recognition of a radical contingency in the relation
> between sex and gender in the face of cultural

configurations of causal unities that are regularly assumed to be natural and necessary.[2]

The travesty of drag can go beyond mere carnival, which can serve in the end merely to shore up the status quo (after all, carnival is really a holiday). It can take the form of an *incitement to rebellion*. It can express a desire to revolt against that most tyrannical of laws, the 'natural' link between sex and gender. This drag-as-rebellion, strange to relate, can even represent a rejection of the denigration of women's bodies on the basis of lack.

Freud suggested that a man's refusal to accept his mother's castration, the improbability of her body compared to his, will often lead to homosexuality. In this castration crisis, he suggests, the non-accepting male's desire for his mother yields to 'ceaseless flight', flight from the 'truth' of her sexual difference. The boy then makes good this lack not through the fetishization of the foot, leg, fur etc., as do heterosexual men, but by substituting his *own body* for the missing phallus.

Caja Silverman in *Male Subjectivity at the Margins* argues that, rather than being simply the result of a horror of women's bodies on the part of gay men, this process might be the result of an identification with femininity that represents a resistance to 'the whole process of devaluation which is made to follow from a woman's "difference"' and 'a refusal to accede to the equation of the mother with insufficiency'.[3] This is perhaps the basis of some kinds of drag-as-rebellion: gay men dress as women, i.e. women with men's bodies, putting on their subjectivity but refusing woman's castration and becoming themselves a kind of phallic mother (i.e. the mother they desire) and avenging themselves on a tremulous world.

In this model of drag, travesty and glamour are deployed in an attempt to erase misogyny rather than the feminine body's threat. This is no doubt the kind of redemptive drag that gay men and lesbians look to with starry eyes, finding in it phallic heroines and goddesses to champion their *demi-monde* against the heavens themselves; in the queer's dream of the mothers' revolt against the fathers, drag queens are prized for their ball-busting terror; they are Bette Davis and Joan Crawford freed from their studio chains and escaped from the Hollywood zoo, causing panic on the streets.

This is also the origin of the mythology of the Stonewall drag queens leading the resistance to the police raid: the first bottle is thrown from expertly manicured and painted fingers and bursts into a thousand glittering shards and suddenly the drag queens are witches casting a glamour over the uniformed representatives of the masculine Inquisition. In redemptive drag, men in frocks are flamboyant, romantic dissidents in the struggle against gender totalitarianism. But most of all this kind of drag has an enchanting glamour of doomed but splendid resistance; these are faggots who demand to be burned with the witches in a fatalistic challenge in which God's law is itself *travestied*, the majesty of His creation transformed into tragicomedy by the sex heretics:

> 'Oh, yes, my dear,' Miss Destiny said, 'there is a God, and he is one Hell of a joker. Just look –' and she indicates her lively green satin dress and then waves her hand over the entire room. 'Trapped! ... But one day, in the most lavish drag you've evuh seen – heels! and gown! and beads! and spangled earrings! – I'm going to storm heaven and protest! Here I am!!! I'll yell – and I'll shake my beads at Him ... And God will cringe!'
> ● John Rechy [4]

'Nature's cruel trick' rebounds on Nature's head in the image of the drag queen's revenge. The '*anima muliebris in virili corpore inclusa*' (woman's soul trapped in a man's body) formula becomes the personal drama of the individual struggle against sex-gender tyranny. In this form of drag a female subjectivity really is embraced, inasmuch as this kind of drag queenery places the man in as 'low' a status in God's creation as woman: synonymous with rebellion and sin. But it is a low status that threatens to turn tables any moment, the world of trash that they are regents over may burst upon the 'high' world at any moment: 'I'm going to storm heaven and then protest!' A brazen act of defiance and deviancy; a 'glamour' of hatred so powerful, a 'charm' of beads and heels so strong, that even God will 'cringe'. The naturalness of the sex-gender causality, the imprisonment of desire, is implicitly accepted

– 'Oh, yes, my dear, there is a God' – *in order to assault it*. The Miss Destiny model of drag is the flagrant, flaming, final embodiment of Foucault's reverse discourse; irresistible in its sheer verve. 'Yes!' screams the drag queen in bitter pride, 'I *am* a woman's soul trapped in a man's body! *Look at your handiwork and weep!*'

The Miss Destiny model of drag is usually associated with street drag and the misogynist-turn model with pub drag (though both have a little of each other in them). But it was ironically the riot that the drag queens led in the imagination at Stonewall which marked the decline of Miss Destiny: the personal drama became a political one, romance was replaced by realism. Even the drag queenery of the early 1970s, the so-called 'rad-fems' in groups like the Gay Liberation Front, demonstrated its travesty of *social* assumptions by carefully including significations of manhood such as moustaches or beards with their alarming apparel. Miss Destiny became Miss Construed. The *heroic* moment of the drag queen had passed: her heroism had always depended on total surrender to drag rather than self-consciously ironic statements (e.g. the carefully staged street drag of the Sisters of Perpetual Indulgence, gay men who dress as nuns, is occasionally amusing but never *moving*).

Post Stonewall, pub drag became the dominant form. As the gay male body pursued its relentless masculinization, drag queenery that was anything other than cabaret was shunned. Sincere identification with woman's subjectivity, however dubious this might be, was now anathema. Drag was taken off the streets and put on the stage. If beer softens the edges of a sharply condemning world, then drag acts blunt the 'sharp' threat of the feminine for the male patrons of the gay pub. We laugh at what we fear, given the chance, and this is what the drag act offers 'her' audience. 'She' knows very well that is 'her' job to send up the feared sexual difference, to place inverted commas around woman. Between performing songs the 'artiste' will make sure that the audience does not forget that, notionally, 'she' has a vagina. Escalating the 'threat' (and thus its defusion), fake whispered propriety about 'down below' and 'women's problems' give way to loud and crude references to 'my fucking twat' and 'my bleedin' fanny'. Jokes then come fast and furious about the loss of an endless stream of increasingly unlikely objects – vibrators, bananas, cucumbers, marrows, gasmen – all devoured without trace by the insatiable vagina, but always failing to take even the edge off its monstrous appetite.[5] The masculine fear of the vagina's ability to swallow up literally everything is avowed through the reference to it, only to be disavowed through the 'joke', through the shared laughter and the shared reassurance that we know very well that this is in fact a man.

This is an inversion of the usual logistics of the disavowal of castration that Freud attributed to children, where the evidence of the child's own eyes about women's bodies is acknowledged on a surface level but denied on another, deeper one. In drag the idea 'all human beings have penises', the primal idea, is no longer held under the secondary, perceptual idea, 'some humans are without penises' – rather the second becomes held under the first: 'I know very well that this person has a penis but I will pretend he is what he appears to be' (this is suspension of disbelief).

The drag queen's invocation of the female body and its terrors in a world of let's pretend is a guaranteed route to comic success. One famous drag queen on the London gay pub circuit exploits this with his famous welcome to lesbian members of the audience: 'Hello all you l-l-l-l-l-l-l-l-l-lesbians!', fluttering his tongue in a grotesque parody of cunnilingus, thus conjuring up the gay man's nightmare of being brought face to face with 'the gash'.

Although the glamour invoked, in the form of 1940s Hollywood film stars, is fetishized, even this ambiguous expression of female power, of female enchantment, needs to be travestied. This is often done through the very frocks that invoke the glamour: the ghoulish mysteries of the female anatomy are pointed up by underwear that never fits and must always be adjusted and complained about, apparently reversing the traditional fetishizing use of Hollywood glamour – but only because we know very well that it is a man's body that lies beneath that corset and hoop skirt.

Dame Edna Everage, a misogynist-turn drag queen par excellence, despite Barry Humphries' indignant protestations, also offers her public an opportunity to resolve fears about the monstrous feminine – in this particular case the maternal body. The tag 'housewife superstar' emphasizes that she is a mother at the same time as pointing up the unlikelihood of this; she herself, with all her famous false modesty, constantly refers to herself as a mother who also happens to be an 'international megastar'; the modesty, it is implied, is as false as her maternal femininity. As a hardly petite man in drag who brings to mind aunts who were suspiciously unfeminine beneath their overly made-up faces and blue rinses, Humphries presents his audience with their worst nightmare of femininity-as-drag in women: the fear that mothers might actually be violent bruisers beneath the day-glo and the sweet smiles. Edna is the phallic mother who is also a bad mother; a bad mother, moreover, dissembling as a good one. For all her talk about her 'little chicks' and her love for them, the joke is that she is clearly a *monstrous* mother. This is the basis of her treatment of her guests: instead of being warm and inviting as her 'feminine' appearance might suggest, she often shocks and humiliates. This is the fear of what Melanie Klein would call the bad mother, the fear that she will not satisfy our needs, that she will instead suddenly become as terrifying as she was once loving. Edna is also the fear of the phallic mother, described by Freud, who at any moment might produce a penis instead of a breast. Edna's successful exploitation of bad/ phallic mother anxieties is perhaps the reason why she has yet to meet that other performer who has made a career out of the same terrors, the scary auntie with a blue rinse to end all scary aunties: Margaret Thatcher.

In the same way the ambivalent attitude towards the womb/ vagina is exploited: her favourite vaginal expression, 'I mean that in a warm, moist, *friendly* kind of way – I do!', is used to envelop the sharpest barbs. This is why criticisms of Edna's racism, sexism and sadism are superfluous. The public want her precisely for her monstrosity and her travesty of nurturing qualities. Again, as a man in a frock these anxieties about the female body are avowed only to be disavowed.

But even the avowal-disavowal of drag is not always enough to eradicate anxieties about the feminine body. The pub drag queen has to cultivate an immobility, an ethereality, in which her body is denied through 'graceful' ghostly movements and she offers up her soul instead through her voice, or better still, through mime (someone else's voice). For the drag queen, movement is internal and spiritual. This stillness and pathos of the drag queen is *deathly* since death is the most 'sublime' state for the female body. Death is there in the immobility of the drag queen on stage, in the rigor mortis of the frocks, in the funereal, other-worldly quality of sex mismatched with gender; there is something just as mournful about men in frocks as there is something comic. Even the grease-paint, in its ghastliness, is an embalmment.[6]

The ultimate statement of drag as misogynist turn, as male appropriation of female glamour, is portrayed in *Death Becomes Her* (1992), a Hollywood comedy which takes the morbid aspect of the drag myth to its logical conclusion. Meryl Streep and Goldie Hawn play glamorous ball-busting bitches whose feminine power 'casts a spell' over the man they fight each other for (Bruce Willis), making him impotent. After being held up as irresistible, their bodies are then brought low through mutilation: Streep's neck is broken by Willis and Hawn's stomach is blown out by a shotgun. But by the aid of witchcraft, in the form of a potion of youth they took to ward off ageing (*the* threat to their glamour), they become undead: alive in dead bodies. But this also deprives them of the 'beauty' that death brings the female body and they are required to literally drag themselves up in embalming fluid and paint in order to maintain their bodies and their glamour. In keeping with the myth of drag this can be done only by a man: Bruce Willis. They now need the powers of the man they unmanned with their glamour to maintain it for them; this reversal has the effect of curing Willis' impotence. In *Death Becomes Her* death is marked as the route by which woman's power – glamour – is passed into the hands of men, saving them from castration, while woman is reduced to a status below that of drag queens (they can at least do their own make-up).

This is the myth not just of drag but of Hollywood itself: male appropriation of glamour is predicated on the death, the lifelessness of the female body – the Medusa's head needs to be cut off before it can be attached to the aegis.

The glamour boys

If the ethos of drag is alive and well in Hollywood, it seems to be on the wane in gay pubs. Changes in the representation of the male body in the 1980s have made it possible for a man to appropriate a stagey desirability to the male body without having to avail himself of feminine glamour. These changes are represented, of course, by the phenomenon of the male stripper – and it is the male stripper who is driving drag out of the gay pubs. In the 1990s the number of gay venues advertising male strippers appears to have 'outstripped' those advertising drag acts; some pubs even offer a stripper every night.

In this new-look gay scene the spectacle of the male body, the showing of that which gay men eroticize – the phallus – has replaced the hiding of that which they reject – lack. This contrast is what appears to define this form of cabaret at every turn; it is almost as if the stripper were saying, 'Look how unlike a drag queen I am.'

Drag is a glorious, glamorous celebration of surface over substance, artifice over nature, pretence over authenticity; the carnival of drag overturns the fear of woman-as-nature and replaces it with woman-as-artifice; appearance is held up for approval and essence mocked. The stripper, on the other hand, ostensibly restores order. He presents us with a ritual of substance over surface, biology over artifice, authenticity over pretence; glamour is shunned and appearance is actually stripped away to reveal ... essence. In the drag act, clothes are as fussy and frivolous as design and funds will allow and are only removed (off-stage) to be replaced by even more ecstatically diverting costumes. In the strip act, clothes and accessories are devout in their simplicity, and despite their canny multi-layering, loyal in their communication of the male body underneath and – so we are led to believe – they are worn only to be removed.

In contrast to the miming/singing and bitchy patter of the drag queen, language itself is rejected as dissemblence, as something untrustworthy, in the stripper's display of 'truth'. The stripper remains determinedly mute during his performance, and ear-splitting dance music plays over the PA forbidding conversation; when he has to give instructions to members of the audience he puts his hand to their ear and covers his mouth, no doubt to make himself heard but also perhaps to hide his moving lips from us. Wordless corporeality is the only way that the ultimate masculine truth can be told. And once that truth is told there is nothing to do but pick up your clothes and body oil and go home. The penis shown – show over.

This is the myth of stripping that we are invited to participate in: what you finally *see* is what you get and what you finally get is what you wanted to see. In fact the myth of male stripping fascinates by its *dissimulation*; it mesmerizes precisely because it contradicts itself with every discarded item; it enchants by denying the very thing it maintains: it disavows what it avows. The only 'truth' of stripping is that the stripper can never be naked enough, never *stripped* enough, because the phallus can never be shown – instead we are palmed off with a paltry penis. No matter how freakish his genital attributes, no matter how craftily engorged and arranged with rings and elastic bands, no matter how frantically it is waved and waggled in front of the audience's faces, the stripper's penis, once naked, *never lives up to the promise of the phallus*: the climactic finale of the strip is . . . an anti-climax. Next to the phallus the poor stripper's penis is almost no-thing; try as he might the stripper cannot 'see or touch anything but his own smooth body'. The removal of clothes and accessories – leather jacket, shirt(s), T-shirt(s), boots, socks, chaps, jeans, boxer shorts, jockstrap, and even the final posing pouch – can never avow the stripper's naked-ness enough. The audience knows this very well and is required (as with the drag act) to suspend disbelief as it watches the strip, as if playing 'Pass the Parcel', knowing that under all the layers of wrap-ping it will be empty. As with 'Pass the Parcel', the enjoyment of stripping is, of course, in the unwrapping rather than the revelation.

But once 'revealed', the stripper has to present 'nothing' as 'everything'. In other words he finds himself in the same position as the drag act who has to present nothing (castration) as everything (fetishistic glamour).

Of course the stripper's nakedness is never 'no-thing', it is always some-thing (though not the thing it is supposed to be). The stripper's body, however stripped, is always clothed with precon-ceptions and conceits. In an attempt to proclaim the nakedness of the male body the stripper accessorizes it. This is the rich irony of male stripping – it is presented as the antithesis of drag *but is in fact part of its thesis*. Surface, artifice and pretence are all celebrated in the strip cabaret. This is, after all, *show-business*, as premeditated, as diverting, as entrancing – as *glamorous* in its masquerade as drag.

The themed outfits (sailor, policeman, leatherman, etc.) frame the stripper in a fantasy that clothes him long after the bell-bottoms and tunic are discarded. The carefully choreographed and rehearsed routines that are the performance of stripping carefully exclude any possibility of 'naked' spontaneity. The artful contrivances on his body, the shaved chest, arms, legs; the clipped balls, whitened teeth; the gym-pampered body, the cock ring, even the glittering oil that he asks members of the audience to spread over his skin, all weave a spell which idealizes him, and lubricates the passage of the audience's fantasies over him. That is to say they accessorize his body and deny it at the very moment that it appears to be offered unadulterated.

In addition to glamour, travesty and carnival are there in stripping too. The phallus is unwittingly brought low at the very moment of its supposed exaltation by the foolish insufficiency of its signification by the penis on-stage, and wittingly in the way that members of the audience are humiliated and debased for their desire for it. So they are persuaded/forced to perform various acts of sleaze, from simulated acts of fellatio to, in one popular London act, removing their glasses from between the stripper's clenched buttocks with their teeth. Another stripper has his victim lie face down on stage with his trousers and pants at half-mast, pour baby-oil between the prostrate man's buttocks and then 'fuck' him with a dildo attached to an inflatable man. The phallus, the male body and those who worship these are ridiculed in the strip act, which abases what it appears to hold up (hen parties know this very well, hence the popularity of male strippers with them). As we have seen, the threat of travesty of the male body in putting on women's clothing is displaced onto the female body. But in stripping, ironically, the male body is travestied in the *showing* of it.

Finally it can be said that, contrary to the supposition that drag and strip acts are dichotomous, we can say that they are *homogenous* (sharing the same ancestry). Drag is a pretence, an ecstasy of surfaces (of frocks), that draws attention to the (feminine) body to distract us from it ('I know very well that person has a penis, nevertheless ...'). Male stripping, it can be seen, is also a pretence, an ecstasy of surfaces (of skins), that draws attention to the (masculine) body and yet distracts us from it ('Is that all there is?'). Thus male stripping works best, and achieves its greatest theatrical and spectacular effect, when it embraces its fate, its continuity with despised drag, and offers the audience self-consciously, not 'nakedness', but *glamour*.

One gay black stripper's act seems to have done just this, and the glorious result is a little epiphany that would surely convince Miss Destiny herself to become a male stripper. The climax of his strip (one of many) is absolutely the finale of a drag act: he presents his back to us, holding out a burgundy red peacock cape at shoulder-length, glittering in the stage-lights. Slowly, slowly, with impeccable grace, he turns towards us, blinding us with an explosion of gold lamé, burning fiery against his ebony skin: the golden wings of Medusa! On his face is a smile that is the soul of glamour, and between his legs, of course, an enormous penis jutting out, pointing at the audience like an accusing priapic finger (a swine's tusk?); this is the male body made improbable, the masculine made Other; naked before us but, in effect, clothed 'in heels! and gown! and beads! and spangled earrings!'

A rush of giddy terror and bliss chills the audience and they know that they are in the presence of the phallic witch-mother, head restored to her shoulders.

And God cringes.

Heavy metal – straight boys discover drag

Stripped to the waist to reveal that fearsome selection of tattoos, drenched with sweat and cycling shorts that leave little to the imagination . . ., Axl Rose [lead singer with Guns 'n' Roses] is a very strong stage character. Kilts, leather jackets and a bandana are frequent accessories . . .
● *Axl Rose fanzine*

Gay men are not the only ones who are attracted to glamour. Straight men are also enchanted by and afeared of it; they are also keen to fix the Medusa's head in the centre of their shield precisely because her gaze freezes their blood: the power of glamour is always in direct proportion to the fear of it. As with the drag queen, the problem for the straight man is how to appropriate the power of its countenance – how to be 'a very strong stage character' – without being frozen himself by its gaze.

Rock and roll, of course, provides the answer – rock and roll *is* male glamour. That it is a form of drag is almost a commonplace. And as with drag, the glamour of rock and roll is controlled by travesty and misogyny. Travesty is there in the carnivalesque world of rock and roll, where Dionysus is worshipped and authority is mocked: glamour is permitted because it is 'far out', and 'zany'; it rebels against humdrum suburban life and upsets your parents. Misogyny stabilizes this male glamour as entertainment, preventing it from spilling over into revolution. This is especially the case in the most 'classical' rock and roll form: heavy metal.

Heavy metal is the most self-consciously Dionysian of all the rock forms and prides itself on what it sees as its 'rassling' non-conformity. In reality the world of heavy metal is a tyrannically conformist one, where rebellion is strictly codified as little more than 'maleness as badness', i.e. the traditional script of fuckin' n' fightin', cussin' n' drinkin'. Most of all, heavy metal is about conformity to the law of the *phallus*. What else could 'cock rock' be but a symphony to phallocentrism?

Ironically it is through masquerade that heavy metal attempts to present itself as a celebration of substance over surface, the phallus over lack. As Kaplan has argued in *Rock Around the Clock*, the male masquerade present in rock and roll differs from that employed in the representation of women in Hollywood in that the accessories do not stand in for lack, rather they attempt to deny that there is any sexual difference that would require the possibility of lack. Thus the dragged-up rock star 'renders the feminine non-male rather than Other ...'.[7] The appeal of heavy metal is that it denies difference at the very moment that it appears to be embracing it: heavy metal fans look to their music not just to celebrate the phallus and repudiate lack but also to make them feel both special and ordinary, unique and one of the boys, exceptional and regular all at once. (The reality of the manic denial of difference in heavy metal is most vividly illustrated by the total absence of any black faces either on or off stage.)[8]

Little wonder then that the most fascinated heterosexual devotees of male glamour in the form of heavy metal masquerade are teenage boys, who make up the vast majority of heavy metal fans. Teenage boys are required to confront the feminine or else jeopardize their successful graduation into manhood. After years of renouncing them (only sissies play with girls), these boys are often faced with the unknown Other in a setting which bears little relation to the phallic fantasy of the all-conquering stud-man in which they would like to see themselves. The mundane fact these boys struggle with is that not all girls are simpering 'babes' who will coo in their arms. This can only amplify their anxieties. As Stan Denski and David Sholle have observed in their study of heavy metal fans in 'Metal men and glamour boys':

> These boys are confronted by girls who may be larger, stronger, and smarter than they are, while at the same time these boys are being socialised into the dominant masculine cultural position of pursuer of the female, thus generating a fear of the feminine.[9]

Although heavy metal may wish to deny the possibility of sexual difference and lack at the moment of capturing feminine glamour as much as any gay drag act, the straight boy's anxiety cannot be dealt with through 'ceaseless flight' (or identification) — unless, as he sees it, he is prepared to jettison his manhood completely. Unlike gay men he is required, by definition, to expose himself to the female body in the most intimate and vulnerable way. Instead of flight he must show mastery; woman is a test of his manhood that must be overcome by domination, by *conquest*. This is why aggression is so heavily eroticized in heavy metal. The Gothic iconography popular with this kind of music provides the teen boy with a fantasy-world where he can be Conan the Barbarian winning his mate or He-Man freeing She-Woman with his mighty sword. The violence is not usually directed at women (this would be unmanly), but towards other men in order to win possession of them. But although women are often represented as damsel babes that wait in their castle for 'Bill and Ted', they are just as often portrayed as 'bitches'. Against the 'babes'/'chicks' there is posited the 'groupie', the Whore of Babylon who threatens to literally gobble men up; in the words of Sammy Hagar from Van Halen, explaining why he steers clear of groupies, 'by the time you meet one of those girls she's already sucked about three yards of dick'.[10]

The ambivalent attitude of heavy metal towards women and the body horror the genre attaches to them ('sucked three yards of dick' connotes perhaps the famous tongue scene in *The Exorcist*) is best summed up in the logo used on the singles review page of the main heavy metal magazine *Kerrang!*: a naked curvacious young woman with a rotted skull atop her shoulders. It is the Medusa's head syndrome again.

Women's bodies are desired for what they can bring a man but feared for what they might take away. A famous gesture of 'cock rock', the mock cunnilingus where the artist tilts his head back and flutters his tongue, invokes the same horror as that employed by the drag queen ('l-l-l-l-l-l-lesbians!'): the horror of being brought face to face with 'the gash'. And yet its equivalence marks the disjunction of the two forms of drag: on the drag queen's face it is a tease, a whiff of fear resolved through ridicule; on the face of the heavy metal performer it is a challenge, a display of bravado, of *gall*. The threat of the female body is denied: 'I am not afraid,' he says, 'I am master of my emotions and therefore master of the female body.' Woman is rendered non-male rather than Other because rock and roll shows that she has no autonomous power: her glamour, her fearsomeness, her body are all appropriated; desire for the mother is displaced into 'sadistic possession'.

In this drag act of rock and roll woman becomes merely the negative elaboration of the masculine subject. Rock and roll's power and appeal to men is that it devalues woman by rendering her non-male in a phallocentric economy.

> When I was 14 I was over at this girl's house I'd been trying to pick up for months and she played 'Aerosmith Rocks'; I listened to it eight times and forgot all about her.
> ● Slash, lead guitarist with Guns 'n' Roses[11]

While 'girls' are very much a part of the rock and roll legend they often come behind drinking, drugs and the music itself in priority and then seem to be valued only in terms of what exchange they bring between 'the guys'; as Denski and Sholle, drawing on Irigary, explain:

> A repressed and, hence, disparaged sexuality (a relationship between men and bonds between men) takes place through

the heterosexual exchange and distribution of women. This is particularly evident in the movie, 'Heavy Metal', and in music videos where groups of men divide the spoils, that is, the women. This is especially evident in the Motley Crue video for their song, 'Girls, Girls, Girls.' In it, the women exotic dancers are obvious targets for exchange, yet function only as visual pleasure. The only physical, bodily pleasure in the video takes place in the exchanges between the male band members.[12]

Rock and roll provides an economy of sameness where rock and roll can itself come to stand in for the usual commodity that prevents the economy lapsing into incest: rock and roll rocks *around* the cock rather than on it.

Put another way, 'cock rock' provides boys with a way to worship the phallus in a fashion that preserves its and their own desired/prized virility – since in Guy Hocquenghem's phrase, the penis is the virile member and what is virile is not queer. So the prick itself cannot be put on display as in the male strip cabaret since this would 'queer' the economy and bring about incest and the loss of what is desired. Instead it is displaced into phallic accessories (as opposed to the ones that accessorize glamour): tattoos, muscles, and, of course, guitars hoisted between legs clad in skin-tight leather or rubber. The guitars are the key phallic trope and are played in a style that it would be something of an understatement to call masturbatory. On-stage the band 'play' their guitars and the male members of the audience join with them, sharing the experience, either there in the stadium or with a hi-fi in the privacy of their own home, playing the famous 'air guitar' – joining up in one vast crescendoing circle-jerk.

The music itself, with its simple four-bar phrases and its crude repetitive chords, effects a solid, monumental phallicism, the most important feature of which is its *volume*, i.e. its size and power. The ground-shaking, pummelling, gut-wrenching sound of heavy metal is the sound of boys enjoying the barely sublimated fantasy of being on the receiving end of the stupendously virile organ they worship. In the end, no matter how frantically the heavy metal fan fiddles with his air guitar it is just air and his enjoyment of the music is essentially passive.

The hysterically over-amplified sound is the equivalent of the stuffed crotch, a legend which is right at the heart of rock and roll. That the penis is never shown, not only prevents the breakout of incest and shame but also prevents the disappointment that is inevitable in the male strip act when the penis fails to represent the phallus; rock and roll is, and must always be, *larger than life*. By relying on phallicism instead of the penis, the heavy metal band goes from one climax to another.

But the teen boy's desire for the phallus is not completely displaced into the music and the props; he also desires the heavy metal star. This is the other purpose of glamour – not just to abjure the possibility of sexual difference but also to affirm the star's desirability. The disparity between the way the metal star dresses up and the fan dresses down shows that no simple identification is at work here: the rock star is, like the male stripper to the gay pub-goer, glamorous and Other, erotic and alluring.

The careful ambiguity of the masquerade of the metal star, the appropriation of masculine and feminine images, is represented most famously and most successfully in Axl Rose. He is 'stripped to the waist', revealing 'that fearsome selection of tattoos'; he is 'drenched with sweat and cycling shorts that leave little to the imagination' – like the male stripper, before his finale, he presents us the male body in a phantasmic, fetishized form. But unlike the male stripper he also accessorizes 'femininity' to himself: 'kilts, leather jackets and a bandana are frequent accessories'. Even his name spells out the ambivalent masquerade (that sends out the unambivalent message: desire me, I am everything): 'Axl' suggests the axle of a truck or car, something rigid which transmits power and causes movement, while 'Rose' suggests sweet-smelling delicacy and beauty. The name is also an anagram of 'oral sex'.

This is the meaning of his 'confessions' about his childhood sexual abuse: we see before us a rock star, rampant with all the power and technology that such status brings, and yet he carries with him a history that is one of victimization, of humiliation, of forced passivity. This is acceptable, marketable even, because his narrative becomes the narrative of phallic triumph over passive subjection; this is what he acts out every time he takes the stage: 'Yes! I am desirable to men; I know you want to fuck me; watch me tease you – but, aha! *I fuck you!*'

Unlike for gay men, the feminine embodies an added terror for heterosexual or would-be heterosexual men – the fear of homosexuality. For the straight boy, failure to conquer the feminine implies homosexuality, which itself implies 'penetration' by the feminine and thus lack. This is a powerful equation for the teen boy whose sexuality is bound to be more fluid than it is supposed to be. Thus the need to confront the feminine becomes also the need to master 'the feminine' in himself: his homosexuality. But like the glamour of woman herself, the fear of homosexuality is in proportion to its allure.

So the glamour of rock and roll in general, and heavy metal in particular, is not just the borrowed illusive magic of woman but also the fear/enchantment of homosexuality. The heavy metal star does not just wish to fix the head of the Medusa to his shield but also the colours of Sodom. Queerness is accessorized to the heterosexual male in the same way as is femininity – employing its power but removing most of its threat. Straight boy rock and roll drag assumes implicitly that there is something glamorous about homosexuality (something that gay men themselves seem to have forgotten). In fact, it might even be argued that in rock and roll glamour the phallocentric economy sees to it that the hyper-masculine and 'effeminate' (rather than feminine) images the rock star employs are simply fetishistic representatives of *active and passive homo-desire*.

Use Your Illusion
● *Title of Guns 'n' Roses double album*

Notes

1. Jane Mills, *Womanwords* (London: Virago Press, 1991), p. 106.

2. Judith Butler, *Gender Trouble* (London: Routledge, 1990), pp. 137–8.

3. Caja Silverman, *Male Subjectivity at the Margins* (London: Routledge, 1992), p. 372.

4. John Rechy, *City of Night* (New York: Evergreen, 1984), p. 116.

5. It is interesting to note that men with a reputation for getting fucked are often teased by their peers about the monstrous appetite of their rectums; gay men, in other words, seem to displace anxieties about the vagina onto 'receptive' gay men's rectums.

6. This was taken to an ironic extreme by a drag act, popular in London a few

years ago, called 'Dead Marilyn', in which a man came on stage dressed as a rotting female corpse.

7. E. Ann Kaplan, *Rock Around the Clock* (London: Routledge, 1989), p. 93.

8. Stan Denski and David Sholle, 'Metal men and glamour boys', in *Men, Masculinity and Media*, ed. Steven Craig (London: Sage Publications, 1992), p. 53.

9. *Ibid.*, p. 53.

10. Sammy Hagar, *Raw*, No. 122 (April 1993), p. 48.

11. Quoted in Denski and Sholle, 'Metal men and glamour boys', p. 54.

12. *Ibid.*, p. 54.

Chapter ten

Rock and Revolution
Business as Usual?

Situationists vacant

An emetically hand-painted Austin Maxi careers around London with the words 'ARREST ME' daubed on the boot. It carries five Situationists who, in only six months, have managed to be the first unsigned band to appear on Rapido; to have their first single acclaimed 'Single of the Week' by the NME; and whose live performances have succeeded in getting them banned from an impressive list of venues, moving the music press to describe them as 'An exclamation mark in a line of commas'. Fabulous are accelerating up the Road of Fame – on the wrong side.

'One university we played at phoned the next gig and warned them to cancel because we'd caused £1000 worth of damage and asked for rent boys and a room to crank up in,' brags Fabulous' lead singer Simon Dudfield. 'We didn't have the money to pay for rent boys or any heroin on us, but just by asking we managed to totally freak them out and they had to think a bit. We can never go anywhere and make it easy for them.'

Rebel rock, ordered, like Lazarus, from its death-bed by the Manic Street Preachers (The Clash in drag), has taken one cocky step further with Fabulous, whose self-appointed mission is to 'bring a little colour and excitement to a scene which is completely grey and turgid', according to James Brown, their manager and ideologue.

If it all sounds a little familiar to those who survived the late 1970s, the echoes are certainly there. In addition to the music itself – savage, staccato, relentless guitar adrenalin spiked with snarling vocals, replete with rolled 'r's – the echoes are there: Fabulous' theft of the reception carpet from EMI (the Sex Pistols were reputed to have stolen £60,000 from EMI); the T-shirts with unfeasibly large penises on them (Sid Vicious sported something similar – on his *T-shirt*); and, most revealing of all, the line, 'I'm a pistol full of sex,' from their first single.

But Fabulous are wary of comparisons. Eager to be seen as parent-less and peerless, Brown dismisses the comparisons ('"I'm a pistol full of sex" was just a good line – better than "come into my bedroom and eat some marigolds".') and emphasizes that the Pistols are part of a past they have no connection with; all the band members were too busy stealing sweets and watching *Magpie* on TV to notice the 1970s riff-revolution going on around them.

Nevertheless, just as punk was not able to acknowledge its roots in early rock and roll, Fabulous cannot acknowledge their debt to punk; deference to the past is no longer cool. And just as punk mobilized against the disco and rock invasion from the United States in the mid to late 1970s, Fabulous are ranged against the 1990s equivalents: the mindlessness of 'E' rave culture ('A generation of cripples!' spat Dudfield from the stage at an audience of saucer-eyed dance-kids recently); the apathy of the indie brigade: 'we're constantly inspired by the screaming *dullness* of the present scene'; and Guns 'n' Roses type ersatz rebellion: 'if you get any prick up on the stage, whether they're from a landed family estate or a housing estate and let them spout their narrow-minded stupid opinions you've got Axl Rose.'

Astutely they have grasped that sex in general, and 'deviant' sex in particular are almost the last weapons in a rebel's armoury that can still wound. Interestingly this is what marks them off from the Sex Pistols and most of the punk experience: the Pistols were curiously *un*sexy – exciting and aggressive, yes, but using theatrical violence, in word or deed, as a sex substitute. Fabulous instead toy with the last taboo – queerness – and ram their sexiness down their audience's throat: 'There's nothing like having your cock felt in a toilet cubicle by a complete stranger,' enthuses Brown, '– that's how I met one of the other members of Fabulous.' But isn't it really all about cynical sensationalism of the Frankie Goes to Hollywood/ Paul Morley School of show-business?

'The only reason that our stance, with the statements about

the sexuality of some band members and the gay porno T-shirts, seems so extreme and sensational is because pop music is now so tame. All the best performers have some kind of bisexuality about them, whether it's Rod Stewart poncing around in lycra leotards or the sly ambiguousness of the Buzzcocks' lyrics,' declares Brown.

Fabulous also believe that their style challenges masculinity. 'We run into trouble because we print T-shirts with erect dicks on them,' says Brown, 'but women masturbating on the cover of magazines is fine. Juggling with sexuality is a valid "tool" for social change because it opens up people's minds. In the last few years everyone's got so frosty and scared of expressing their sexuality that it just seems to have stopped being a part of rock 'n' roll.'

'We all like dressing up, and that's got a lot to do with rock 'n' roll too,' says Simon. 'One of the first big influences on me was David Sylvian – mainly because he just looked so fantastic,' enthuses Simon. 'So I started dressing like him and that caused a lot of problems, because in Morecambe, where I'm from, you don't deviate: you just work the week, go down the pub on Friday and go to the Match on Saturday. If you're a man and you dare to be different you get shouted at in the street and called "poof".'

'It's strange,' ruminates James. 'I remember wandering around Leeds with pink hair and earrings being called a poof by blokes in pink v-necked sweaters, with jumbo red cords, Kickers and bouffant hair-dos.'

'Yeah,' agrees Simon. 'Being attacked like that has more to do with embracing femininity than homosexuality. That's what makes real rock and pop stars; even someone like Jason Donovan: you can see that with his pretty-boy looks and his slightly camp style he's got something; whereas someone like Chesney Hawks is just so ordinary in every respect that there's just nothing there at all. As soon as you break out of the confines of what's supposed to be masculine you double your personality.'

'Look,' says James, 'you can go and watch the glorious spectacle of a Kinky Gerlinky Ball [a glam transvestite club in London], or some tedious rock band grinding out their latest single. If you compare the two to the greatest moments in rock 'n' roll it's quite obvious that a gang of TVs rolling around the centre of London has got a lot more to do with the likes of Elvis Presley, James Brown, Little Richard, Marc Bolan – at their slimmest and meanest; just oozing sexuality in the way people at the height of their creativity can.'

And Fabulous are oozing, all over stages up and down the country in their highly rated live acts, in which Dudfield portrays a demonic possession of Mick Jagger by Johnny Rotten with the Iggy Pop stage technique: teasing and tormenting the audience before hurling his half-naked body into the crowd, inviting adulation or punishment – anything that smacks of passion. And his strategy is working – student unions are resounding to the clatter of thousands of pimply jaws hitting the floor.

Meanwhile their first single, *Destined to Be Free*, does not so much ooze as spurt, the refreshingly egotistical chorus drenching the gentle listener with seminal stickiness: 'I don't give two fucks about ya / I just want to shove it up ya!'

It's a line which has a message for their audience: 'Fabulous is pop which is sexy and colourful and in your face – and we'll continue to polarize opinion; whether it's hatred and contempt or love and inspiration. As the band gets better, bigger, badder those opinions will become even more polarized,' says Brown, without even a shade of self-consciousness.

(Originally published in *The Guardian*, 12 March 1992)

Useful sluts

'No! You won't fool the children of the Revolution ...'. It's the soaraway seventies and Marc Bolan, the Sun King of glam is on *Top of the Pops* and the dowdy, buck-toothed peasants that pass for an audience are shuffling in an agony of self-consciousness at his feet, pretending that they can dance with all the weight of generations of British *dullness* on their shoulders.

But look at their *eyes* – they shine up at Bolan with an intensity that hurts; they want so much to escape their pasty prison and their pale past and they live a dream of revolt against it all through Bolan and his masterful blend of camp and rock and roll: these are the children of the 1960s revolution of aspirations and they dream of a better world of colour and sensation, where to feel is to mean; naive, pathetic, wonderful creatures that they are, they believe that Rock can take them there.

Twenty years later *Top of the Pops* is about to have its life-support system turned off. In a postmodern world where heroes, meta-narratives and utopias have all been kicked over or deconstructed who needs pop? Look at the 'performers' and now at the audience: can *you* tell them apart? The anxious and inhibited bundles of hope in the TOTP's audience of 1972 have had children and they are on the stage playing techno. The children of the children of the revolution have been fooled.

Out of all this polystyrene rubble of pop music struts a band that wants to be *worshipped*, a band that wants to explode over our head in a brilliant, brief starburst of something that used to be called rock and roll.

'*You* love us / You love us / You love us / You *love*.' At a gig in Brighton the Manic Street Preachers take control. They know that these kids have to be grabbed by their twitching techno shoulders and shaken until their complacency falls to the floor like torn panties. Through sheer will-power and glitz the MSP's are determined to violate the CNN/MTV virtual reality womb-world that is modern life. Like a pastiche of the New York Dolls with their rock vixen attire and eye-liner applied with a trowel, they look strangely anachronistic and yet offer a promise of something gushingly momentary, something arrogantly *now*.

Nicky Wire, bass guitarist, is wearing Ray-bans, ski-pants and hennaed hair; Richey James, rhythm guitarist and lyricist, sports a Madonna crucifix and a T-shirt with 'I'm too dead' spray-stencilled on it. Bitterly sweet in their cheap and priceless presentation they offer snarls like bouquets and blow promiscuous kisses to male members of the audience like a gauntlet across the face. Rock and Roll! – all the discomfort and provocation of a salami-in-your-Spandex, but with none of the disappointment.

'I like it when it's cold and wet. I don't like warm weather at all.' Well, the sentiment is perverse enough but is this *really* Richey? Short and wiry he's almost ordinary looking. Only his eyes offer a hint of the terror of his stage persona. And he's drinking Diet Coke. Whatever happened to the fucking and fighting alcoholic haze most rock bands seem to regard as *de rigueur*? His accent is another surprise – whoever heard of a rock star with a *Welsh* accent? But perhaps this is the secret of the Manics' unfashionable zeal: coming from a small-town background in a part of the world as uncosmopolitan as Wales fills you with a desperate, frightening faith in the transforming power of rock and roll.

As guitarist Nicky Wire told *Gay Times*, 'If you're hopelessly depressed like I was then dressing up is just the ultimate escape. When I was young I just wanted to be noticed. Nothing could excite me except attention so I'd dress up as much as I could. Outrage and boredom just go hand in hand.'[1]

Richey admits that forming a band was a 'first step towards becoming something – some*one*'. Rock and roll for them was about excitement and romance right from the beginning; their dreams were stadium-sized from the start. Not for them the ritual indie band invocation of the 'sincerity' and 'spontaneity' of poverty, the yawnsome 'slumming it' with the lads for 'authenticity'.

'When we began touring in a crappy minibus, changing in pukey dressing rooms and eating cold pizza on a beach in Hartlepool at 2 a.m. with a hangover, we never kidded ourselves or anyone else that this was "cool" and what being in a band was all about. Of course, that's blasphemy: you're supposed to brag about not washing for a week and blocking dressing room toilets.'

Richey has no time for the naff boys' club mentality of much of the music press and the indie scene. 'The whole Crusty image [increasingly fashionable squatter and traveller attire], like the Levellers [a self-professed anarcho-syndicalist band], is all about being dirty and slovenly and that's such an offensive middle-class idea of what it means to be "working class" and "authentic". Where I grew up the first thing a miner would do when he got home was *scrub himself thoroughly* and put on some decent clothes. Only middle-class college boys on a three-year rebellion kick could think that dirt was revolutionary.'

Uninterested in conforming to indie formalism, sartorially or musically, it seemed only natural to these Welsh boys, who began with an interest in punk, to gravitate towards the heavier sounds and more grandiose gestures of heavy metal that stud their debut album *Generation Terrorists* like rhinestones on black velvet. On that album the MSP project, which seemed to begin as a reckless imitation of the Clash and Guns 'n' Roses, gorgeously, glitteringly transcends both. From the reeling firestorm of 'Slash and Burn' to the paean to capitalist alienation that is 'Motorcycle Emptiness', *Generation Terrorists* manages to equal the anger and frustration of punk and, remarkably, marry it to the glitz and glamour of old-style rock and roll. Even the intellectual terrorism of quoting passages of Nietzsche, Confucius and the Futurists on the album sleeve in a kind of jumble sale of modernism seems to work.

But the most exciting feature of the album is the prospect of the reaction of the gender-anxious, overweight, male supremacist boys of middle America who think that it is less likely that rock and roll will surprise them than that McDonald's will turn vegan. Watch them scream and run for the lifeboats when this sequined depth-charge of an album detonates against the rusty hull of heavy metal, sinking all their assumptions.

The mindless conservatism and prejudice of heavy metal is legendary. What does Richey think about the homophobic ravings of its stars, including his hero Axl Rose?

'Yes, of course Axl's a prat,' says Richey, 'and he spouts all sorts of rubbish. But I think there's a lot of hypocrisy around this issue. A lot of artists are prejudiced one way or another. I mean the *NME*'s pounding away at Morrissey for being "racist" is just absurd; he hasn't suddenly changed – he has always offered a nostalgic view of "Englishness", even when he could do no wrong by the music press. Or take the Happy Mondays fiasco where the *NME* suddenly "discovered" their homophobia after ignoring it during the Madchester craze; but when the Happy Mondays were going out of fashion it became "an issue".'

The Manics themselves have had a chequered relationship with the *NME*, being fêted at first and then slated for 'selling out' by signing to Columbia Records, and then being fêted again. But far more interesting than the cynical self-righteous machinations of pop journals are the teenage scribbles from boys and girls who have seen the light shining from out of the MSP's arses and foaming diatribes from boys who collect beer mats: 'They're wearing fuck-ing *eyeliner* – they should be fucking kicked in.'[2]

It's easy to see why they should attract so much masculine venom: they don't *compensate*. So many heavy metal artists look like your worst nightmare of an amateur drag queen, or plumber's mate tranny, but they are careful to atone for this by cussing and swearing, pulling 'babes', drinking cold tea out of Jack Daniel's bottles at breakfast and being unable to form a sentence without the customary phrase 'fuckin' faggot!' Not the MSPs. Instead of macho gestures they pout, and the lead-singer, James Dean Brad-field, has been known to ask if there are any pretty boys who want to bugger him. The challenge to the conventions of rock mascu-linity that the Manics represent suffuses their new single, 'Little Baby Nothing' which lyrically kneels at the feet of exploited femi-ninity: 'You are pure, you are snow / We are the useless sluts that they mould.'

Are they a feminist band?

'I believe very much in Valerie Solanos' view that "the male chromosome is an incomplete female chromosome,"' enthuses Richey. 'In other words that the male is a walking abortion: aborted at the gene stage ... maleness is a deficiency disease and males are emotional cripples.' Strong stuff indeed. But does not this self-abnegation have some rather musty aroma of incense about it? Something almost Marian? Richey confesses freely: 'Much of our music is Catholic influenced. That's why there is so much reference to death.'

The Manics are good Catholic boys gone bad, but like all lapsed children of the Church of Rome they still hanker after some-thing to take the place of lost faith. 'Little Baby Nothing's' final lines offer the most pithy exposition of their rock and roll credo: a means of transcending the meaninglessness and mundaneness of everyday life as well as their own 'worthlessness'; a credo in which rock and roll is the sigh of the oppressed, the search for a 'soul in a soulless world': 'Rock 'n' Roll is our epiphany / Culture, alienation, boredom and despair.'

Whether there remains any room for such big, glam hopes in such a small, plain world crowded with mediocrity disguised as savant cynicism remains to be seen.

(Originally published in *Capital Gay*, 13 November 1992)

Frightening the horses: Bowie and Suede

All rock and roll is homosexual.
● *Manic Street Preachers*

The heterosexual rock fan idolises his star, and pays for his success because he believes that only a star can get fucked and still look the world in the face. Like a mirror surrounded by glitter, the rock idol reflects the fascinated light of the homoerotic libido that his audience project onto him. The cult of the gay superstar is the reverse side of the two-faced attitude that heterosexuals have towards homosexuality. Their more customary face is immediate disdain and disparagement for the queer who stands at the crossroads of life and dares to smile at them in the underground.

● *Mario Miele on David Bowie*[3]

I've read a lot of goddamn issues of the NME in my time, but you left-wing homos have gone too far this time. Plastering half-naked pictures of that effeminate guy from the Lemonheads all over the paper, including the cover, and for what? What are we supposed to get from looking at them?

Then Suede: mentioned on the cover, a full ad on the back (two guys kissing),[4] *the band pouting on page three and then a full review of their LP. Personally, I find all this 'homoerotic' and 'limp-wristed' stuff disgusting. If there are people who want it, then let them buy Gay Times or something.*

I'm not asking you to start sticking naked girls in the paper ... but at least head back to normality, where men are men, and women are women.

Think about it, and then ask yourselves the question: is the NME trying to queer the nation?

● *Letter to the New Musical Express (10 April 1993)*

As Miele has suggested, rock and roll, as part of capitalism, can be characterized as part of the process of repressive sublimation that immediately resublimates desire while rechanneling it to a consumerist outlet. This is why 'the heterosexual fan of the gay rock star idolises him and pays for his success'.

While this analysis is true, it is also untrue. Like the queer, rock and roll stands at the crossroads of life – or at least tries its damnedest to – facing towards both 'repressive resublimation' and dissidence, dissidence of a kind that can cause enormous instability, threatening, or so it would seem, to 'queer the nation'.

The leading edge of rock and roll must always be searching for the faultline of sexuality, the cusp of gender, where the connections between the two are most fraught and thus most dynamic and most *productive*. In order to be able to channel desire into consumerism, rock and roll capitalism has first to locate the richest sources of desire, the most untrammelled and polymorphous longing in young people. This requires a continuous probing and testing of boundaries to discover just precisely where these flaws and fissures can be located.

As Foucault has observed, sexuality is not a 'natural fact' but instead something that has to be *manufactured* and should be seen as the 'set of effects produced in bodies, behaviours, and social relations by a certain deployment deriving from a complex political technology.'[5] This 'deployment' always attempts to demonstrate that 'masculine' and 'feminine' proceed from male and female and in this way heterosexualize desire, making it depend upon sex and gender.

Rock and roll as part of capitalism is part of that 'complex political technology' that *attempts but fails* to heterosexualize desire; sites of power can also be sites of resistance. In her book *Gender Trouble* Judith Butler argues that since gender norms are impossible to embody they become the 'stylized repetition of acts' – Foucault's 'effects produced in bodies'. Thus 'the possibilities of gender transformation are to be found precisely in the arbitrary relation between such acts . . . that exposes the phantasmic effect of abiding identity as a politically tenuous construction.'[6] At its leading edge, in order to have any credibility with and appeal to young people, rock and roll has to appropriate images and acts that are unstable and expose the 'arbitrary' nature of gender performance, revel in the 'phantasmic' nature of identity and thus cause some disturbing feedback in the transmission of the 'complex political technology'.

Eventually, of course, they stabilize (e.g. heavy metal), but that is also the moment when they go out of fashion – i.e. lose their power over (hip) young people. To be effective rock and roll has to appeal to 'the kids'' desperation to escape the mortifying *square-*

ness of heterosexism, a route out of the crushing sex/gender Scylla and Charybdis that await them on their voyage into adulthood.

As the political technology changes, as it always does, so rock and roll has to renegotiate its relationship to it, trying to ensure that it remains not completely within it, always keeping its outsider edge, and trying to elaborate the idea that masculine and feminine do *not* always proceed from male and female. So when the 'feminine' glamour of 1970s androgyny turned into football favourites Sweet, sharp rock and roll abandoned it and took up instead the outsider/hustler offensiveness and ripped jeans of punk;[7] when that became the Boomtown Rats, 'feminine' glamour came back in the form of the New Romantics and the *Blitz* look; and when eyeliner became blokish again it was time for the obscenity of Frankie Goes to Hollywood.

Thus rock and roll becomes a faultline itself. Like the now-defunct street drag queen which it has replaced, *vibrant* rock and roll is itself both an abdication to power *and* an incitement to rebellion, drawing attention to the performative nature of gender and saying, 'Oh Bondage! Up Yours!' (X-Ray Specs).

And like drag, rock and roll is fascinated with trash, with those things that society has labelled worthless and discarded. It is a protest against the technology of power which assigns all value and which young people feel descending upon them as their teen years tick away: the 'grid' which will mark their position and measure out their potential precisely, counting out their years all the way to the grave, differentiating desire and separating them from one another and their bodies. Thus to be determinedly worthless in the adult scheme of things (punk) is a resolution to evade entrapment.[8]

If the phrase 'All rock and roll is homosexual' means anything, it is that young people and homosexuals are all outsiders, criminals waiting for their sentence to be passed but doing their best to make a run for it. The difference is, of course, that ultimately the straight rock fan/star wants rebellion *but not damnation*.

> *It seemed to be the one taboo that everyone was too afraid to break. I thought – well, if there's one thing that's going to put me on the edge, this is it. Long hair didn't mean much any more. So I thought – right. Let's really go into*

> *the gay lifestyle and see what that's about and see how*
> *people relate to me. If they can.*
> ● *David Bowie, Arena (Spring 1993)*

Rock and roll, with its ceaseless turnover of images of gender revolt, from the foppish quiffs of the 1950s to the scandalous long hair of the 1960s, from the faggoty fashion of the Beatles' collarless suits to the *Cage Aux Folles* wardrobe of winged lamé outfits of the 1970s, knows very well that the signs of sexual identity and 'masculine' and 'feminine' are as unfixed as the desires of its audience. What rock and roll shows, in its ravenous appropriation of revolt, is the way in which these signifiers have no referents, that there is, ultimately, no substance to what they are meant to signify. If the signs of deviance turn out to be not so very deviant after all, this is both a victory for the status quo and a defeat: if there is no substance to the signs of deviance then there can be no substance to the signs it refuses.

So, by the early 1970s long hair, once the touchstone of revolt for men, 'didn't mean very much any more'. And Bowie decides to associate himself directly with the deviance long hair had hinted at but not embraced: *sexual* deviance (other than heterosexual promiscuity). But it is something that he 'goes into': he does not become part of it: he refuses 'damnation'.

Bowie's famous announcement to *Melody Maker* in 1972 that he was 'bisexual' and enjoyed dressing up in women's clothing was part of this 'going into'; a kind of sexual tourism: 'let's see what this is about'. His bisexuality was a physical expression of the two-faced aspect of rock and roll itself, neither completely inside *nor* completely outside the 'complex political technology'; it was 'just' more dressing up (and interestingly, his penchant for women's clothes actually marked him apart from most gay men at the time, who by then were beginning their process of resolute masculinization).

Hope on the part of many gays that he was going to be the 'gay Elvis' was understandable if rather naive. Miele's 'gay superstar' may reflect his audience's homoerotic libido but the irony is that this is more often done by the star who is *not* 'gay'. The world does not need a 'gay Elvis', for the original, with his black leather suit, pomaded pompadour, come-fuck-me eyes and radiant narcissism, was quite queer enough.

Bowie came to regret his bisexual statement because it was not taken as 'facing both ways'; in a homophobic society 'bisexual' can never be balanced: any *confessed* deviation from heterosexual identification tends to collapse that identification altogether (this is why 'bisexual' is not an identity taken on by the vast majority of men who are bisexual in behaviour: they regard themselves as straight men who happen to have sex with other men).

But it is instructive of the fraught position that rock and roll occupies in our culture that even the 'gay superstar' who left his androgyny and platform shoes behind and reinvented himself as a 'lad in a suit' in the 1980s, still struggles to escape the embrace of squareness. So in 1993 when Bowie tells *Arena* that he no longer considers himself bisexual he is nevertheless careful to avoid using the word 'straight' to describe himself.

Explicit androgyny and sexual ambivalence are once more the height of fashion, as evidenced by groups like the Manic Street Preachers and Fabulous, but most particularly the phenomenal success of a group called Suede who make no secret of their admiration for Bowie's work in the 1970s. So in the *Melody Maker*, twenty years after Bowie, the lead singer Brett Anderson announces that he is 'bisexual' – 'but, I've never had a homosexual experience'.[9]

While the statement might be taken as rather coy and pathetic, it is also smart rock and roll: it is the Bowie formulation but with the 'homosexual' part removed, effectively maintaining his 'two-faced' aspect where Bowie failed; a psychic but chaste dalliance with queerness. This is, after all, the classic position of the rock and roll star: he tells the world, either by impression (Elvis) or confession (Anderson) that he would *like* to get fucked in the arse but has not actually managed it yet (nor will he). The rock and roll star's appeal to his straight audience, their point of identification, is not so much based on his posing as a sodomite as his *failure* as a sodomite; his ability to look towards the Cities of the Plain without turning into a pillar of salt.

Understandably this new rush to appropriate what are taken to be signs of homosexuality and the gay 'subculture' has provoked cries of 'exploitation' from some gays themselves. One gay music journalist was prompted to complain: 'When such things get taken up by those who aren't fully immersed in the culture from which they've sprung, they never get it quite right. Camp goes from being something quite specific but indefinable to something meaningless.'[10] But if rock and roll shows anything it is that there is nothing which is not open to appropriation, and that this appropriation does not represent anything but itself: it is only 'meaningless' to talk about 'getting it right'. Hence Bowie not only appropriated 'gay styles' but also black culture: he reinvented himself as a 'soul singer'; neither his 'gay' persona nor his 'soul' persona actually referred to anything 'specific'.

And, as we have seen, is not the whole giddy glory of rock and roll precisely that it renders all these signs insubstantial – summoning up, for at least the length of a three-minute single, a foolish but splendid vision of a world of meaning without reference, longing without object, a world where there is no 'sexual aim' – just endless desiring?

'Suede' by Suede

Forget 1970s revivalism and androgyny – polymorphous perversity is what the 1990s are dressing up for, and Suede are the most 'bestial' outfit going. Breathlessly awaited for over a year in what must be the most hyperventilated press anticipation ever, their eponymous debut album is, alas, all that was hoped for and more.

Suede, the unnatural offspring of Bowie and Morrissey, present us with a haughty lopsided smile induced by crap drugs and cheap cider; spoilt, sullen faces that peer awkwardly from under irritating long fringes and demand everything: proudly narcissistic babies that need your love – all of it.

If pop has been reborn then it has been born degenerate in a decadent nation. Suede take you on a tour that celebrates the squalor and despair that is Britain. In a wasted landscape of the burnt out grandiose pretensions of the Thatcher revolution, sex and excitement are to be got where and when you can; in Suede country meat, violence, drugs, dogs are all equally valid sources of pleasure, of escapist passion. The songs – 'Animal Lover' and 'Animal Nitrate' – and the lyrics – 'she's got a big black dog in her' – turn the very quintessence of homely Englishness, the domestic pet, foaming and slavering onto the suburban dream. In the amyl prostrate world of Suede, rough trade 'jumps on your bones', semen and poppers mix on your shiny nylon sheets, in the squat next door kids 'chase the dragon', and down the road up on the common, girls fuck with men in cars, engines still running, 'exhaust in their hair'.

Lead singer Brett caterwauls like a depraved Terry Hall over driven guitars about a glorious grubbiness of the soul for which grunge was just a (bad) dress rehearsal. And unlike Morrissey, who was strangely *wholesome* in the fever of his hypochondria, Brett and his swinish friends are incurably *louche* in their sickly, sibilant sounds.

(Originally published in *Him*, November 1992)

Notes

1. Richard Smith, *Gay Times*, August 1991.

2. *Ibid.*

3. Mario Miele, *Homosexuality and Liberation* (London: Gay Men's Press, 1981), p. 129.

4. In fact they are two women.

5. Michel Foucault, *The History of Sexuality* (London: Penguin, 1990), p. 172.

6. Judith Butler, *Gender Trouble* (London: Routledge, 1990), p. 141.

7. 'Punk' in American usage means both 'trash' and the passive partner in sodomy (Jonathan Green, *The Slang Thesaurus*, London: Penguin, 1988).

8. The popularity of grunge in the early 1990s was due to the same effect: American teenagers revelled in flouting that most important part of the US Constitution – the belief in cleanliness (although, of course, they embraced only the signifiers of uncleanliness – unkempt hair, tatty woodsman clothes – never dirt itself).

9. *Melody Maker*, 12 December 1992. Another member of the band has described himself as 'a bisexual who has never had a heterosexual experience'.

10. Richard Smith, 'Ambisexuality', *Melody Maker*, 12 December 1992.

Chapter eleven

Don't Die on Me, Buddy
Homoeroticism and Masochism in War Movies

Yet each man kills the thing he loves,
   By each let this be heard,
Some do it with a bitter look,
   Some with a flattering word.
The coward does it with a kiss,
   The brave man with a sword!

● Oscar Wilde, 'The Ballad of Reading Gaol'

In the dominant versions of men at war, men are permitted
to behave towards each other in ways that would not be
allowed elsewhere, caressing and holding each other,
comforting and weeping together, admitting their love. The
pain of war is the price paid for the way it expresses the
male bond. War's suffering is a kind of punishment for the
release of homosexual desire and male femininity that only
war allows.

● Anthony Easthope, What a Man's Gotta Do

THE war film is perhaps the richest of all texts of masculinity. Escape from the feminine, bloody initiation into manhood, male bonding: these are all themes which the traditional war film employs. In a sense, the war/military film is hardly ever about anything other than what it means to be a man and how to become one.

This is often quite clear not just on a narrative level but also on a symbolic level. Psychoanalysis suggests that the traditional war film can be described as the (positive) Oedipus complex made social. Central to the Oedipus complex, the process by which, according to Freud, boys become men, is the fear of castration. When realization of his mother's 'castration' sets in, the boy becomes aware of the possibility of his own castration. This threat is seen as coming from his own father, his rival for his mother's affections. It is through this threat of castration that the boy comes to transfer his affections from his mother to his 'bride' (as with all the terms in psychoanalysis this is merely symbolic, not necessarily his wife). Now the castration threat is resolved, since there is no longer rivalry between father and son, and the boy is able to identify with his father: this is the moment that Freud describes as the 'triumph of the masculine ego'.

In the classic narrative of the war film this drama is acted out when the boy leaves home to face death (which represents castration – or rather, death is but a shadow of the fear of castration), wins the war (victory is the triumph of the masculine ego), returns to claim his bride and is congratulated by the generals/his father. The medals pinned to his chest betoken nothing so much as his successful attainment of heterosexuality and the appreciation of this by patriarchal society.[1]

Even the post-Freudian view of how a boy becomes a man, which rejects castration anxiety as an insufficient explanation for this process, can be accommodated in the war film. Post-Freudians suggest that boys have to separate socially as well as psychically from their mothers in order to become men. A tendency towards regression to narcissistic 'blissful oneness' with the mother, a sense of omnipotence based on the failure to separate from this dyad, is postulated as the chief obstacle to 'personhood' for a boy. In other words, he has to leave the womb-like warmth of the home and strike out into the world to perform some 'test' that will set up an autonomous identity.

Ignorant of the Freudian or post-Freudian interpretation put upon the narrative of war films, boys keen to become men as fast as possible constitute the most avid audience of these films, enthusiastically learning the 'lessons' such films have to teach them about masculinity and acting them out with their friends by playing 'war' themselves.

Arguably it is *in spite* of the Oedipal and post-Freudian message that such films appeal to many boys. The war film not only offers a text on masculinity and how to take one's place in patriarchy, it also offers a vision of a world in which the privileges of heterosexual manhood can be combined with a boyish homo-eroticism – a purely masculine world awash with femininity. In other words, something of an *escape* from the Oedipus complex.

This is undoubtedly the secret of the special appeal of the buddy war film, the war film which concentrates on the close friendships that develop between men in wartime. The buddy war film offers boys a dream, a dream of an impossibly masculine world in which boys become men and yet remain boys, an alternative to the peacetime route to manhood of marriage – every boy's dread.

But it is worth remembering that these films are made by men. If boys dream of growing up but escaping from the future, men dream of never having grown up and escaping from the present. This leads to the irony that when boys play games of 'war' based upon films they have seen, they are, in effect, boys playing men playing boys playing war. War films may be texts of masculinity but the biggest lesson they have to teach is that being a man is a game, albeit a deadly one.

In war films of the buddy type the deadliness of war is not glossed over. But it is portrayed not in the death of the enemy, who are often faceless or even unseen, but in the death of comrades and buddies. Classically, the moment when the buddy lies dead or dying is the moment when the full force of the love the boys/men feel for one another can be shown. And, for all the efforts of the conscientious film maker, the deadliness is thus attached not so much to *war* as to the queer romance of it all. An intimate relationship between death and the expression of homo-desire is set up in the war film. Easthope, Russo[2] and others have pointed out how the most physical expressions of masculine femininity have to pay the 'ultimate price'. But pain and death are not just a price that has to be paid – it is as if the caress, the kiss, the embrace *were the fatal blow itself*. The lesson that the buddy film has to teach boys (and remind men) is that 'war' is a place where queer love can not only be expressed but *endorsed* – but only when married to death. Death justifies and romanticizes the signs but not the practice of queer love – death, as we shall see in the following four buddy war films made in the last decade, is itself the consummation, the cathartic masochistic climax that satisfies the audience and keeps the desublimation of homo-eroticism on the battlefield.

Stanley Jaffe's *Taps* (1981) shows what can happen when homo-erotic love between boys breaks out in peacetime. The cadets at Bunker Hill Military Academy for Boys led by 'Major' (head boy) Moreland (Timothy Hutton) take it over to prevent its closure to make way for condominiums that the Academy's board of trustees have decided will make them more money. The concept of 'honour' is constantly invoked by the boys, particularly Moreland, and their belief in it is contrasted with the outside world's apparent lack of it.

The system of honour their military academy depends upon involves respect of rank, but in contrast to the real military, this army of young boys (for that is what a military academy is) considers honour more important than respect. And what is this 'honour'? Why nothing more nor less than boyish love. General Boche (George C. Scott) tells Moreland on his promotion to the rank of Major that the boys will respect his rank but the man behind the rank has to earn respect for himself; in other words he has to earn the boys' love. This he does in the course of the occupation. It becomes clear that what sustains the boys in the face of the National Guard and their hysterical parents who lay siege to them is their love for their Principal, General Boche; for their ranking boy, Major Moreland; for their platoon commanders; for each other and for the boys of yesteryear who passed through the Academy's walls and fought and died for their country. Boyish love/honour is thus initially presented as being stronger than the forces of family and society.

It also becomes clear, however, that there is something more than a little suspect about this boyish love. The unmarried old General who inculcated this love in the boys is, quite properly, removed from the picture very early on by the local sheriff's department (ostensibly on a firearms charge). He is later finished off by a heart attack, leaving the boys to honour one another without his problematic presence. It is also worth noting that the General's exit is brought about while he is trying to end a brawl brought about by the local rowdies shouting 'faggots!' at the soldier boys, spruced up in their dress uniforms for their end-of-term ball. This is also the only scene in which girls make an appearance, demure alibis on the arms of the boys attending the ball (the only other females we see in the film are distraught mothers trying to persuade their sons to abandon the occupation and return home).

But with the General gone, Moreland's swooning devotion to him only increases: 'I felt privileged to be in his presence', he sighs. Moreland's buddy and roommate Dyer (Sean Penn) begins to smell something odd and expresses the audience's discomfort when he accuses Moreland and Boche of being wrapped up in a romantic dream about the Academy, 'as cosy as two bugs queer for each other!' The inevitable fisticuffs that follow this accusation is designed to dispel our fear of the love that has been named. Ironically it is actually a lovers' tiff: the relationship of Moreland and Dyer is the central love-affair of the film, even if Moreland is hung up on Boche. Moreland's devotion to Boche is coded queer in order to throw his affair with Dyer into a 'natural' and 'healthy' light. Dyer is also the voice of reason, opposing the occupation all along, but not taking up the opportunity to leave because of his sense of 'honour' towards his buddy and CO. Moreland ignores Dyer's entreaties (to end the siege/to love him) and prefers to watch old home movies of the General.

The death of a young cadet leads to a tearful scene between Dyer and Moreland in which Moreland abandons the memory of Boche and chooses Dyer instead, calling off the occupation. But before the surrender can happen and the Dyer/Moreland marriage be consummated, a gung-ho/psycho character played by Tom Cruise lets rip with a heavy machine gun from the second floor of the Academy. Moreland rushes to stop him but both of them die in a hail of bullets, witnessed by Dyer. In one satisfying burst of gunfire the audience's queer anxieties are erased: Cruise, the cadet with a suspicious fascination with bodybuilding and easily the shortest hair in the Academy, and Moreland, whose peculiar love for Boche led to this rebellion against family life. Equilibrium is restored after its disruption has allowed the audience to enjoy the manifestation of queer love.

The film ends with Dyer weeping over the body of his dead

buddy and carrying his corpse, draped over his outstretched arms, Achilles carrying Patroclus, out of the entrance to the Academy – the only way their love *could* enter the civilian world.

Stand By Me (1986), directed by Rob Reiner, is another buddy war film set in peacetime, this time disguised as childhood rites-of-passage nostalgia. This conceit actually points up the 'text of masculinity' status of buddy war films and the way in which they tend to be about men dreaming they are boys again. Four twelve-year-old boys are trying very hard to be men and separating themselves from 'girly' things ('pussy' is the worst insult in their vocabulary – one that curiously does not seem to run to 'fag'). The 'enemy' is a band of older boys who humiliate them and call them 'girls'. As in many war films, 'the feminine' is a purely symbolic presence, a problematic presence in *boys*. There are no girls to be seen anywhere, even the older boys who *talk* about girls and what they do to them a great deal are never actually seen with anyone other than their male friends. The 'far-offness' of the 1950s in which the film is set is the alibi for all this homosociality: the past – particularly the nostalgic variety – is as 'other' as wartime.

And just as war provides a pretext for evading women and seeking out the company of men, something to 'do' with other boys, so *Stand By Me* offers a common task for the boys: a journey to see the corpse of a young boy they have heard is lying by a railway line. This plot line is in fact the very distillation of the buddy war film theme: leaving home and 'the feminine' behind to be with your buddies and look death in the face. The boys themselves, living in the shadow of the Second World War in which their fathers served, are very keen to play up the warlike nature of their 'great deed'.

It is made clear that the narrator, Gordie (Whil Wheaton), and Chris (River Phoenix) love one another very much. But, in classic war film tradition, this tenderness cannot be expressed physically until they encounter death in the form of the boy's corpse. Gordie breaks down in tears and shouts, 'It should have been me!' His fascination with seeing the corpse has been a fascination with confronting his older brother's death. In flashback we have seen his brother as strikingly handsome and astonishingly affectionate towards Gordie, asking for hugs and showing an interest in his life that his parents fail to show.

No brother is like this – not even in Hollywood. This is the dream of an older boy lover made possible because it is just that, a dream: his brother was dead before the film began. The 'brother' motif is played again and again throughout the film in contradistinction to the 'father' motif. The boys have reason to hate their fathers who are alcoholics (Chris), violent (Teddy) or resentful (Gordie). Boyish, brotherly love is offered as a more attractive alternative to the disappointment of paternal love. Chris, attempting to console Gordie who is anguished about his father's hurtful treatment of him, says, 'If I were your Dad things would be different.'

Beside the symbolic corpse of his brother, Gordie grieves and is hugged by his buddy Chris. The older boys obligingly make an appearance so that Gordie can brandish a huge pistol that he has brought with him, scaring them off and passing the 'test': he has overcome castration anxiety, 'let go' of his brother and his feminine attachment to him and proved his manhood.

The intimation that these boys have a queer passion for each other is hermetically sealed in the past by the final scene. The narrator Gordie is now a middle-aged writer who has been typing this reminiscence onto his word processor. We learn that Chris is dead, killed in a 'fast-food joint brawl that he tried to stop' – a poignantly heroic, and literally *convenient*, death. The horror and the violence of it, 'stabbed in the throat', is shocking but consistent with the deaths of 'war buddies': Gordie has stepped out of Bunker Hill Academy with Chris in his arms. Nicely completing the sterilization of the queer contamination of adult life represented by childhood sweetheart Chris, the door of Gordie's study opens and we see his young kids waiting for him to take them out. For all the film's exploitation of homoerotic brotherly love and the sympathetic opposition of this to 'the fathers', family life wins out, the homoerotic is outgrown; Chris is dead and Gordie has become a father himself.

Now safely established in the heterosexual present, Gordie can afford a reverie about his boyish past (which is what the whole film, of course, has been): 'Although it has been ten years since I saw Chris I will miss him forever,' he writes. 'I never had any other friends like the ones I had at twelve,' he adds, sailing a little close to the wind. Hastily he recoups by swearing and moving from the personal to the general: 'Jesus, who does!'

Memphis Belle (1990), directed by Michael Caton-Jones, unlike either *Taps* or *Stand By Me*, is actually set in real wartime as opposed to a symbolic one. But despite this the film is even more nostalgic and sentimental about boyish love than either.

It tells the story of the crew of an American Army Air Force B–17 bomber named Memphis Belle, operating out of Cambridge-shire in 1942, who have only one more mission to fly before being shipped back to the US. If they survive their final mission they will be the first crew to complete their tour of duty intact.

The film begins with loving footage of the (enlisted) crew playing touch football: vital American youth on fine English grass under a mild summer sun. A male voice-over introduces us to each of the men as the camera follows them running, shouting and laughing. Their attractive qualities are listed by the voice-over, finishing with, 'Yes, I think we can do something with these boys …'. The voice could easily be that of God or the director but it turns out to belong to an oily PR man who wants to make war heroes out of our boys for propaganda purposes. 'The nation's gonna fall in love with these boys,' he tells the base's CO.

In fact it is *us*, the audience, that falls in love with these boys. The Army PR acts as a foil; his self-serving and crude attempts to exploit these golden boys distracts from the director's own manipulative techniques.

The scene following our dreamy introduction to these youths reminds us what this beauty is based on: a winged bomber landing with only one wheel down crashes and explodes.

In the opening line-up two lover boys are reserved for special treatment: Rascal (Sean Astin), 18, a stocky little gunner, baby-faced and with curly hair, but all boy; and Danny (Eric Stoltz), also 18, a tall, red-blond, clean-limbed radio operator with a face ordinarily attractive but with a hint of extraordinary sensitivity. In visual shorthand Rascal is introduced to us as 'lust' and Danny as 'love'.

Although it is a warm summer's day and they are playing football, Rascal is the only boy presented to us without a shirt, revealing a smoothly muscled chest that is far from unpleasant to look at. He is also the only one whose bodily measurements are offered: '5'4", 120 lbs', and whose sexual potential is made explicit: 'with a reputation as a ladies' man – at least that's what he *says*.' As we hear these words we see Rascal standing behind a bent-over boy, swinging his hips around in a sexy circle in a mock-swishy fashion (boys' boys are allowed the luxury of camping it up: we later see Rascal jitterbugging and 'screaming' with Danny at the dance before their last mission).

So sexy is the little tyke that the other boys seem unable to keep their hands off him, especially his curly locks. In one scene Rascal is eating breakfast before their last flight when the co-pilot, Luke (Tate Donovan), walks up behind him and grabs his head in a friendly arm-lock and runs his fingers vigorously through Rascal's hair. 'Stop that!' cries Rascal, embarrassed but obviously enjoying it. 'You won't have a chance to do that after today, sir,' he adds half challengingly, half wistfully. 'I wouldn't be too sure about that,' warns Luke, grabbing Rascal's head again.

Given Rascal's role as a spunky, irrepressibly physical guy, 'the body of the boy', it is entirely appropriate that we should discover that his gunnery position in the bomber has him crouched in a retractable spherical turret slung beneath the aircraft, from where he spits fire at enemy fighters: Rascal is the 'balls' of Memphis Belle.

If Rascal is 'down below', then Danny is 'the higher things': love, romance and soul-mateship. He is introduced to us as 'Danny Daley: as Irish as you could get.' And, as we all know, in Hollywoodland the Irish (when not playing salt-of-the-earth, bull-necked NYPD employees) are the 'romantic', slightly other-worldly, 'poetic' types. Sure enough, Danny turns out to be a poet, reading out a poem he has penned before the crew take off on their final flight. And like Rascal, Danny's job positions him in relation to the rest of the crew and to male qualities: as the radio operator he is language, culture, communication, sensitivity: the means by which the other men are brought together; he transmits and receives love. The way in which Danny becomes a conductor for all the emotion that the boys are generating is graphically demonstrated in a remarkable scene at the dance where the tail-gunner Clay (Harry Connick Jnr) sings 'Danny Boy' on stage at the dance and the others join in with the final line, 'Oh, Danny boy – I love you', delivering it directly at Danny, dressed up as ribbing of course, but all the more sincere for that.

The love that Danny broadcasts is picked up by a jittery young rookie, also a radio operator, who has just arrived from the US. Teased at the dance by the more experienced men about getting his 'ass blown off', he rushes into the toilets to throw up. Danny follows him in, helps him clean up and pep talks him. Then he tells the white-faced boy to close his eyes and produces a four-leafed clover; he touches it to the boy's nose, who then opens his eyes. 'It's good luck', he says, and puts his arm around the boy and leads him out of the toilet.

During the exchange Danny tells the nervy boy, who just wants to get his tour of duty over with and go home, 'Sometimes I wish I could stay ... these guys are like brothers to me. I never had any – had *four* older sisters ... I don't know when we're ever gonna get together again – we come from all over. I guess that's why I keep taking their pictures.' Danny expresses here the tacit premise of all buddy war films: that war is not really so bad – at least when compared to family life (which is represented as suffocatingly feminine: '*four* older sisters'). In itself this is something of a departure. This idea is hardly ever articulated in words, and that is the point of the whole buddy war film genre, something told visually because it is an idea that cannot be named.

Danny's sadness at the knowledge that this escape from the family and heterosexuality into the arms of brotherly love is doomed has encouraged him to try to possess the boys for ever with his camera, so that he can enjoy the dream of boyish love nostalgically in a heterosexual future, like Gordie in *Stand By Me* with his writing. Of course the irony is that Danny with his camera is capturing the boys for *us*, the audience trapped in the heterosexual future, enjoying this daydream of homoerotic love. Like Danny we have the bitter-sweet feeling of wanting the film and their love to go on for ever, knowing full well that it cannot and must not.

The voyeurism of the camera (Danny's/ours) and its implicit homoeroticism is self-consciously highlighted by a scene that comes shortly after Danny's confession. Southside Chicago reform-school boy Jack (Neil Giuntozi) is shaving in the barracks while Danny takes his picture. 'Oh no!' exclaims Jack. 'I can see it now. I'm back home banging my wife and the door opens and there's Danny taking my picture!' The preposterousness of the image encapsulates the impossibility of their love continuing after the war and underlines the homo/hetero opposition between the life they lead now and the one they have to return to.

The only girl to make an appearance in the film is unsuccessfully chatted up by 'ladies man' Rascal (who consoles himself by dancing with Danny). Later she does have sex with one of the minor characters from the crew, but his main concern appears to be shaking off the teasing moniker assigned by the other boys, 'Virg'.

'Women' figure mainly as a superstitious fetishism that takes a female form. Their bomber is called 'Memphis Belle', after a girl Captain Dennis (Matthew Modine) met in Memphis, Tennessee, and has the traditional busty 'centre-fold' picture airbrushed onto the fuselage beneath the cockpit. The four-leafed clover Danny gives the rookie radio-operator is found between the leaves of a girlie book. And like women they are fetishes to be exchanged between men.

But luck also takes a feminine form because it expresses a maternal quality: 'lady luck' looks after her men. Dennis talks to his plane and says, 'You know how to take care of your men. I guess that's the best thing a guy could say about any girl.' In fact he is the 'girl' that takes care of his men. We see him constantly concerned about the welfare of his men. During the flight he tells them when to take oxygen, when to connect the heating elements in their suits, when to eat and when to catch some sleep. As Captain this is his responsibility, but his clucking ministrations go far beyond his job description. The men pretend to resent his womb-like care but actually thrive on it. Rascal reluctantly attaches his safety harness in his turret only after Dennis scolds him for not using it. Shortly afterwards an enemy fighter blows the turret away and it appears that Rascal has gone with it. But then we are relieved to see him dangling in the air, suspended by the safety belt – Dennis' umbilical cord.

All the boys look after one another and the lucky charms are *love tokens*, representing that care, their 'feminine' aspect. During the last flight, Eugene (Courtney Gains), a goofy-looking Catholic boy, has a row with his best buddy, fellow gunner Jack, who grabs his medallion and throws it out of the plane. Eugene is hysterical and beside himself with grief, '*Why did you do that!*' he screams, more in horror and incomprehension that his buddy would do such a thing than concern about the loss of the object itself – the fabric of male love has been rent, leaving him exposed to a hostile world. Danny comes to his rescue, slipping over his wrist his own lucky charm, a rubber band. 'It works,' he assures Eugene who is consoled because he has been told that he is loved again: the rubber band holds closed the hole opened up by the loss of the St Christopher. Later Jack is hit by an enemy round and Eugene rushes to his aid, forgetting his previous hurt. It turns out that Jack is only grazed, but he is sufficiently moved by Eugene's display of concern to reveal that he still has the medallion in his hand – their love was never in question.

The power of masculine 'femininity' is shown to be the only thing that can survive war and death. Danny's four-leafed clover was found in the belongings of one of the crew who died in the crash we witnessed at the beginning of the film (somebody asks if his things should not be going back to his family rather than being cannibalized by the boys, but it is clear that it is assumed that the boys *are* his next of kin, his nearest and dearest).

And the charms *do* have supernatural powers. By the end of the film we are left in no doubt that the crew of the Memphis Belle have cheated death by virtue of the love for each other that the charms represent.

In the final reel Danny, beau of the Belle, is hit by shrapnel and appears to be dying. The whole crew is instantly more concerned about Danny's fate than their own (they are limping home on a wing and a prayer). Eugene slips the rubber band back over Danny's wrist and as they come into land on one wheel they begin to whistle, 'Oh Danny Boy' (echoing the scene at the dance: but now there is no joshing). Miraculously they manage to lower the other wheel and survive, avoiding the fate of the plane at the film's start.

Danny's survival is especially miraculous. Like Moreland in *Taps* and Chris in *Stand by Me*, we would expect that Danny has to die, to protect the civilian heterosexual world from queer contamination (Jack might be interrupted while banging his wife) *and* to preserve the magic of the queer romance, keeping it within the sepia-tinted photograph album of popular memory marked 'War

Years'. But Danny's life has a cost. The rookie radio operator he showed such tenderness towards, passing on his four-leafed clover, dies in his place. An Me–109 slices the tail off his B–17 and Danny hears the terrified shrieks of the boy spinning to his death on his wireless.

There is another reason for Danny's escape from crucifixion: the makers of the film did not want to trap its 'moral' in the past. The producer, David Putnam, who won an Oscar for his other boys film *Chariots of Fire*, is well known for his support for the Labour Party, having made widely admired Party Political broadcasts for them gratis in British general elections. These were noted for their 'slick' image and appeal to emotions instead of the traditional 'serious' political rhetoric. In the same vein, *Memphis Belle* avoids the usual anti-war stance ('isn't it horrible') and instead offers us unabashed sentimentalism which promotes Putnam's vision of socialism: men working and pulling together in a world based on love of their fellow men. Putnam originally intended to make the film about a British Lancaster bomber crew, but the financial realities that meet all British film-makers soon forced his hand and the film was made with American money and focused, naturally, on American boys. Nevertheless, the film is a nostalgia piece for wartime collectivism that exploits homoeroticism to portray an almost Edward Carpenter image of socialism. It even has a 'lesson' about Thatcherite/Reaganite individualism. The only truly individual member of the crew is the co-pilot Luke, a stocky reddish-blond with a pleasant enough face but an unattractive smile. When the very 1980s Army PR man tells the officers that he is going to make them famous he is the only one to react enthusiastically. His selfishness is shown as 'anti-love' and alienating: it has the effect of isolating Dennis, the captain; Luke should have been his 'special' buddy (the brotherly love community of the bomber is based on couples) but is too wrapped up in himself. But Luke redeems himself at the last moment by managing to hand-crank the second wheel down in the nick of time, saving everyone aboard. Even Thatcherites can find their place in the socialist utopia through 'boyish love', it seems.

In eulogizing man's love for man the film also ends up inadvertently eulogizing war, undermining the political message. Although it endeavours to equate the Army PR with the military/

capitalism and offer this as the 'anti-war' message, (distracting from its own manipulations), the world that is held up for admiration is a world that, on its own terms, is only possible in wartime.

As Danny puts it in the final line of the poem he reads before the last raid to his buddies that he does not want to leave: 'In balance with this life is death.'

The dependency of 'this life' of boyish love on death exemplified in *Memphis Belle* is taken to its (un)natural conclusion in Keith Gordon's *A Midnight Clear* (1992), written by William *Birdy* Wharton, where the juxtaposition of masculine love and sudden death is explicitly turned into a religious sacrament. But this is done with an irony that implies a critique of the mechanism of the traditional buddy war film, as well as war and masculinity itself.

This irony becomes apparent early on in the film in a scene where the men are on leave after basic training before their posting. They elect for one of them to go out and find them a prostitute who will service them all, setting up the typical war film male 'bonding' mediated by a whore; literally men coming together through the act of fucking a 'low' example of 'the feminine'. But instead of this familiar cliché unfolding, the boy brings back not a hooker but a girl who has just heard that her soldier sweetheart has been killed and she is contemplating suicide. Instead of gang-banging her they talk for hours and fall asleep. Just before dawn she comes to each of them individually, bestowing a kind of maternal benediction on them through sex, a benediction which places *them* rather than her in a supplicant, passive position.

In the same way, the boys' experience with the enemy is the reverse of what convention dictates. Their first encounter with them is hearing the words 'Schlaf gut' (sleep well) whispered across the gardens of the chateau; a tender greeting instead of a hail of bullets. Later the Germans pass up another opportunity to shoot the Americans. At first confused by this behaviour, our boys eventually learn that the Germans wish to surrender. When they finally meet, the negotiations are tortuous and tense, and the language barrier and ingrained distrust prove almost insurmountable problems. In effect the film portrays the dilemma faced by men who lower their guard with other men – can they be trusted not to do what they have been trained to do and take a 'pot shot'? It transpires that the Germans wish to protect their families from retribution by staging a mock ambush to make it appear as if they have been taken fighting. In other words, t. ey want to pretend to fight in order to protect their families, thus satirizing the logic of the war film 'dream of war', where boys play war to 'protect their families'.

The surrender ends in disaster – 'Mother', a soldier ignorant of the plan, wanders across the 'ambush' and joins in, turning it into a real firefight in which an American soldier called 'Father' and all the Germans die: one boy's failure to distinguish pretend from real results in a massacre.

Father is the most 'sensitive' member of the platoon and his role directly corresponds to Danny's in *Memphis Belle*. His nickname refers to his training to be a priest before the war: he is very much the 'queerest' and – because this is a buddy war film – the most popular boy. Which is of course why he has to die. But his death immediately takes on the most explicit religious 'redemptive' overtones instead of the usual implicit ones. Father is shot running between the Germans and Americans, begging them to stop firing; his dying breath is used to ask the sergeant of the platoon to protect 'Mother' from the knowledge of his mistake: 'Promise me you won't tell Mother.'

Back at the chateau the boys bathe one by one in a tin bath in front of the fireplace. Then together, in an astonishingly moving scene that takes the homoerotic masochistic 'ecstasy' of war and death to its limit and beyond, they bathe the body of Father, lovingly holding his limp corpse in their hands. As they wash clean the large hole in his back made by the bullet which killed him, their fingers seem to linger caressingly around it, echoing strongly the earlier sex scene with the girl. Father's death has brought the boys together in a physical expression of their love for him and each other. His Christ-like significance takes the ultimately self-conscious form when they tie him to a wooden cross in order to fit him into the jeep when effecting their escape from the advancing Germans. Later he becomes the means by which they save themselves when the jeep runs out of petrol; in a bizarre 'communion' (though perhaps no more bizarre than the real thing) they squeeze congealed blood from his mouth to make red crosses on their white snow camouflage capes, passing themselves off as members of the Red

Cross as they make their way across hostile territory to their lines, carrying his frozen body on their shoulders.

And like Jesus, Father represents the 'feminine' in man: he becomes a 'love token' in the way that lucky charms did for the boys of *Memphis Belle*, symbolizing a masculine femininity that protects them from masculine hostility even from beyond the grave.

The Jesus myth, like the buddy war film, teaches the deadly sublimation of homoeroticism. The figure of Jesus stands outside the Oedipus complex and yet at its heart. He has a 'feminine' attitude towards his Father and is submissive towards Him ('not my will but thine') and accepts his castration; but it is through his death that the Oedipal sublimation of homoerotic love is symbolized: he saves the world and his love lives for ever, symbolized by the 'love token' of the crucifix ('I worship the crucifix because there is a naked man on it'). In 'Mourning and Melancholia' Freud shows how the loss of the deceased loved one is denied through identification with him or her. Later, in *The Ego and the Id*, he describes the process by which this brings about the creation of the super-ego; the boy sacrifices his father as a love-object but consoles himself by setting up his image in his own ego where he can love him for ever. Flesh must be exchanged for spirit, homoerotic object-love for the eternal love of the super-ego (ego narcissism). The Passion is thus the enactment of the sublime agony of the super-ego: 'As a substitute for a longing for the father, ... [the super-ego] contains the germ from which all religions have evolved.'[3]

Buddy war films are gospels of masculine love that is 'betrayed by a kiss'. They are tales set in far-off lands in times past, about a band of boys who leave their families behind and create their own (homosocial) community. They live by love, but one of them, the most 'sensitive' and the 'queerest', must die to save the others and the world from the practice of it, and also to demonstrate the 'proper' way it should be sublimated: 'Greater love hath no man than this, that a man lay down his life for his friends' (John 15: 13). Like Moreland in *Taps* and Chris in *Stand By Me*, 'Father' sacrifices himself trying to save the lives of others, selflessly accepting his castration: 'Promise me you won't tell him'.

Death in these films is a sacrament: it makes love between men eternal by removing it from the male body; by cancelling forever the threat of its consummation it ensures that boyish love is immortal, and that queer love, transformed into a cadaver, is buried on the battlefield:

> They shall grow not old, as we that are left grow old:
> Age shall not weary them, nor the years condemn.
> At the going down of the sun and in the morning
> We will remember them.
> ● Laurence Binyon, Poems for the Fallen

Notes

1. This exposition is contained in Anthony Easthope's *What a Man's Gotta Do* (Winchester, MA: Unwin Hyman, 1990), p. 63.

2. Vito Russo, *The Celluloid Closet* (New York: Harper and Row, 1987).

3. Freud, *The Ego and the Id*, Penguin Freud Library, Vol. 11, p. 376.

Chapter twelve

Top Man
Tom Cruise and the Narcissistic Male Hero

'DO you think your name's gonna be on that plaque by the end of the year?' Viper, the chief instructor at the US Navy's elite fighter school, asks Maverick (Tom Cruise). The plaque on the wall he refers to lists the names of each year's best pilot, or Top Gun, all of whom have the option to come back to the school as an instructor.

'Yes sir!' he pipes up in his spunky way.

'Considering your present company, don't you think that's just a little bit arrogant?'

Maverick looks round the room at the assembled young pilots and grins at the camera sideways on. 'Yes sir!'

'I like that in a pilot,' affirms Viper. *We* like that in Tom Cruise and the 1980s likes that in men.

Top Gun (Tony Scott, 1986) was perhaps *the* 1980s film. Like Reaganism it promoted a new brazen individualism as a return to old fashioned values. Made with massive assistance from the Pentagon and self-consciously retro in its reference points (interiors carefully try to reproduce those of a 1940s fighter pilot film like *The Flying Tigers*[1]), the film appears to endorse the patriotic macho masculinity of the Second World War, a masculinity based on the collectivist notions of teamwork and self-sacrifice. In fact the film is a stage for the realization of male narcissism in which the 'old-fashioned values' are just as much designer accessories as the 1940s flying jackets and sunglasses.

Tom Cruise was the perfect man for the lead role in *Top Gun*. Even his name has a curious symmetry with the title, typographically and connotatively. The most famous and impressive piece of military hardware in the 1980s was the Cruise Missile. These nuclear-tipped phallic hi-tech weapons were designed to fly alone, slyly beneath enemy radar, penetrating their defences.

Like his missile namesake, Tom Cruise in *Top Gun* plays an arrogant pilot called 'Maverick' (a popular tag for cowboy characters in the 1950s and the name given to another 1980s missile), who reasserts individualism and the potency of the American war machine and the American male, linking all these institutions in one self-loving grin.

Tom Cruise was the perfect cinematic embodiment of the new male narcissism that emerged in the mid-1980s. *Top Gun*, the film that introduced him as a star to the cinema-going public, made him just as surely as *Top Gun* was made for him. His all-American brand of boyish *bodily* sexiness, a cinnamon-flavoured studliness – a pure and wholesome indulgence – made him the American Dream dish of the 1980s.

But more than just a pretty face, he was the contradiction of 1980s masculinity made appetizing flesh. Stocky and square-jawed he gives a semblance of no-nonsense masculine virtues, while his round face, baby blue eyes and surprisingly high-pitched voice send out an ambiguous undertow; an undertow that is the real appeal of his screen presence, which makes him both desired and desiring: a Dream Boy that both men and women can entertain in their slumber. It is as if Montgomery Clift or James Dean were playing John Wayne – a very *gay* machismo, contrived and paradoxical; (over)stating one thing and promising another.

That he manifestly takes himself as his own love object merely enhances his appeal. His self-love is taken as evidence of his self-confidence – *the* sexual magnet of the 1980s. His buffed body and the display of it become paradoxically both the proof of his virility – what a *guy*! – *and* the very thing which turns him into a passive thing-to-be-looked-at. More than this, his compelling self-love allows men (and women) in front of the cinema screen to take him as their own idealized reflection and love him/themselves narcissistically.

Of course, Cruise's narcissism, enjoyed by the world in

wide-screen Technicolour, cannot be *too* blatant: the admission of self-consciousness of his self-love in his performance before the camera would threaten his virility. So, the male film star, the ultimate 'poseur', has to affect an unaffectedness in front of the camera. Cruise's happy-go-lucky, boisterous style is vital to the successful acceptance of his narcissism. His famous smile expresses the Hollywood masculine myth in one dazzling grin: easy, spontaneous, irresistibly *natural* – the result of the best dentistry that money can buy and countless hours of face-aching practice in front of the mirror.

The Grinning Machine's appearances in two other military roles, *Born on the Fourth of July* (1990) and *A Few Good Men* (1992) since *Top Gun* has had much to do with the attempt to normalize his evident narcissism and homoerotic appeal. These films have not been classic war films – rather they have been films about the military that self-consciously offer a message about the civilian world in general and masculinity in particular. But the military setting suits Cruise, not just because his all-American-boy looks sit easily with the public perception of the military as the repository of an idealized American masculinity (doesn't he look *dashing* in uniform?), but also because the military setting provides an opportunity to focus on Cruise with a gaze unobstructed by wives or real girlfriends in a way that would be unsettling in civilian life. The military provides both an alibi against charges of narcissism ('active duty') and self-obsession ('serving his country') and a guarantee against anxieties over his ambiguous presence: what could be more *regular* than a military guy?

Cruise's achievement has been to pass off passivity (narcissism) as activity (the military), exemplifying the recent revolution in masculinity at the same time as masking it. Nevertheless his screen personae give us an insight into the changing response to male narcissism of Hollywood and, as we shall see, an idea of just how 'irregular' a regular guy can be.

The best

In *Top Gun* Cruise is placed in the centre of a world which seems to exist only to satisfy his needs: the narcissist is located in a narcissistic universe. Ernest Becker has argued that narcissism is at the root of the human urge to heroism. 'When you combine natural narcissism with the basic need for self-esteem, you create a creature who has to feel himself an object of primary value: first in the universe, representing in himself all of life.'[2] In *Top Gun* the urge for heroism is linked very closely with narcissism and the satisfaction of desire: Maverick repeats again and again, 'I'm used to going out and getting what I want.' The goal of the film is to be 'the best': because only the best can be at the centre of the universe where all his needs will be satisfied.

Competition, the mechanism which decides whose needs are satisfied in a free market economy, who will be 'the best', is itself explicitly sexualized. During practice dogfights Maverick says of other 'enemy' pilots, 'I want him.' The dogfights, the main form of competition (of a Darwinian variety), are presented as highly sexual with fast-cut techniques that won the film an Academy Award nomination for editing, conveying the motion and power of modern jet flight as a white-knuckle and damp-crotch ride. This is war film as pop-promo. We watch enthralled as leather-clad men, eyes obscured by dark visors, throw their state-of-the-art killing machines around the sky. The language, verbal and visual, breathes hotly on our necks: 'thrust', 'G-force', 'blackouts', 'spin', 'dive', 'going ballistic'; the techno-sexy dirty talk works up to a climax in which the men shoot their snow-white missiles across the blue skies in an ecstatic arch, blowing apart their target.

In his *Interpretation of Dreams* Freud suggests that dreams of flying represent a phallic fantasy of power and mastery. *Top Gun*, a film about *air-superiority*, misses no opportunity to exploit this significance, lovingly emphasizing the phallic attributes of the 'things that go' operated by visibly aroused macho men who themselves are phallicized by their flying gear, suits and helmets.

Immediately Maverick's cigar-chewing, coach *manqué* CO (the film is replete with images drawn from the blessed iconography of American sport) tells him he is going to Top Gun, a driving MOR power-rock track used for the flight sequences, 'Playing With the Boys', kicks in. Cut to Maverick astride his top-of-the-range BMW motorbike, clad in his jeans, leather jacket and sunglasses, throttle wide open, powering down a road parallel to the runway where an F–15 is taking off, afterburners afire. The camera frames them together, foregrounding Maverick and his bike, while in the background the huge jet roars up, into the sky. The music crescendos and Maverick whoops and punches the air with his fist. Cut to footage of dogfights in the Korean War: a MiG is being shot down. We are in the lecture theatre at Top Gun. One of the pilots in the audience, blond and hunky, leans over to his companion and whispers in his ear 'It gives me a hard-on.' 'Don't tease me!' his buddy joshes.

In this sequence of shots, lasting less than a minute, the film slickly establishes the erotic aspect of both flying and men's enjoyment of it – even going so far as to hint quite strongly that there might be something really rather queer about it all ('don't tease me!'). This latter idea is played with by Maverick who, sitting in the front row like the keen student he is, keeps looking over his shoulder, apparently cruising the collection of preposterously attractive men assembled in the room.

And who could blame him? The desirability of the men in this film and the sexualized nature of their competition is made palpitatingly explicit. Steamy locker-room scenes offer us the pilots in a state of near-nudity discussing the 'flying' they have just taken part in. In war films of a more innocent age this kind of dialogue would have taken place in the safety of the base bar where manly modesty could keep its shirt on. But in *Top Gun* the shaved, centrefold bodies of America's finest pilots are served up to us in a format that is utterly *indecent* (in one memorable locker-room scene a young man wearing nothing but a towel lies on his back on a bench, waving his legs in the air while the other men stand around him peppering their conversation about the day's action with expletives: 'my dick! my ass!'). In fact the director is so keen to show off his boys' attributes that he seems frustrated by the practical necessity of filming the pilots *clothed* whilst they are 'dogfighting'; he gets around this practical problem by inserting, in addition to the locker-room sequences, a scene where they play volleyball on the beach, stripped to the waist (Levis, natch), wearing their 'shades' (representing the dark visors on their helmets), while 'Playing With the Boys', the dogfight anthem, rages on the sound-track.

Back at the lecture theatre Maverick and a tall blond pilot (who we learn later is called 'Iceman' [Val Kilmer]) with hair so impeccably gelled/moussed that it never loses its shape once during the whole film, exchange long cruisy looks.[3] Goose, Maverick's navigator, is unnerved by/jealous of these queer goings on: 'Maverick, what are you doing?' he asks. 'Just wondering who is the best,' Maverick replies. Masculine competition is presented as erotic, and masculine eroticism as competition (something any *habitué* of a metropolitan gay disco will confirm).[4]

All this 'queer business' points up again the manner in which the film appears to endorse a 'timeless' masculinity but is actually doing something more ambitious. It is not the homoeroticism of *Top Gun* that is at variance with the traditional war film with its buddy-love theme, but its *stridency*. *Top Gun*'s brazenness and the explicit sexual tension between the men that this provokes would be disastrously disruptive of the 'pure' manly love of *esprit de corps* in the traditional war film (see Chapter 11). This departure stems from the individualism and narcissism at the heart of the film which actually encourage desire (especially for the male body) which would be taboo in earlier films. Maverick is allowed a certain polymorphous perversity, to appear to desire everything and everyone, because he is at the autoerotic centre of the universe, 'representing in himself all of life.'

Where *Top Gun* is more traditional in its presentation of war film masculinity is in its attitude towards the feminine: it is something to be conquered. This is dramatized in Maverick's courtship with 'Charlie' (Kelly McGillis) whom he meets in a bar he describes to Goose as a 'target-rich environment'. In a scene that was to loose Karaoke on the world he serenades her along with Goose by 'singing' 'You've lost that loving feeling' (his first meeting with the lead girl takes a narcissistic form, a performance of 'personality'). His ballsy-but-casual pass at Charlie fails, but by allowing her to appear as just some broad that Maverick fancies, the audience is set up for the scene the next day. At a briefing of Top Gun pilots an expert who is 'top in her field' is introduced – it is Charlie. Suddenly our hero is in a submissive position; the girl he chatted up so contemptuously the night before has become his superior (and we suddenly realize that she is an *older woman*).

For a breathless moment it looks as if *Top Gun* is actually going to negotiate the changing role of women, that its nostalgia for a mythical 1940s style male aviator is in danger of being surprisingly modern in its treatment of gender. Fat chance. What develops is a film that merely plays with the semblance of a challenge to phallic male authority (in the same manner as the slightly gender ambiguous name 'Charlie' on a very 'femme' looking woman). Straightaway Charlie's 'authority' is overturned by Maverick who contradicts her civilian/academic statement about the specifications of a MiG with his first-hand experience *in combat* – the man's world. After all, Charlie is only a civilian and the anxiety that women might be invading the masculine world, here represented by the military, is abjured. Despite their numbering tens of thousands by the mid-1980s, there is not one woman in uniform in the whole film. The sky and its thrills remains an unchallenged boys-only world, uncontaminated by women.

The 'conflict' is cranked to an artificial climax in a later scene when Maverick is humiliated by her in front of the other boys in a debriefing session in which she criticizes his 'unorthodox' tactics. He leaves the room in a sulk. But this upset is just to set up some 'drama' to arrange for Charlie's total capitulation in the scene that immediately follows. In a pathetic echo of the dogfights, she chases after him (she in her 1950s Porsche convertible; he on his BMW)[5] and confesses that she could not say what she really felt: 'that your flying shows signs of real genius and I think that I've fallen for you.' The challenge to his power turns directly into a submission to it and he clinches with her. Cut to torrid sex scene. Maverick triumphs, he is literally Top Man, and there is no further 'struggle' for dominance – on the ground.[6]

In the air, the struggle/courtship with the Iceman continues. Significantly, the sex scenes are in fact less 'sexy' than the flight sequences, and the music used for these scenes, 'Take My Breath Away', underlines this irony – it is the *flying* that takes your breath away. Competition, the desire after desire, lust without consummation, is where the excitement is, and the competition in the air is *real*: it is between two men, Iceman and Maverick, both determined to be 'top' – neither wants to take a 'feminine' submissive position (homo-desire is endless and shown to be the eternal basis of the masculine economy).

Of course there is one man who is quite happy to take that position – Goose. As Maverick's devoted navigator who rides behind him, Goose is his 'wife' in the boy's world of air combat. Charlie's arrival makes his role clear and also no longer tenable. At a bar she joins in Maverick and Goose's duet and then leaves with Maverick, riding pillion for the first time on his motorbike – in Goose's position in the F–15. At the end of this sequence she implores him to 'Take me to bed and make love to me, you great big stud.' *Top Gun* is murderously direct in its message about what happens to men who willingly adopt this feminine position: a couple of scenes later Goose is dead, killed in a flying accident. Reminding us of Goose's 'submissiveness', we see his widowed wife tearfully affirm, 'God, he loved flying with you, Maverick!'

But Goose's death serves a larger purpose: to provoke a struggle within Maverick against his own 'feminine' feelings. His attachment to Goose is *itself* suggested as 'feminine' and therefore inappropriate; 'You're the only family I've got,' he says to Goose just before the accident (his mother and father are dead).

Heartbroken, Maverick plans to leave Top Gun and the Navy. Viper, the father figure, tells Maverick that he must 'let go', as he did in Vietnam when his buddies were falling around him – loss is the price that must be paid for male love: the 'feminine' must be overcome. If you refuse to pay that price you forfeit your right to play the game of war/manhood. The castration threat represented by death (of buddies here) has to be disavowed. The 'mother' that has to be separated from (sexually and socially) is the 'family' that Goose represents. Right at the beginning of the film we see a pilot named Cougar lose his nerve in a dog-fight after gazing at a photo of his wife and kids pinned to his instrument panel. His failure and resignation led directly to the *single* Maverick going to Top Gun.

Further enhancing his paternal significance, Viper tells Maverick that he flew with his father, also a Navy pilot, and that he died honourably (there has been a question mark over the circumstances of his death). Thus his father faced down castration anxiety, performed a heroic deed which guaranteed him immortality and so must Maverick. He decides to stay on but loses the 'Top Gun' title to Iceman (Iceman's name will go on the plaque and so he will achieve immortal hero status: fame is the narcissist's victory over death).

In the final reel, Maverick is 'put to the test' during a dog-fight with MiGs over the Indian Ocean. He still has not 'let go', so he initially loses his nerve. But after looking at Goose's dog-tags he is holding in his hand he successfully overcomes his fear of castration/death. Maverick honours the memory of his dead father and partner by attacking the enemy and winning the day, saving Iceman's life. (Later he throws Goose's dog-tags into the sea: he has no use for them any more; he has abandoned the love-objects of Goose and his father, incorporating them into his ego.)[7]

After winning the dogfight Maverick lands back at the carrier and *the* relationship of the movie is consummated before a cheering audience of perfectly coiffed male models posing as pilots (who are supposed to have just taken part in a desperate dogfight). '*You*!' Iceman shouts, pointing at Maverick. 'You are still dangerous!' Breaking into a warm smile and gripping Maverick's shoulder, he announces, 'You can be my wing-man any time!' 'Bullshit!' grins Maverick. 'You can be mine!' They embrace passionately to the jubilation of what seems like the entire (male) crew of the carrier. The new love-affair may be consummated but neither individualist will take a submissive position towards the other (unlike Goose). Despite the blatant homoeroticism of their screen affair the 'feminine' is kept at bay – both men have conquered it and yet have won one another. War/success in *Top Gun* has proved a route by which the oppositions of individualism and teamwork, homoeroticism and manhood can appear to be reconciled: both men can play 'top' and neither has to play 'bottom'.

The narcissistic dream of celebrity is also realized. Maverick's CO tells him that his face is on the cover of every newspaper in the English-speaking world. Summing up the backwards-looking modernization of masculinity that *Top Gun* represents, Maverick has achieved through old-fashioned heroism the status that has come to replace it – fame. As others have observed: 'Today our heroes are no longer warriors, conquerors, or generals ... the criteria for success have been re-defined with the advent of the pervasive influence of the media.'[8]

Maverick, now successful and famous, is able to choose any posting he likes anywhere in the world. He chooses to be an instructor at Top Gun, thus winning the prize that was set up at the beginning of the film: he has achieved the dizziest heights of manhood, the focus of other men's admiring gaze, and is now in a position to instruct others, to take on the paternal role.

Cut to him sitting in a bar (another 1940s retro scene) and the juke box begins to play 'You've Lost that Loving Feeling'. He turns and sees Charlie. Consonant with the traditional war film script he has faced down castration anxiety, passed his test and now he is able to claim his bride: the masculine ego has triumphed. This combines with the modern career/ambition theme of the film: now that he has achieved success he can settle down.

But there is an ambiguity to the dialogue here. Maverick talks about 'crashing and burning' in his first relationship. Is he talking about Goose? Certainly the music reminds us of his duet with Goose as much as it reminds us of his meeting Charlie. And rather than showing Charlie and Maverick embrace, the scene fades out with them standing looking at one another across the room. The credits roll over a shot of two F–15s taking off and rolling together in the air: is it Maverick and Iceman? All we can be sure of in the end is that no one can truly possess Maverick – he remains the narcissistic centre of his own universe and the voyeuristic property of the audience. In the military you need never say to yourself, You've Lost That (self) Loving Feeling.

We dreamed of being men

Born on the Fourth of July (Oliver Stone, 1989), Cruise's first military role after *Top Gun*, gave him his first Academy Award nomination and was just as resolutely anti-war as *Top Gun* was pro. Whereas *Top Gun* said that war and the military were boys' clubs that made boys into potent individualists at the centre of the world's attention, *Born on the Fourth of July* said that war castrated them and left them alone and unloved. Where *Top Gun* emphasized the fantasy and phallic glamour of warfare, *Born on the Fourth of July* emphasized its nightmare and horrific humiliation.

Oliver Stone almost certainly chose Cruise for the part precisely to contradict the message of *Top Gun*; and yet his choice also highlights what the films have in common: both represent Cruise as the all-American boy and in both films the narcissism of the American male/Cruise takes centre stage, crowding out the political message.

More than just another 'anti-war' film, *Fourth of July* gives an account of a crisis of masculinity that began in 1960s America and one man's struggle to adapt to it. The opening sequences masterfully evoke the 1950s America that Kovic grew up in and took his standards of masculinity from.

The film begins with an eight-year-old Ron Kovic playing soldiers with his friends in the forest. Cruise's soft voice-over tells us that he and his friends would 'dream of being men'. We then see young Kovic watching the Fourth of July parade, especially the soldiers and veterans. We see Kovic kissing a girl uninterestedly and then doing press-ups instead. While playing baseball, he sees her holding hands with another boy, but just strikes the ball high into the air while his father whoops for joy. Thus Kovic is shown to be more interested in his dream of being a man than in girls.

We are shown that his dream of manhood is not his own: rather that of his devout Catholic mother. Sitting in front of the television watching Kennedy's inauguration speech – 'Ask not what your country can do for you, but ask what you can do for your country' – she turns to Kovic and says, 'Ronnie, I had a dream last night that you were addressing a big crowd like that and you were saying great things!'

Now we see Kovic as an adolescent (played by Tom Cruise), who is training hard to be a first-class wrestler. His coach is a sadist who calls the boys 'Ladies'. But when the big day comes, Kovic fails and is pinned to the ground by his opponent. His parents, especially his mother, are ashamed, and he is inconsolable (and no one attempts to console him). Men must always be on top. In the next scene we see him at a USMC recruitment meeting where a Marine sergeant (Tom Berenger) tells the assembled boys that the USMC 'Only takes the best.'

In these opening sequences Kovic's decision to join up is portrayed as an inevitable consequence of his upbringing, an upbringing very ordinary for an American boy at that time. He feels that he is doing his duty to defend his country, defeat godless communism and prove the mettle of his manhood.

In Vietnam all his assumptions about manhood and its 'duties' break down. He discovers that there is nothing Christian or manly about the war: his platoon is ordered to open fire on a village full of women and children. In the confusion brought on by this discovery, Kovic shoots dead a rookie private from Georgia. An anguished Kovic tries to turn himself in, but his CO refuses to hear him. Good and bad, them and us, cease to exist. The sniper's bullet that rips through his chest in the next scene, snapping his spine and crippling him, is merely a physical metaphor for the collapse of his 'language' of manhood.

Hospital is total and unrelenting humiliation. It is staffed entirely by underpaid blacks who are unimpressed by the white man's war: 'You can take your Vietnam and shove it up your ass!' Here there is no stage for the triumph of the masculine ego. As a paraplegic, Kovic's impotence, literal and symbolic, is shown in the gruesome morning ritual where the shit is washed out of him by black male nurses. He lies naked on a rack surrounded by other men, all with enema bags piping water into their colons. Kovic complains that he is 'done', but an orderly sadistically reminds him of his total helplessness by making him wait before attending to him. The white Marine war hero, America's finest, the ultimate 'fucker', has to endure the shame of his rectum being at the mercy of a black man who is literally shoving Vietnam up his ass.

On returning home Kovic has an angry confrontation with his brother, who with his long hair and printed shirts looks like a fag – he has embraced the counter-culture. The row is ostensibly about his brother's opposition to the war – 'What, you don't believe in the war!? ... What, you believe in demonstrating and burning the flag!?' – but is really about completely antagonistic credos of masculinity, Kovic representing the old, his brother the new. The word 'believe' is repeated again and again. In the end Kovic's brother shouts 'You believe in war? Look at what the war did for you! I mean *look* at you, man!' Kovic goes berserk. '*What do you mean look at me? Is there something wrong with me? I fought for my country!*'

But Kovic is furious because he realizes that he cannot win. However faggoty and unpatriotic his brother is, he still has his 'biological' manhood, while the war has castrated Kovic. His masculine ethic has cost him the body pictured in a photo in his high school wrestling suit, which he looks at forlornly when he returns from the hospital. The military which was to make him 'the best' has pinned him to the ground far more effectively and humiliatingly than the wrestler in the earlier part of the film. He has lost everything he worked so hard to get and narcissistically desired as a child, when 'we dreamed of being men'.

Eventually Kovic makes a break with the past in a drunken scene with his mother. 'God and country? They don't exist!' he yells at the top of his voice. 'They're bullshit!' It becomes clear that Kovic has finally rejected his mother's view of the world and what a man should be. He accuses her of castrating him: at the climax of the scene he fiddles with his trousers, trying to take something out, shouting to her, 'Here's my penis!' She moans and yells 'Nooo!' as he hauls out his catheter. She shouts, '*I won't have that word in my house!*' He yells so loud that the whole street can hear, '*Penis!* Huge, fucking, erect, goddamn *penis!*'

His father, an inept and shadowy figure, whose weakness is implicitly blamed for Kovic going to war and becoming a cripple, helps Kovic to bed and tells him that it would be better if he left home. 'What do you want from us, Ron?' he asks. 'I want my body back!' he cries. 'Who's gonna love me?' But it is not simply an anxiety that, like his mother, women will no longer desire him: Kovic's underlying fear is that he cannot love himself. The whole credo of masculinity he had been brought up on depended at root on a narcissistic love for one's own 'manhood', a love-affair with the strong, dominating masculine body that he had been taught to desire for himself as a kid. As a cripple he has no body, no phallus, so he can have no self-respect/love.

The narcissism at the root of his masculine sense of self is clear: Kovic has been 'mamma's boy' all along. But as Leslie Fiedler puts it, '*all* American boys belong to Mother.' As little Ronnie Kovic's mother tells him at the beginning of the film, he is 'my own Yankee Doodle Dandy boy', born on the Fourth of July: America is Kovic's mother just as surely as he represents the American boy.

And for the American boy, being 'mamma's boy' does not necessarily mean being soft or sissy – quite the reverse. Kovic's life has been characterized by an evasion of the feminine and a gritty determination to prove his masculinity. He has no girlfriends because he is too busy playing sport, and when it finally seems that he might get involved with a girl he must leave to join the Marine Corps. The dream of manhood set up by his mother keeps him separated from other women, in love with *her* masculine image of *him*self and he remains 'mamma's boy'. Kovic is still wrapped up in a narcissistic dream of manhood that ironically draws him towards childhood and away from the challenge of an autonomous manhood. In the case of Kovic the 'great deed' that post-Freudians such as David D. Gilmore believe the boy must perform to 'break the chain with his mother' is not going to war (the traditional movie dramatization of the Oedipus complex) but fighting *against* the war. By shouting 'Penis! Huge, fucking, erect, goddamn penis!' in front of the mother who searched his room religiously for girly mags, Kovic is asserting his autonomous manhood and ending the narcissistic romance with his mother and America (the 'Motherland').

Determined now to prevent his castration from keeping him from being anything else but 'mamma's boy' for the rest of his life, Kovic travels to Mexico, where the women at least respect his dollars. We see him have sex with a whore whose sensitivity and understanding seems almost to overcome his impotence. In other words, she represents the final break with his mother.

In Mexico Kovic falls in with a group of other disabled vets who are taking advantage of Mexican poverty to inflate the value of their pensions. They cuss and drink like stevedores and brag about using their tongues in place of dicks on the whores. But this hypermasculine bad-boy performance is just a charade, Kovic soon realizes. He gets into a fight with another paraplegic vet over a false bragging match about who 'killed the most babies' in Vietnam. They fall out of their chairs onto the ground and struggle for a while in a pathetic echo of Kovic's wrestling days before the absurdity of the situation dawns on them both. Kovic returns to the United States and visits the family of the Georgian private he shot in Vietnam and confesses his crime. This is a symbolic recantation of his Mexican fantasy – the last gasp of his outmoded masculinity.

But it is also the beginning of his 'new' masculinity. It is equivalent to Maverick's action in the final dogfight: Kovic 'lets go' of the private (in a sense, *becoming* him) and faces up to his own castration anxiety. And as for Maverick, this moment allows Kovic to take up the fight with renewed zeal: with a difference. Now he is fighting the war/the mother that crippled him (and killed the private).

He becomes involved in anti-war protests. We see him at the 1970 Republican Convention in Miami trying to interrupt Richard Nixon's acceptance speech. He is thrown out by Secret Service men, one of whom is played by Tom Berenger who also played the recruiting sergeant who persuaded Kovic to enlist, underlining that Kovic is now taking on the conventional masculine order that mangled him. Outside, the police charge the demonstrators but Kovic leads, military-style, a counter-charge of disabled vets and draft-resistors in army surplus camies. The image is rich in irony: the 1960s counter-culture, those who say 'no' to America's martial manhood, an army of cripples and 'degenerates', takes on the baton-wielding uniforms of Miami's finest.

The final scene shows him about to address the 1976 Democratic Party Convention. A black woman reporter asks him how it feels to be about to speak to the nation. 'It feels like I've finally come home,' he says. As he approaches the platform we see his mother in flashback telling 'little Ronnie' about her dream. We are left in no doubt that 'little Ronnie' has now become a man by separating himself from his mother, making his own 'dream of manhood' and performing his own great deeds: learning a new way to love himself. But the *assumptions* on which this 'new' dream of manhood is based are the same: manhood can come only through struggle.

Nevertheless Kovic's dream of manhood and America is still not entirely his own: it is implicitly one belonging to black men. Although there are no central black characters in *Born on the Fourth of July*, black men are faceless angels who make regular appearances to help our hero on his journey to manhood. It is a black soldier who carries Kovic's wounded body out of the firing line at great risk to himself. It is a black nurse who is the first to tell him the truth about Vietnam. It is a black protester who carries him to safety when he falls from his wheelchair outside the Republican Convention. Black men offer the alternative masculine paradigm for Kovic. Black men's bravery in the face of racism and oppression is more manly than white men's soldiering; they present Kovic with another America to love and fight for. In fact the only romantic continuity in the film is Kovic's love-affair with black men, a love-affair that has to remain in the background and unconsummated (except for the enema scene in the vets' hospital). He is Huck Finn, saved by his devoted Jim. And like Jim, the black man in this film is, as Leslie Fiedler puts it, 'sometimes more servant than father, sometimes more lover than servant, sometimes more mother than either!'[9] Kovic looks to black men for not just another masculine paradigm but another America-as-mother. It is 'the American dream of guilt remitted by the negro' again.[10] Thus before Kovic speaks at the Convention we see a black politician giving a speech about fighting for an 'America' that embraces *all* its people: blacks, whites, women, disabled.

Born on the Fourth of July, for all its radical aspirations, is an anti-war film that employs *conventional* war film mythology to bring about a successful transition from boyhood to manhood: 'War' loses but masculinity is victorious. This continuity is shown in the opening and closing images of the film, which begins with Kovic playing at being a man, a little boy playing at being a great soldier, and ends with him as a war protester approaching a stage from which he will deliver the performance of his life. And as in *Top Gun*, hero status has been replaced by celebrity status as the ultimate narcissistic goal. The masculine ego triumphs again – this time in a wheelchair instead of an F–15.

'You fucked with a Royal Marine!'

A Few Good Men (1992), directed by Rob Reiner (see also *Stand by Me*), is the second film featuring the USMC in which Tom Cruise stars and this is worthy of some comment. The USMC has a special status in the United States as not only the élite regular outfit of the armed forces, but also as the keeper of the flame of America itself; they are the front-line troops upon which the American Way of Life depends. They are the modern equivalent of the US Cavalry; prairies were replaced by oceans as America's frontier closed and its overseas empire opened up. And like those boys in blue on horseback the USMC symbolize in Hollywood a 'timeless' type of masculinity, one that remains unchanged and unimpeached through the ages, one that represents the most acceptable homosociality: an escape from 'civilization' and 'the feminine' in order to protect it. 'The Marines are looking for a few good men' runs the famous recruiting slogan; the Marines only take 'the best', as the recruiting sergeant in *Born on the Fourth of July* tells Kovic.

The pro-war film *Top Gun* took the idea of 'the best' and turned it into narcissistic individualism, while trying to preserve its 'timelessness'. The anti-war film *Born on the Fourth of July* employed the same strategy, merely reversing the official politics. *A Few Good Men*, a pro-military film which goes out of its way to emphasize its respect for the USMC,[11] the men who 'stand on the walls', ends up *reconstructing* masculinity in a way that is more radical than either of the other two films.

The film begins at Windwood USMC barracks, Guantanamo Bay, Cuba (the 'front line/frontier'), with the victim of a 'Code Red' (an unsanctioned disciplinary action) being bound, gagged and beaten. During the course of this 'training' the 'trainee' inadvertently dies. We learn later that the base commander, Colonel Jessep (Jack Nicholson), ordered this attack on the young marine as a punishment for breaking the chain of command and for consistently failing in his performance. The boy showed weakness and disloyalty to his masculine world and must be punished by traditional masculine justice – a summary beating by his peers. The defence of the two marines who administered the beating depends upon the officially non-existent 'Code Red' being exposed. But what is on trial in this film is not just the brutal tradition of unofficial disciplinary action, but the kind of brutal traditional 'frontier' military man exemplified by Colonel Jessep. The man who puts him in the dock, Lieutenant Kaffee (Tom Cruise), is not merely his prosecutor but an alternative paradigm. *A Few Good Men* is not so much a military courtroom drama as a battle between two men and their conflicting beliefs of just what makes a Good Man.

The publicity for the film includes a close-up of Lieutenant Kaffee and Colonel Jessep, both in full dress uniform (worn for 'public' occasions), Jessep in his Marine Corps black/dark blue and Kaffee in his Navy Whites. Their heads are framed side by side, facing forwards as if at attention, faces half-lit on opposite sides, suggesting that they are two halves of one man: dark and light, old and young – yin and yang, masculine and feminine. Kaffee's face is inviting where Jessep's is forbidding, soft where Jessep's is lined; his lips are full and sensuous where Jessep's are thin and cracked; his eyes warm and liquid where Jessep's are fish-cold. Jessep is a man; Kaffee is a boy. Jessep is a Marine Colonel, with all the masculine tradition of the Marine Corps behind him; Kaffee is a Navy pen-pusher just out of law school. In Marine Corps folklore Marines are 'hard-case jarheads'; Navy boys are 'pussy squids'.

These opposites which place Kaffee in a traditionally 'feminine' position are summed up by Jessep the first time Kaffee tries to assert himself by requesting to see a key document. 'You stand there in your faggoty white uniform and with your Harvard mouth telling me what to do!' spits Jessep, demanding *respect*. The syntax of patriarchy has been elided.

The courtroom confrontation in the final reel is not simply Kaffee's opportunity to face down the castration threat (although interestingly in this military film it is his career rather than his life which is on the line) and gain manhood – i.e. take up his position in patriarchy – but also an opportunity to reform it; literally to introduce justice into a system (military masculinity) that operates on 'codes' of rank and 'respect'. Goading Jessep into a trap, Kaffee manages to elicit an admission – a *brag* – that he gave the order for the Code Red. Contrary to Jessep's expectations the court does not 'respect' his reasoning. Sensing this Jessep announces he is going back to his base but the judge orders him restrained. Purple-faced, grappling with two MPs, Jessep calls on his masculine tradition, yelling at Kaffee, '*You fucked with a* Royal Marine*!*',[12] adding, 'Son, *I oughtta tear your goddamn eyes out!*' Kaffee angrily rebuffs this 'castrating' attempt to put him in his place and asserts his new-found status and self-respect. 'Don't call me son. I'm an officer and a lawyer and you're under arrest – you sonofabitch!'

Jessep's use of 'son' has another resonance. In taking on Jessep, Kaffee was also taking on the memory of his father, the great Navy lawyer whose shadow he has been living in, 'keeping him emotionally distant and devoid of purpose' (production notes): Jessep represents 'the fathers'. In *A Few Good Men*, unlike the traditional war/military film, the boy wanting to become a man needs to be separated not from the mother but from the father. In *Top Gun* the motherless Maverick overcomes castration anxiety by overcoming/introjecting his 'feminine' attachment to his dead father and navigator. In *Born on the Fourth of July actual* castration is overcome *symbolically* by separating from the mother. In *A Few Good Men* Kaffee faces down castration anxiety not by bravery in the face of the enemy or by 'letting his comrades go', but by confronting and vanquishing the DI/Dad who is the author of it.

Jessep as played by Jack Nicholson is all the DI's and all the fathers rolled into one terrifying Colonel with a castrating gaze. (Kaffee's narrative is that of the Ethical Oedipus – the same as that told by Democratic Candidate Bill Clinton on the nation's TV screens in his bid for the White House: how he stood up to his brutal step-dad who beat his mother.[13])

This new ethic is learnt by the two marines who administered the 'Code Red'/paternal law. The jury acquits them of murder but finds them guilty of conduct 'unbecoming a Marine'. They are desolate – the Marine Corps is their entire world. One turns to his buddy and asks 'What did we do wrong? We just did our duty!' 'No,' replies his comrade. 'We failed. We failed to protect those weaker than ourselves.'

The film closes with a classic courtroom drama shot of Kaffee, the victorious crusader for justice alone in the courtroom, camera pulling away and above: one man *can* make a difference in a democracy, the same celebrity/narcissistic resolution of *Top Gun* and *Born on the Fourth of July*. All that is missing from this rousing scene is a final close-up of the Stars and Stripes fluttering proudly in the wind. The Established Order of the military and masculinity has been subjected to ruthless criticism but it has been restored in the end. This is Barthes' 'Operation Margarine' resolution, described in *Mythologies*:

> Take the Army again: lay down as a basic principle the scientific fanaticism of its engineers, and their blindness; show all that is destroyed by such a pitiless rigour: human beings, couples. And then bring out the flag, save the army in the name of progress, hitch the greatness of the former to the triumph of the latter ...[14]

The Established Order of the military/masculinity may have been restored but *at a cost*. *Top Gun* conquered the feminine, *Born on the Fourth of July* evaded it, but *A Few Good Men* incorporates it. The triumph of 'progress' in this case is the triumph of 'the feminine' *within* 'the masculine'. The 'greatness' of masculinity has been hitched to the triumph of 'the feminine' – dramatized here in the masculine body of the military and Lieutenant Kaffee. For all the flag-fluttering finale, this is no simple classical triumph of the masculine ego: 'the feminine' has been admitted into the citadel.

Nor is the presence of 'the feminine' in the military disso-ciated from 'woman'. Unlike in *Top Gun*, women are actually to be seen in uniform: Joanne Galloway (Demi Moore) is a military woman who, as a Lieutenant Commander, occupies a superior rank to our boyish hero. Here we find no *Top Gun faux* struggle for dominance which proves to be nothing more than elaborate fore-play, the cinematic equivalent of a husband asking his wife to wear leather boots and use a riding crop. In *A Few Good Men* Galloway *is* his superior. And most remarkable of all, Hollywood resisted its compulsion to bring such women low and kept Demi Moore both vertical and fully clothed. Thus, sexually speaking, Cruise does not get to be Top Man in this picture. Further, Galloway is not just his superior in terms of rank – she is *morally* superior to Kaffee: it is her courage and professional commitment that finally persuades Kaffee to fight the case instead of resorting to his customary sleazy plea-bargaining.

The audience's expectation of a *Top Gun* type romance developing between Kaffee and Galloway is flung in their faces. This is achieved by putting the assumption that Galloway is just another 'love interest' into the mouth of the most reprehensible character. On meeting Galloway and Kaffee for the first time, Jes-sep ignores Galloway and directs his remarks to Kaffee. Suddenly he realizes with offensive amusement that Galloway is Kaffee's superior. 'I envy you,' he leers to Kaffee. 'You just haven't lived until you've received a blow-job from a superior officer.' This cal-culated insult to Galloway predicated on the knowing assumption that 'we're all boys together' ironically shoots the legacy of *Top Gun* out of the air: Maverick 'crashes and burns'.

Rather than represent the Other to be negotiated, Galloway seems to represent an aspect of Kaffee himself, an aspect that once energized enables him to defeat 'the fathers'. This can be read in the uncanny similarity between their faces on-screen. Both wearing naval officer uniforms and both with short dark hair, their soft skin, round faces and wide cheek-bones seem to blur together. (This is most apparent in another publicity shot in which the heads of Jessep, Kaffee and Galloway are placed in line, with Jessep's leathery features separating Kaffee and Galloway.)

So indeterminate is the gender relationship between Kaffee and Galloway that they might easily be queer. Not only do they not fuck, but, more strikingly still for Hollywood, no serious attempt is made to establish them as having a heterosexual preference despite the absence of a triumphal bed scene. The only 'date' scenario turns into a friendship tryst. Even Kaffee's love of baseball, demonstrated by his incessant playing and watching of it, is not all that it should be. On the one hand it might help to characterize him as a healthy American male, warding off any queer suspicions, but on the other it seems suspect *itself* – a refusal to put away 'childish' things.[15] At home he is never seen without his bat clutched in his hand, even during meetings with Galloway to discuss the case. 'It helps me think,' he explains. On one occasion we see him without his phallic pacifier because Galloway has put it away in a closet. 'Don't *ever* do that again!' he tells her, gripping it firmly in both hands.

In *A Few Good Men* the boyish narcissism of Tom Cruise and the audience's relationship to it finally come out of the closet. In *Top Gun* he *appeared* to be romantically involved with all his co-stars: Charlie, Goose and Iceman. But despite a sex scene with McGillis and erotic flying sequences with Goose and Iceman he never quite gives himself to any of them: *he* remains the real object of his affections, leaving him to the rapacious gaze of the audience. In *Born on the Fourth of July* he is kept from romantic involvement before his wounding by his narcissistic devotion to playing sport and war; and after by his impotence (even his love affair with black men is kept off screen). But in *A Few Good Men* the 'beards' of *Top Gun* and the devices of *Born on the Fourth of July* are abandoned: he, his autoeroticism, his cheeky grin, and his baseball bat are openly and exclusively available for the consumption of the audience, from whichever subject position they prefer.

His narcissism, now that it can be open, seems less paranoid than in the earlier versions. The 'feminine' is no longer Other so much as an aspect of himself that he (and we) can love: this is the meaning of the date scene where, instead of putting out, Galloway expresses her enormous admiration for Kaffee; in *Top Gun* this was a cue for Maverick's phallic victory, here it seems a signal for Kaffee – the boy who lacks confidence because of his father's shadow – to love himself and his 'feminine' side.

It is to be hoped that *A Few Good Men* represents an evol-

ution of male narcissism in Tom Cruise that is very contemporary
in its gender and sexual indeterminacy, a narcissism that supports a
masculinity that is no longer destructive (*Top Gun*) or misogynistic
(*Born on the Fourth of July*) but instead one that turns boys into
ethical Oedipuses, facing up to patriarchy.

While undoubtedly all three types of narcissistic masculinity
displayed in Cruise's film career will coexist for some time to come,
perhaps *A Few Good Men* will turn out to be *the* 1990s film in the
way that *Top Gun* was *the* 1980s film. In the early 1990s a real-life
'Maverick' became famous, a *Top Gun* F–15 pilot whose face
appeared in 'all the papers'. But this pilot with the same call-sign as
Cruise's *Top Gun* character was *female* – the first woman to be
given a combat post with the US Air Force.[16] In the 1990s Charlie
no longer rides pillion.

Postscript

Charlie may now be allowed in the pilot's seat and Hollywood
might be moving towards an accommodation with sexual indeterminacy but, as events were to demonstrate graphically, the Pentagon and Colonel Jessep are still fighting a bloody rearguard action
which is costing thousands their careers and some their lives.

Released as it was in the run-up to the 1992 presidential
election in which the Pentagon's gay ban came under attack by the
Democratic Candidate Bill Clinton, *A Few Good Men* could be
read as a perhaps unwitting allegory for lesbians and gays in the
military. The issues of the film, maintenance of good discipline and
morale and the relation of these to difference and rights, are precisely the issues cited by the Pentagon in its defence of the ban:
lesbians and gays are 'detrimental to good order and discipline and
the performance of the military mission'. Military life, they maintain, is different from civilian life; in an environment in which large
numbers of lives are at stake, military personnel cannot be afforded
rights in the sense in which civilians understand them. This is the
line that Jessep presents in support of his brutal regime and 'Code
Red'. 'There are ten thousand Cubans on the other side of that
fence trained to kill me,' we are reminded.

And like the issue of gays in the military, the case of the
marine who died while being 'disciplined' had the effect of making

the private rules of the military public and bringing its practices into the court room. Both 'Code Red' and military homophobia depend for their continued existence upon remaining private military affairs, like wife beating; hidden mechanisms that manifest themselves only to their victims (this is the character of masculinity itself – it must remain unexamined if it is to keep its power). In *A Few Good Men* this silence is broken by the Marine 'breaking the chain of command' and writing letters complaining about his ill-treatment.

The fictional experiences of this marine were to be eerily echoed in the short real life of a US sailor whose treatment at the hands of his comrades was also to become a media event a matter of months after the film's release. On 27 October 1992 the badly beaten corpse of 22-year-old Seaman Alan Schindler was found in a park toilet near the US Naval base at Sasebo in southern Japan. Unlike the fictional marine at Guantanamo Bay, this real boy's death was very much intentional: his body had been so methodically and violently worked over that his mother could recognize him only by his tattoos. Letters Schindler had written before the incident revealed that he had been subjected to terrible harassment for his homosexuality; complaints to his superiors, including his chaplain, had no effect. While there is no evidence that his superior officers were implicated in his killing, their apparent indifference to the attacks on him taken with the Pentagon's codified homophobia gave a signal to Schindler's killers just as clear and just as irresistible – and in this case even more violent – than the 'Code Red' ordered by Jessep in *A Few Good Men*.

Notes

1. *Flying Tigers*, United States, 1942 (Edmund Granger).

2. Ernest Becker, *The Denial of Death* (New York: Free Press, 1973), quoted in *Psychiatry and the Cinema* by Krin Gabbard and Glen O. Gabbard (University of Chicago Press, 1987), p. 205.

3. This scene and the theme of male narcissism is commented on by Judith Williamson in *Deadline at Dawn* (London: Marion Boyars, 1992), pp. 29 and 37.

4. In fact immediately after the lecture theatre scene the boys go to a bar in which Maverick 'picks up' Iceman: Goose points him out to Maverick as 'the best' and introduces them. Out of all the impressive young men in the lecture theatre only

Iceman is 'good enough' for Maverick. Thus the narrative of 'the best' becomes the narrative of their being *destined for one another*.

5. These designer consumer durables are undoubtedly part of the glossy consumerism of the film, but perhaps they also offer, in retrospect, a message about the real state of the American economy and the Reagan military purchase-led boom.

6. So anxious were the film-makers to allay any real threat to Maverick's dominance that Kelly McGillis later complained of a bad back brought on by all the crouching she had to do to hide the fact that she was a good few inches taller than 'Top Man' Cruise.

7. See 'Don't Die on Me, Buddy', p. 227.

8. *Psychiatry in the Cinema*, Gabbard and Gabbard, p. 205.

9. Leslie Fiedler, *Love and Death in the American Novel* (New York: Stein and Day, 1975), p. 353.

10. *Ibid.*

11. In the production notes the director Rob Reiner is attributed with describing *A Few Good Men* as 'a plaudit for the military justice system because it shows that the system works and is capable of policing and administering justice on its own.'

12. In using the adjective 'Royal', Jessep is here invoking a military tradition so old that it stretches back to pre-Revolutionary times.

13. See Naomi Wolf, 'Battle on the home front', *New Statesman and Society*, 6 November 1992.

14. Roland Barthes, *Mythologies* (London: Paladin, 1973), p. 45.

15. 'Although Kaffee is possessed of a brilliant legal mind he prefers softball to the hardball game of law' (production notes).

16. 'High-flying women set to take off', *Guardian*, 1 May 1993.

Chapter thirteen

Iron Clint
Queer Weddings in Robert Bly's Iron John and Clint Eastwood's Unforgiven

*In the seventies I began to see all over the country a
phenomenon that we might call the 'soft male'. Sometimes
even today when I look out at an audience, perhaps half
the young males are what I'd call soft. They're lovely,
valuable people – I like them – they're not interested in
harming the earth or starting wars. ... But many of these
men are not happy. You quickly notice the lack of energy
in them. They are life-preserving but not exactly life-giving.
Ironically you often see them with strong women who
positively radiate energy.*

● *US men's movement guru Robert Bly*[1]

*Listening and talking little was the one non-convict in the
group, Harris Breiman, a specialist in the men's movement
who made contact with the prison through the movement
council he runs in Woodstock ...*

*'It's the warrior notion of the youngsters,' said Mr Velez,
37. 'So much focus on being a warrior. When I was first on
Rikers Island [the prison], you had to have the right walk,
the right display of aggression'.*

*As the group focused on prison swagger, Mr Harris
cautioned that 'the warrior can have a positive direction,
too. The warrior in and of itself is part of what we are. If
you give away the warrior energy you're going to be a
passive victim.'*

● *New York Times (23 February 1993)*

IN his book *Iron John* (1990), a Jungian mythopoeic allegory-with-commentary extravaganza based on the Brothers Grimm fairytale 'Iron Hans', the poet and self-styled spiritual leader of the US men's movement Robert Bly has argued that the problem facing men today is that they have become too soft, too concerned about their 'feminine' side. They are, he says, too eager to please women, with the result that they are out of touch with the 'deep masculine', the 'warrior' who is an essential part of their psyche, making them miserable, passive and unsure of their identity. The story of Iron John is interpreted by Bly as an instruction on how to reclaim that 'deep masculine' and the male energy that is said to go with it.

The story tells of a wild man covered from head to foot in hair (whose rusty iron colour gives him the name 'Iron John') who is kept in a cage in the courtyard of a castle. The key to the cage is kept by the Queen under her pillow. The young prince, playing in the courtyard, loses his prized 'golden ball' through the bars of the cage. Iron John persuades the boy to steal the key and release him in exchange for the return of his ball. But once Iron John is released, the boy is frightened of being punished by his parents and runs off to live in the forest with Iron John. Their partnership does not last, however, and the boy returns to civilization (in fact a kingdom adjacent to his parents') disguised as a peasant. Nevertheless he is able to call on Iron John's assistance from the edge of the forest whenever he needs it, and in this way wins great battles and eventually the hand of the princess.

Bly stresses the timeless, pre-Christian origins of the story and offers it as an antidote to what he sees as the present-day dearth of images of 'real men' in popular culture and the prevalence of 'stereotypical sissies like Woody Allen – a negative John Wayne'.[2] It becomes apparent that Bly's obsession with ancient narratives of manhood is a liking for a kind of heritage masculinity, an Olde Worlde natural virility with added bran: 'One of the things we do is to go back to the very old stories five thousand years ago when the view of a man, what a man is, is far more healthy.'[3]

In effect Bly is telling us that the 'unhealthy' soft men, constipated on their modern diet of processed, domesticated manliness are in *sore* need of a change in their intake of role models; what is needed is the raw *fibrous* manhood of Iron John (Ⓣ Robert Bly Bakeries Inc.) to restore their 'authentic' regular maleness and relieve them of their haemorrhoidal 'feminine' condition.

To restore his strength, Bly suggests, the soft man must stop taking his cue from 'mother', ignore the negative John Waynes and 'descend down into the male psyche and accept what's dark down there':[3] get in touch with the 'wild man', the 'hairy man': release Iron John from his cage.

Bly's ideas, which may appear bizarre and even comical to an English readership, have gained a remarkable popularity in the United States. Since the mid-1980s tens of thousands of American males have attended weekends in the forest based around his Wild Man masculinity and the 'need' to counteract the 'feminization' of modern men. As *Iron John* became a best-seller, the American men's movement went mainstream and gained respectability, its representatives often consulted on the burning men's issues of the day and even involved in prisoner rehabilitation schemes (Bly's ideas are shamelessly employed to explain the opposite phenomenon of 'soft men': the violently non-feminine behaviour of maladjusted males, suggesting that they are overcompensating).

American popular culture too began to show evidence of being influenced by these ideas, most notably Clint Eastwood's *Unforgiven* (1992), which is analysed below and compared with the Bly philosophy as told in *Iron John*. The two texts are examined alongside one another not simply to demonstrate the permeation of Bly's ideas in American popular culture but also to illustrate their remarkable *symmetry* with the work of Eastwood (a masculinity 'guru' from an age before the men's movement) as well as the secret of their appeal and the reason why they will probably not export well: their intimate connection, not to 'ancient' conceptions of manhood, but to the New World and the American Western tradition.

Unforgiven features Clint Eastwood as William Munny, a widowed Kansas pig farmer struggling in the 1880s to raise his two children single-handedly and live by the values which his dead wife, a strong Christian, instilled in him – putting his murderous past as the 'meanest sonofabitch in the West' behind him. We see him trying unsuccessfully to separate his pigs which are dying of fever. Into this scene of uneasy domesticity rides an impetuous young man by the name of The Schofield Kid (Jaimz Woolvett). In awe of Munny's reputation as a gun-slinger he tries to persuade him ιο be his partner for a contract killing in Big Whiskey, Wyoming, a revenge killing of two cowboys for 'raping and killing a prostitute' (in fact her face was slashed). Munny refuses. 'My wife,' he says, covered in pig shit, looking tired, old, and defeated, 'cured me of my sinful ways.'

Munny has become a sad, soft man, trying to please his dead wife. The boy rides off disgusted: 'You're not William Munny!' he shouts, rejecting this 'negative John Wayne'.

Munny looks at his dying pigs (are they dying of shame?), his hungry children and his filth-covered clothes and realizes his failure as a 'soft man'. Finally the need to feed his children sends him out after the Schofield Kid and his disowned past. But he still has not 'accepted what is dark down there', he is still in thrall to his dead wife: he is still without masculine energy. So we see him fail to hit a single bottle when practising with his revolver and his horse shies away from him when he tries to mount it, causing him to fall flat on his back (the horses, like the pigs, instinctively *know* when their master is a weak, soft male). His young son looks on ashamed.

Mounted at last – but looking very *queasy* in the saddle – Munny looks up Ned Logan (Morgan Freeman), his black partner from the bad old days and persuades him to join him while Ned's Indian wife looks after Munny's children; the pair of them catch up with the Kid and ride on to Big Whiskey.

In Big Whiskey the fragile Munny has caught a chill as a result of the heavy rain during the ride (and quite possibly his Christian refusal to partake in the cockle-warming liquor the other men drink to keep the rain out). True to the memory of his wife he remains downstairs in the saloon while the other two visit the whores upstairs. In swaggers Sheriff Little Bill Daggett (Gene Hackman) with his deputies. He has heard about the bounty and is determined to keep hired guns out of 'his' town. Daggett demands and gets Munny's weapon and then proceeds to kick seven shades of shit out of him. Munny does not resist Daggett's boot as it drives into his chest and stomach. Later he is found by his partners and carried away to a barn where the whores nurse him. 'I can't believe he didn't do anything,' exclaims the Schofield Kid.

Munny still has no energy, he is still passive, he is without his 'golden ball', because he has yet to steal the key from under his wife's pillow, escape her power and set his wild man free. In Bly's words:

> We see more and more passivity in men. .... If his wife or girlfriend, furious, shouts that he is a 'chauvinist', a 'sexist', a 'man', he doesn't fight back, but just takes it. ... If he were a bullfighter he would remain where he was when the bull charges, would not even wave his shirt or turn his body, and the horn would go directly in. After each fight friends have to carry him on their shoulders to the hospital.[4]

In 'hospital' Munny develops a terrible fever and nearly dies. But when the fever breaks and he recovers, it transpires his skills and self-assurance are returning; he has begun to accept his 'true' nature; and with that acceptance comes his *virility*. With The Schofield Kid and Logan he corners the partner of the cowboy who mutilated the whore. Munny asks Ned to do the shooting because, as we know, he is now such a poor shot. Ned only manages to wound the boy and, hearing his moans and pleas, cannot bring himself to finish him off. Taking Ned's rifle Munny kills the boy – with one shot. He has become a killer again and a *man*. But his restoration is still not complete: he shows far too much compassion for the boy, allowing his friends to bring him water before murdering him. It takes another 'fever', another 'kicking', to send him into the very darkest depths of his psyche.

That 'kicking' comes in the form of Ned's death. Distressed by the killing of the cowboy and his loss of nerve, Ned tries to return home to his wife. He pays dearly for his attempt to renounce his past and his 'warrior' inside. On the way he is captured by a posse and handed over to Daggett who tortures and then kills him.[5]

When Munny hears this he is grief-stricken but instead of showing it he finally takes the elevator ride to the basement of his psyche and embraces whole-heartedly its darkness. He rides into town, single-handedly killing Daggett and most of his deputies, ordering the quaking survivors to bury Ned's body which has been propped up in an open coffin outside the saloon with the sign 'This is what we do to assassins' around his neck. They obey him, now recognizing him at last as William Munny, *'the meanest sonofa-bitch in the West'*.

In terms of the film's development he is finally restored as 'William Munny', having decided to embrace his dark destiny; in terms of the audience's relationship to the film he is Clint Eastwood again, a reassuring Good Bad Guy, replacing the tormented, inef-fectual, *embarrassing* Good Good Guy; and for Bly he is a soft man made hard, a Woody Allen self-doubting figure transformed into John Wayne, no longer life-preserving but life-taking and thus life-giving (it is the destroyer, the warrior who has the power to grant life just as surely as to take it). He is imperfect, certainly; pained, definitely, but he is an authentic man, no longer trying to please women, true to *him*self. As Eastwood himself has said, 'Munny gave her his word that he wouldn't pick up the guns, but it's what he knows; it's the accident of who he is.'[6]

In his preface to *Iron John* Bly goes out of his way to reassure that his masculinism does not present a threat to women.

> I want to make it clear that this book does not seek to turn
> men against women, nor to return men to the domineering
> mode that has led to repression of women and their values
> for centuries. The thought in this book does not constitute
> a challenge to the women's movement. The two movements
> are related to each other, but each moves on a separate
> timetable.[7]

Unfortunately the 'separate timetables' are very much in conflict: there is only room for one train on Mr Bly's railroad, something that he is not afraid to admit out of print. At a two-day lecture at the Jung Centre in San Francisco he harangued a mixed audience shouting, 'There's too much passivity and naivete in American men today. There's a disease going around, and women have been spreading it. Starting in the sixties, the women have really invaded men's areas and treated them like boys.'[8]

Women *are* the problem. It is women's influence and power

that must be destroyed in order to free Iron John and save the 'soft' men. Bly's 'ancient', 'healthy', 'warrior' masculinity is one that women will recognize as not so very ancient or healthy at all; just the social imperative for male dominance/domination at any cost ('If you give away your warrior energy you're going to be a passive victim' – i.e. a 'pussy') that they only very recently began to roll back. Bly's prescription of how men should escape the 'power of mother's bed' is also familiar: employ the threat of violence. In his book he advises men to show women 'the sword', being careful to add, 'But showing a sword does not necessarily mean fighting. It can also suggest a joyful decisiveness' – the joy of a bully, in other words.

The bully's power, as any woman or man who has suffered under one will tell, does not rest upon his *use* of his fists, so much as the threat of them. This seems to be what Bly is encouraging men to do. But of course the threat of violence eventually has to be backed up by something more substantial than 'mythopoetics'. According to Susan Faludi, at a 1987 seminar Bly revealed just what 'showing the sword' meant. A man in the audience complained, 'When we tell women our desires they tell us we're wrong.' 'So, then bust them in the mouth,' Bly instructed. After someone pointed out that this promoted violence against women Bly modified his statement, 'Yes. I meant, hit those women verbally!'[10]

Bly's *Iron John*, for all its careful prevarication and prefaces, its airy-fairy 'mythopoetics' and its earnest scholarliness, is really a paean to male violence: 'show the sword', 'get in touch with the wild man', 'accept what's dark down there', 'bust them in the mouth!'

Unforgiven, made by a director/actor famous for his use of violence to achieve his ends, is a better story than Bly's *Iron John* and better told. Somehow a lesson in violence comes across better as a taciturn visual tutorial from The Man With No Name than the wordy, flighty 260-page volume written by a soft-bodied, white-haired, cravat-wearing poet trying on Whitman's clothes and playing with Hemingway's hunting rifle.

What is interesting about Eastwood in *Unforgiven* is the way in which, like Bly, he seems anxious to present violence no longer as a Spaghetti Western hedonistic experience, but rather as something fated: in place of the Spaghetti Western we now have the Gothic Western. 'Violence always hurts,' he told the *Guardian*. 'The new thing about *Unforgiven* is the way it hurts the per-petrators too.' Violence is no longer celebrated for its fun but for its 'nobility', its 'human tragedy'.

And like Bly's book, *Unforgiven* has a preface that appears to pre-empt any reading of the film as misogyny. At the beginning of the film a young prostitute has her face slashed for laughing at a cowboy's penis. The sheriff initially wants to horsewhip him but the brothel-owner demands compensation instead: 'After all, it's my property that has been damaged.' Daggett orders the cowboy to hand over his horses to the man. But the prostitutes refuse to accept this male 'justice' and decide to pool their savings to hire a gunman who will dispense their *own*. 'They might ride us like horses,' vows the whore 'mother'. 'But we'll show them we're not horses.'

But this nod to feminism, as in *Iron John*, is rapidly taken over by the internal logic of the plot of a film that demands that women be characterized as 'the problem'. Initially treated sympath-etically, their grudge against the cowboys turns to vindictiveness. They refuse the attempts of the slasher's cute young partner to make amends by keeping his best horse from the brothel owner and offering it to the scarred girl instead. In fact the first cowboy killed is the nice boy, whose agonizing death Logan cannot stomach. Women, whether Madonnas (Munny's wife) or whores, bring trouble into this Wild West world, trouble between men and trouble with men: 'there's a disease going round and it's spread by women' (and it kills pigs).

This is why Bly's famous weekends in the forest are men-only affairs. Forget Odysseus and the Iliad; the age-old 'universal' myths of manhood that he lays claim to in an attempt to legitimize his philosophy, are as local, as close to hand, as *American* as the myth of the Western. Bly's *Iron John* is nothing more than a bad Western: 'bad' because it looks to Europe to 'authenticate' a myth-ology that is as home-grown as John Wayne and Huckleberry Finn. The 'healthy man' that Bly looks for in high-falutin' translations of fancy European folk-tales and Greek myths is right on his doorstep in good ol' American chaps and stetson, thumbs hooked over his gun-belt, chewing baccy. Eastwood, in his leathery, old-timer way, knows this, and that is why he won Best Picture and Best Director from the Academy Awards for his retelling of this myth.

Both men are American romantics (but give me Eastwood's grim romanticism any day over Bly's lush prose trying to be plain), in love with the wilderness Eros, an Eros founded on the exclusion of women and the 'pure' love of male for male, the object of which is, as Leslie Fiedler put it, 'to *outwit* woman, that is to keep her from trapping the male through marriage into civilization and Christianity. The wilderness Eros is, in short, not merely an anti-cultural, but an anti-Christian, a Satanic Eros.'[11] The Queen must be outwitted and the key stolen from under her pillow to allow the Wild Man to escape from the cage of marriage and civilization and flee with him into the forests. Bly's emphasis on the pre-Christian status of his myths is a belief in their pagan/Satanic power to roll back the 'feminization' of man in Western Christian civilization, in the same way that in the Western the frontier is 'unsettled' and beyond the rule of law; Bly looks to the past while the Western looks to the horizon to achieve the same ends. (Of course, the Hollywood Western also looks to the past: the horizon is that of nineteenth-century America before the closure of the frontier.)

In *Unforgiven* the pure love of male for male, the romance of the West, is that of 'partners': it is taken for granted that *both* cowboys, rather than just the slasher, should pay the penalty: the bond between such men is closer and even more indissoluble than marriage. This is also the story of Munny and Ned: Ned leaves his wife the moment his old partner comes riding by.

And as so often happens in American dreams of the wilderness, the 'partner' sought by the white man 'lighting out for the territory' is black. For once 'civilization is disavowed and Christianity disowned. ... The wanderer feels himself more motherless child than free man. To be sure, there is a substitute for wife or mother presumably waiting in the green heart of nature: the natural man, the good companion, pagan and unashamed – Queequeg or Chingachook or Nigger Jim.'[12] Ned is Munny's first port of call on leaving his farm. Ned appears to agree to his request only because his old flame has asked him to, rather than out of any real desire for the bounty. In the tradition of masculine passion denoted by its very understatement the film makes clear their deep and 'pure' love for one another, one that is unspoken but fought to the death for.

This is precisely what Munny is prepared to do when he learns of Daggett's killing of Ned (whose own death can be read as a punishment for turning his back on Munny). This is the diabolical denouement of this Western: in embracing 'what is dark down there', calling Iron John from the edge of the forest, Munny is making a Faustian pact. Munny rides into town at night and sees Ned's corpse propped up in a coffin outside the saloon lit by flickering candles, ghastly and satanic: as Fiedler points out, 'the dark-skinned companion becomes the "Black Man", which is a traditional name for the Devil himself'. In avenging/saving Ned, Munny is making an infernal vow, putting him forever outside the reach of his wife, Christianity and civilization. He is Huckleberry Finn, determined not to give in to Aunt Sally's threats and reveal the whereabouts of his beloved Nigger Jim, embracing damnation.

> 'All right, then I'll *go* to Hell' ... It was awful thoughts and
> awful words, but they was said. And I let them stay said;
> and never thought no more about reforming. I shoved the
> whole thing out of my head, and said I would take up
> wickedness again, which was in my line, being brung up to
> it, and the other warn't.[13]

'It's what he knows, the accident of who he is.' The Faustian pact is a 'queer' marriage. Munny is Ishmael clinging to Queequeg's coffin in *Moby Dick*, saved but damned by Ned's corpse, married to him forever in a way that the living Ned would not or could not allow; it is a marriage that puts Munny forever outside civilization, sends him to Hell – but in his own way.

But however 'queer' the marriage, it must never be physically consummated: the diabolical, pagan homosocial world of men is atoned for in the 'purity' of their love for one another. Ned's death guarantees the chastity of Munny's marriage to him.[14]

Likewise in *Iron John* the preface tells us that 'Most of the language in this book speaks to heterosexual men but does not exclude homosexual men.'[15] In fact *all* of the language speaks to heterosexual men; homosexuality is as *necessarily* invisible (but always present) in the world of Bly as that of Eastwood's West; 'the past' is used as a circumvention of the irresolvable problem of homo-desire: 'It wasn't until the eighteenth century that people ever used the term homosexual; before that time gay [*sic*] men were understood simply as part of the community of men.' In other words, 'I deal in timeless mythologies of masculinity and since homosexuality is not timeless I shall ignore it'.

As usual Bly employs disingenuousness dipped in an 'inclusive' aniseed liberalism to throw his enemies off the scent. Despite the claim to a 'universal' myth, he makes a very clear distinction between homosexual and heterosexual men. His whole mythology, like that of the West, depends upon it – but only to *exclude* homosexual men. Bly's masculinism and the tale of Iron John depend upon the implicit myth of 'pure love' between men: explicitness – i.e. actual homosexuality in general or the homosexual in particular and especially – threatens to bring it low and spoil it for everybody. This wilful blindness becomes laughably clear in Bly's analysis of the ending of the Iron John story:

> The young man's father and mother were among those invited to the wedding, and they came; they were in great joy because they had given up hope that they would ever see their dear son again.
>
> While all the guests were sitting at the table for the marriage feast, the music broke off all at once, the great doors swung open, and a baronial King entered, accompanied in procession by many attendants.
>
> He walked up to the young groom and embraced him. The guest said: 'I am Iron John, who through an enchantment became turned into a Wild Man. You have freed me from that enchantment. All the treasures that I own will from now on belong to you.'[16]

What could be clearer? The real romance of the story has been consummated. But Bly, the expert mythologist and translator, cannot recognize a queer wedding when he sees one. The ending tells us, he writes, that we need not only to 'free ourselves from family cages and mind sets' but also to free 'transcendent beings from imprisonment and trance'. Yes. ... But what about the symbolism of the wedding scene, the embrace, the sharing of worldly goods? And any child could tell you how you turn a frog into a prince. 'I think that we have said as much as is proper here about the Wild Man,' is Bly's final word on the matter. Perhaps Bly should be less concerned about 'transcendent beings' and work on freeing himself from his own 'imprisonment and trance'. His insubstantial analysis reveals the bogus notion that is at the very heart of Bly's credo: 'descend deep down into the male psyche and accept what is dark down there' is a call to end repression if it is anything at all – and yet Bly's interpretation of the most crucial scene in the whole Iron John story is itself a lesson in disavowal, a refusal to accept 'what is dark down there'.

The end of the Iron John story shows that, just as in the Western, the overriding romance was homosexual: 'woman' has been outwitted again, prevented from 'trapping the male through marriage into civilization and Christianity' even at the very moment of the boy's readmission into the family ('they had given up hope that they would ever see their dear son again') and holy matrimony: instead of the bride, Iron John comes through the 'great doors'. Freed from his enchantment by the boy's love, Iron John is 'tamed'; he loses his hair and becomes a baron (in effect he turns 'white') and thus can return to civilization to join the boy, to save him from it in the nick of time.

The ending also demonstrates that Iron John is more than just an aspect of the boy's own psyche, as Bly would have it. The romance has been a mutual attraction of opposites: the soft boy's attraction to Iron John's toughness and *Iron John's attraction to the boy's softness*; in the end the romance had the effect of both giving the boy just enough 'wildness' and giving Iron John just enough 'civilization': a perfect exchange, a perfect couple. Thus the ending appears to balance the incompatible: marriage and queer romance, familial acceptance and masculine freedom, civilization and the forest.

But this is just a fairy tale. In the 'real' world of adult literature and cinema these opposites cannot be reconciled and the resolution must be darker: there can be no 'queer wedding' or Fiedler's 'holy marriage of males'. Instead there is the usual fatal sublimation: the dark-skinned Queequeg dies but lives on through white Ishmael's love for him, adrift in an endless blank wilderness of ocean; black Ned dies but lives on through white Munny, an outlaw cast adrift in a wilderness of crime.

Notes

1. Robert Bly, *Iron John* (New York: Vintage, 1992), p. 2.

2. Quoted in Susan Faludi's *Backlash: The Undeclared War Against Women* (London: Chatto and Windus, 1991), p. 340.

3. Bly, *Iron John*, p. 6.

4. *Ibid.*, p. 63.

5. 'An intelligent man with no stomach for killing, despite his proficiency with a rifle, his distaste for the job at hand is obvious and his reluctance to participate ultimately proves his undoing.' – production notes.

6. The production notes offer this succinct and revealing description of the Munny character: 'William Munny is a complex, taciturn man whose perspective is tempered, not only by his past, but by the love for his late wife and his children. He becomes caught between who he was and who he is, struggling with the knowledge that he can make himself solvent by calling upon the very darkest elements of his personality.'

7. Bly, *Iron John*, p. iv.

8. Faludi, *Backlash*, p. 345.

9. Bly, *Iron John*, p. iv.

10. Faludi, *Backlash*, p. 345.

11. Leslie Fiedler, *Love and Death in the American Novel*, p. 212.

12. *Ibid.*, p. 26.

13. *Ibid.*, p. 352.

14. In *The Eiger Sanction* (Eastwood, US, 1975), Eastwood gave us an unambiguous example of his attitude towards homosexuality. In it he plays an expert mountaineer and part-time CIA operative whom a mincing queer villain, complete with a lap-dog by the name of Faggot, tries to have killed. Rather than demean himself by killing such a monstrosity he merely leaves him out in the desert to die – he lets *nature* wreak its revenge on this freak. Even heterosexual men cannot be trusted. Another character, a friend of Eastwood's, oversteps the limit of friendliness; 'Don't go sloppy on me,' Eastwood warns disgustedly. So it comes as no surprise to learn later that he is the enemy agent Eastwood has been looking for all along.'

15. Bly, *Iron John*, p. v.

16. *Ibid.*, p. 232.

Chapter fourteen

Popular Men
Manly v. Unmanly

Working-class heroes

ON the letters page of the *Guardian*, housewives have cried
into their washing-up and 'stereotypical' Tory voters have fulmi-
nated. *The Times* and the *Telegraph* reported how Cheltenham
took to the streets and the Gucci-heeled women of Kensington
cheered the miners. Suddenly the 'enemy within' of 1984–5 are
'our miners'. But someone forgot to inform one old lady in
Kensington about this lightning rehabilitation; according to the
Telegraph, she threw a bucket of water over marching miners from
her first-floor flat, shouting 'animals!'

The press treatment of the pits crisis has unearthed more
than pent-up frustration with the government's incompetence. Nor
can the crushing sentimentality of the right be explained simply as
paternalist bingeing on their first 'caring' pub-crawl after the long,
dry years 'on the wagon' with Thatcher. As Simon Jenkins worried
in *The Times*, why this fuss over mining communities and not over
the redundancies in, say, retailing or financial services?

Unasked, the miners have been assigned the burden of representing authenticity in an inauthentic Britain; real British men
from real communities doing real work. Their labour – hard, masculine and productive – is an antidote to failed, frivolous and 'feminine' service industries. Heavy industry, once as unfashionable as
Old Spice, is now the subject of a nostalgia that cuts across class,
party and even gender lines.

'A family gone to waste' is the *Mirror*' headline over a

picture foregrounding a retired miner surrounded by his sons, their wives and children out of focus in the background. The reporter tells us that the sons were sent down the pit by their father: 'It's been dirty, dangerous work, ten hours at a time on hands and knees working at a four-foot high seam ... But they loved it.' Thus we are invited to admire the manly embrace of dirt and danger in the last corner of Britain where men are men and women are wives.

This kind of fantasy is projected again and again onto the miners by all sections of the press. Just when Tony Parsons' lament for the decline of working-class decency was getting a head of steam, the media 'discovers' workers who have kept alive pre-consumer society notions of masculinity based on duty, discipline and team-work. The miners, traditionally the vanguard of the proletariat, now find themselves portrayed as the rearguard of a vanished world.

Michael Parkinson, in a *Telegraph*[2] piece on football, eulogizes and patronizes miners as if pits were bottomless wells of virility. 'The pits provided a certain kind of player. He was likely to be of medium height, of sturdy build and uncompromising in tackle ... they were unending in supply. All you had to do was peer down any pit-shaft and whistle and one came up, ready to go to work.'

The equation of the pits with a reservoir of men's men, sporting and spunky, is also exploited by the *Star*[3] in a startling picture of the British rugby league team wearing their British Coal strip. They march grimly towards the camera shrouded in the smoke of battle with a war-torn Union Jack at their head. The headline barks, 'Best of British, lads' (the comma is clearly optional), while the copy pants about 'fully grown, hard-bitten, genuine, tough guys.'

The sporting motif ties in with the renaissance of one of the oldest male fantasies: the nation state. With Britain out of the ERM, Maastricht in doubt, and a trade war looming, old-fashioned manly virtues are required to make our nation strong again.

As John Major said, 'It's a cold, hard world outside the ERM,' and real men are needed, not 'sensitive' wimps like him. Major having shown weakness, his manhood is questioned; either slyly, in *The Times*'s rumours of a crack-up, or bluntly, as with the *Star*'s[4] description of him as a 'wimp'. The same issue bellows to its readers: 'You demand real men in power – not a bunch of failed wimps.' Even the *Guardian*[5] cannot resist the gender slur: Simon Rae implies that Major is 'Jane' to Heseltine's 'Tarzan'. Everywhere our ineffectual and effete leaders are compared with the macho miners and found wanting.

Those tempted to consider any stick worth beating with, so long as it hurts, should consider the way that the masculine mystification of the miners is used to point up the 'unmanliness' of left-wing intellectuals. The *Telegraph*[6] report of the march contrasts 'burly' miners with 'wispy peddlars of left-wing papers' and 'radical students ... weedy with glasses'.

But it is a *Star*[7] leader that makes explicit the reduction of 'the workers' to 'the real men'. In a crude style not without resonance on the left, it jeers: 'If Labour cannot do better for the miners, the founding fathers of the movement, it will prove conclusively that the party is now fit only for polytechnic lecturers, leftie lawyers and twittering women teachers – NOT the workers.'

The bitter irony is that media eulogies of the miners have only been possible because they are now so *weak*, and traditional masculinity so enervated. The *Mirror*[8] offered a poster of an attractive, exhausted young miner slumped on a bench in a locker-room, posed in his sweaty singlet with a ghostly winding tower super-imposed, emerging from his leg as a kind of hazy memory of the phallus. In inviting pity, this male image also invites the gaze in a way that would have been impossible without the very changes in gender roles that it seems to lament.

(Originally published in *New Statesman and Society*, 30 October 1992)

Swish that back end, Bill!

Is there a fag in the White House? If you followed the accounts of the US election campaign in the British and American press you might be forgiven for thinking so.

According to New York magazine *QW*, Ray Scott, a fishing buddy of Bush, told an audience of 10,000 in Montgomery, Alabama, that Clinton's mannerisms are effeminate. 'He's a sissy,' Scott said. 'You can tell how he walks. Watch how he swishes his back end.'

The Republican Party declared war on queers and women at its Houston Convention last year. A return to 'family values' was a widely understood code for a war on gender nonconformity, to restore patriarchal norms. Let's be rid of feminists with moustaches, single mothers, and sodomites! they cried, and then our men will be men again! 'The Grand Old Party has declared war on the war against men,' commented US feminist Naomi Wolf.

America responded by electing to the post of Most Powerful Man in the World a 'sissy' who swishes his rear end. And that *face*: so plump and soft you might expect to find bum-fluff growing there instead of beard. Worst of all he is said to actually like women's company and his wife is generally acknowledged to be much smarter than he *and* a self-confessed feminist ('that smiling barracuda', according to the *National Review* – talk about castration anxiety).

In fact Clinton is so unmanly that the British male left can't bear him either. Marxists like Alexander Cockburn of *New Statesman and Society* or left-liberals like Andrew Stephen of the *Observer* find their balls retracting into their abdomen at the merest mention of his name. What galls them is Clinton's 'duplicity', his 'desire to please' which (of course) conceals something very *un*pleasant indeed: Bill Clinton as *femme fatale*. His lack of phallic certainty, his inability to face 'hard' choices and take 'firm' stands brings these men out in a rash – an allergic response to the presence of the Other?

Cockburn reverently quotes a passage from the *Arkansas Gazette* that could easily be a description of a homosexual from a forties novel: 'Finally, and sadly, there is the unavoidable question of character. ... There is something almost inhuman in his smoother responses that sends a shiver up the spine.'[9] For 'inhuman,' of course, read 'unmanly'. Women, by and large, had the opposite reaction and voted for 'Slick Willy' in droves (45 per cent as against Bush's 38 per cent).

In the same vein Andrew Stephen tags him 'Bill the Pleaser',[10] a tag with a fascinating aroma of sexual passivity, and devotes a whole page to bar-room psychology which reads like the kind of explanation of homosexuality you might have found in *Reader's Digest* twenty years ago. 'Clinton is the product of a strong mother and a weak father. ... From the time of his birth onwards it is as though Clinton embarked on a search that continues to this day for the strong man in himself – as if he has to prove something.' But what about his reputation as a ladies' man? The Gennifer Flowers case, for example? Surely *there* is irrefutable evidence of a *real* man? 'The truth seems to be that, sexually, he is more talk than action. In this, as in other things, Clinton is no Jack Kennedy.'

Like many British journalists covering the election campaign, Cockburn and Stephen repeatedly told us that Clinton was 'no Kennedy': he was a 'third-rate man' and couldn't win. Even when they were proved spectacularly wrong the credit could not go to Bill. His stunning victory was for any reason other than his breathtakingly well-managed campaign, his promise of a 'gentle revolution' and his direct appeal to women and homosexuals. Instead it was 'the Bush factor'. 'Sissies' like Bill, by definition, cannot succeed at what is supposed to be the butchest sport going.

That now famous appeal to 'our nation's most gifted [gay] community we have been willing to squander' and his high-profile pledge to end the Pentagon ban on lesbians and gays, which has already dominated his time as President Elect, is the sign of brave, visionary politics – ironically what Cockburn and Stephen would call 'balls' if they weren't so full of spleen.

And no sooner has Clinton won one poll than he tops another, almost as prestigious: the London weekly, *Capital Gay*'s Man of the Year Reader's Award. But the accolade was not without its provisos: 'This is the first time that anyone has won the title without actually doing anything', *Capital Gay* added.

Excuse me, but did he not stop the war chariots of the fundamentalists who were rolling out of the South and across America in their tracks? Did he not throw out a Republican administration that has been an on-going holocaust for gay Americans? Was he not the first presidential candidate to bring lesbian and gay issues into the mainstream? And, most importantly of all perhaps, has he not shown that a man who 'swishes his back end' can be President? Even if Clinton reneges on every single election promise he made to lesbians and gays he cannot undo what he has already done.

As Clinton runs up against seemingly intractable problems over the coming months and years and, in Perot's memorable phrase, into 'deep doo-doo' – as he must – many will gloat about how right they were about Clinton and his 'duplicity'. As the betrayals begin and the agony piles on, perhaps we ought to bear in mind the other observation about Bill our Alabaman sissy spotter is reported to have shared with the world: 'I've seen them both in the washroom, and let me tell you, Bill ain't like George Bush!'

But then again, they do say that small ones hurt more when they start to stick it to you.

Within days of his inauguration, Clinton was subjected to a barrage of criticism, from both Republicans and Democrats, unprecedented for a president so soon into his term, for sticking to his campaign pledge to repeal the Pentagon ban. A British television news feature on the brouhaha ended with a clip showing Clinton the baby-faced 'draft dodger' sitting down at a table faced by the combined might of the Pentagon. Po-faced five-star generals and admirals confronted 'Elvis' across the table; sitting stiffly in their starchy uniforms beneath a carapace of medals and ribbons, the very epitome of the *ancien régime* of masculinity.

The reporter laid it on with a trowel: 'And it is symbolic of Clinton's troubled young presidency that at his first meeting with the Chiefs of Staff he discussed not Somalia, not the war in Bosnia, not Iraq nor the proposed cuts in the defence budget but *gays*.'

That the President of the United States and his generals should be preoccupied with this issue rather than the business of projecting US power across the world *was* extraordinary and inconceivable just a few months previously.

Nevertheless the scene of Clinton v. The Generals had a certain familiarity about it: you felt you had seen it somewhere before but you could not quite put your finger on it ... that boyish face, that cute, dazzling grin, that earnestness, those twinkling eyes – *yes* this was life imitating Hollywood again. President Clinton played Tom Cruise playing Lieutenant Kaffee opposite General Colin Powell's and Senator Sam Nunn's joint rendition of Jack Nicholson's Colonel Jessep with Hillary as Demi Moore's Lieutenant Galloway. Once again the boyish man stands up to the fathers, egged on by a resolute woman whose relationship with him is sexually indeterminate. Sadly, life failed to produce the same uplifting ending as *A Few Good Men*: the Pentagon ban stayed in place (albeit modified), while Clinton's future was put in doubt.

(Originally published in *Gay Times*, February 1993)

Funny men: Laurel and Hardy and a queer affair

Stan: Well, what's the matter with her anyway?
Ollie: Oh, I don't know. She says I think more of you than I do of her.
Stan: Well, you do don't you?
Ollie: We won't go into that!
Stan: Y'know what the trouble is?
Ollie: What?
Stan: You need a baby in your house.
Ollie: What's that got to do with it?
Stan: Well, if you had a baby it would keep your wife's mind occupied; you could go out nights with me and she'd think nothing of it.

● *Their First Mistake, 1932*

Suggesting that cinema's most cherished comedy duo might be homosexual is not something you are likely to be thanked for. But this is precisely what Vito Russo does in his book *The Celluloid Closet*. Boldly claiming Laurel and Hardy for the history of gay cinema, Russo points out that in films like *Their First Mistake* (1932), the fat man and the thin man exemplified the 'perfect sissy-buddy relationship, which had a sweet and very real loving dimension' with 'unmistakably gay overtones.'[1]

Could 'buggery-pokery' *really* be at the root of Stan and Ollie's relationship – a relationship which has endured as the most fondly regarded cinema partnership of all time? Could their videos, amongst the all-time best-sellers and considered perfect children's entertainment, be promoting some kind of queer Eros? Or is this rather the result of over-heated analysis, the product of the perverse imagination of gay critics?

Laurel and Hardy's classic silent short *Liberty* seems to confirm the Russo reading, in the most explicit way. Stan and Ollie play convicts on the run, who, in their haste to change into civvies, manage to put on each other's trousers, which, given their famously contrasting shapes, proves somewhat impractical. There then follows a sequence of events that will be only too familiar to many gay viewers. Frantically, they try to swap their pants in an alleyway, behind some crates and in the back of a taxi. Each time they are frustrated by being discovered by some horrified passer-by, including: a housewife, a shopkeeper, a young heterosexual couple and a policeman. Sheepishly they scurry off in search of some other intimate place to effect their transaction (a building site, as it happens). Even critics unsympathetic to homosexuality have noted the sexual script here: as French film critic André S. Labarthe observed: '*Liberty* offers to anyone who can read, the unequivocal sign of unnatural love.'

But others have reacted indignantly to the suggestion that there could be anything 'unnatural' in the fat man and the thin man's relationship. 'There is something rather absurd about discussing this seriously at all,' writes Charles Barr in his book *Laurel and Hardy*, responding to Labarthe. What is revealing is not so much Barr's response as the example that he selects to refute the imputation: '"Their First Mistake" surely gives, to anyone who can read, an explicit rebuttal of Labarthe.'[12] In Barr's analysis the signs of 'unnatural love' represent in fact, through infantilization, the very naturalness and purity of Stan and Ollie's love: 'since their mental processes, particularly Stan's, are those of nursery children, one takes it for granted that they should share a bed as in the nursery.' Their infantilism, in other words, guarantees their 'pre-sexual' status.

This response by Barr is little more than the patriotic repulsing of an invasion by filthy foreign slanders, reminiscent of Leslie Fiedler's remark that, 'In our native mythology, the tie between male and male is not only considered innocent, it is taken for the very symbol of innocence itself.'[13] In effect, Barr is defending the myth of America itself, positioning the purity of the Great American Childhood between Laurel and Hardy and those who would seek to corrupt their legacy. 'After Mark Twain,' writes Fiedler, 'one of the partners to such a union is typically conceived of as a child, thus inviting the reader to identify with the Great Good Place where the union is consummated with his own childhood ...'

Infantilism is not, of course, 'pre-sexual'. Like the myth of childhood innocence itself, Laurel and Hardy's own 'innocence' serves to keep the critical lid on a veritable Pandora's box of forbidden desires. We laugh at their 'queer' antics to relieve our discomfort at their associations. But we also *enjoy* that discomfort. This is why *both* Barr and Labarthe are correct.

In *Their First Mistake* Ollie is sued for divorce by his wife (with Stan named as 'the other woman'). The action then centres around Ollie's incompetent attempts to run a house and look after an infant. Eventually he and Stan end up in their bed with the baby. Ollie falls asleep but is awoken by the baby's cries. Half asleep, eyes closed, Ollie reaches over with the feeding bottle, but it inevitably ends up in Stan's mouth who is sleeping alongside him, cuddled in his arm. Stan instinctively sucks it dry in his sleep.

The scene's humour depends precisely upon reading this as both 'innocent' and 'queer', with the second reading held under the first. In other words, the signified 'pre-sexual' status of Stan and Ollie defuses the threat of the bed scene but does not remove the charge – if it did, where would the gag be? The disavowal of Stan and Ollie's queerness does not erase it, otherwise they would never have cut it as a comedy duo and would have long been forgotten. Ollie's oral gratification of Stan is 'funny' precisely *because* to take it any other way would be shocking and indecent. The absurd protects itself against enquiry by salvaging the disturbing reading beneath the innocent one – by humorous 'contamination'; thus 'there is something rather absurd about discussing this seriously at all', i.e. Barr continues the disavowal through the idea of the 'joke'.[14]

Of course, Laurel and Hardy are not 'gay'. But they are clearly not 'straight' either. Attempts by gays to claim them as 'the ultimate gay couple', as some have done, are as legitimate or illegitimate as any other claim on them. But no one can successfully claim *exclusive* ownership. Laurel and Hardy's dalliance with perverse signifiers – their 'queerness' – is actually a measure of their gender nonconformity as much as, if not more than, a sign of sexual deviation. Their refusal/inability to perform heterosexuality and play the role of 'men' is what defines them. This is the other meaning of their infantilization, their escape from the usual masculine standards. Unable to hold down a job for the length of a film, irresponsible, cowardly, living in the shadow of their Amazonian wives and regularly given a good pasting by them, our heroes are wonderfully, thrillingly *catastrophic* failures as men. Which is of course why we love them – gay or straight.

In her book *Gender Trouble*, Judith Butler argues that from a queer perspective heterosexuality prescribes 'normative sexual positions that are intrinsically impossible to embody'. These in turn become 'an inevitable comedy,' and heterosexuality becomes a 'constant parody of itself'.[15] But comedy duos like Laurel and Hardy show that this perspective is not exclusive to lesbians and gays. The particularly rigid enforcement of gender roles that accompanied the arrival of capitalism and the sexual division of labour still rankles in the popular subconscious, and any 'safe' revolt against them, especially the transformation of 'straight' roles into pantomime, is enthusiastically welcomed.

Laurel and Hardy base their own brand of sex-role panto on the impossibility of the demands of manhood. The joke, so to speak, is on masculinity. This is even suggested in the title of their first headline movie together, *Putting Pants on Phillip* (1927). In it Stan plays a kilt-wearing Scotsman visiting his American uncle Ollie, who is embarrassed by his nephew's unorthodox leg-wear. Despite Stan's portrayal as – of all things – a woman chaser (a peculiarly jarring image) most of the jokes revolve around Stan's 'skirt'. At one point Stan even treats us to a bizarre premonition of Marilyn Monroe's trademark by standing over a ventilation grille, with predictable results. At this, women in a crowd that has been attracted by Stan's strange apparel faint and a policeman warns Ollie, 'This dame ain't got no lingerie on.' It is not Stan whom we laugh at, but the social agonies of the respectable gent played by Ollie who desperately tries to get his nephew kitted out in some 'proper' masculine attire, to no avail.

In a later silent, *You're Darn Tootin* (1928), the trouser motif, or rather the lack of them, is taken to glorious extremes. The duo's infectious mayhem embroils a whole street full of men in one of their tiffs (brought about by their failure, once again, to successfully perform a job). Soon trousers sail through the air in a 'debagging' orgy. No man, however dignified, is safe: workmen, businessmen and even policemen succumb to the chaos Laurel and Hardy have brought to the masculine world – and quite literally lose their trousers. The gag is simple but universal in its effectiveness, relying on one basic assumption: men and the way they take themselves so seriously are actually the biggest joke going – just pull their trousers down and you'll see why.

Stan and Ollie, meanwhile, waltz away from this scene of masculine devastation sharing a pair of trousers. Unmanly men they may be, but together they have just enough dignity to go round after the 'real men' have been stripped of theirs.

'Pants' also symbolize the civilization and refinement of the 'nether regions'; their loss stands for disorder. For the Russian critic and medievalist Bakhtin, laughter brings the mighty low and turns the natural world upside down – returning us to the body. The carnivalesque in our comic duo's films resides most obviously in Ollie's belly and bottom: soft, wobbly, outsized and irresistible, they are hardly ever out of frame. Especially that bottom.

The arse is the first line of defence in the paranoid masculine struggle against being 'unmanned'. It is the inevitable site of floods of jokes designed to allay fears about being penetrated, sexual passivity and ridicule. And in case we should forget Ollie's laughable arse and all that it represents, a stream of missiles launch themselves with unerring accuracy at his flabby flanks: water jets, nails, arrows, pitchforks, shotgun pellets and pins 'prick' his bottom in a sadistic torture that makes *us* squirm while we guffaw.

And, true to Bakhtin's carnivalesque characterization of popular humour, everything these 'crap' men touch turns to shit. Objects exist only to be broken; conventions, to be flouted. Now wincing, now cheering, we follow their sniggering trail of destruction to a millionaire's trashed mansion, to a banquet become a battlefield, or to the remnants of a grand piano – the ultimate symbol of failed bourgeois pretension. In the anally-fixated, scatological humour of popular comedy, shit, bottoms and mess are gleefully celebrated as an antidote to the repressive strictures of high-minded middle-class respectability: bathos triumphs over pathos; the ridiculous over the sublime. Mess, destruction and disaster, epitomized in the custard pie fight, are *fundamental* fun.

If their humour is medieval, then Stan and Ollie's relationship is more modern. Inhabiting a resolutely hostile world where nothing goes right, the inadequate co-dependents that are Stan and Ollie have only each other to count on or blame: 'That's another nice mess you've gotten me into!' We identify not only with their hopelessness but with their *love*. We can laugh at their spiteful, shin-kicking, eye-poking squabbles only because we are sure that their love will endure. We know that out of the rubble of a Beverly Hills villa, the heap of torn trousers and the sea of 'custard', Stan and Ollie will emerge unscathed and indissoluble; survivors of everything the world can throw at them.

So admirable is their love that very often it is set against conventional male heterosexuality, as both a resistance to it and, for all our silly pair's 'crapness', as a favourable contrast. *Pack Up Your Troubles* (1932) begins with war being declared and Stan and Laurel unsuccessfully trying to evade conscription by faking invalidity (again their unmanliness allows them to display traits, in this case cowardice, that other men are forbidden). Once inducted into the army, they continually demonstrate their hilarious inability to perform the martial myth of manhood. In drill they are, needless to say, disastrous. Stan cannot get the hang of left and right and so hooks his arm around Ollie's. True to form they *both* end up marching in the wrong direction – arm in arm. They are sent to the trenches, where their love continues to defy the expected manly performance: we see them at reveille in the same bed, arms wrapped around one another with their feet pressed against a hot water bottle. A sergeant major barks at them and orders them to capture some Germans. Their bungling ineptitude saves them from certain death and wins the day without the death of a single soldier, American or German.

One American soldier, however, is captured by the Germans. Stan and Ollie resolve to visit his baby girl on their return home. On their visit they discover that she is being ill-treated by her foster parents. We see the girl being deprived of love and affection by uncaring husband and wife, especially the husband who is tyrannical and sadistic. On this scene of glum misery the door opens and it is good old Stan and Ollie, clearly representing 'love'. Naturally they rescue the girl from her ogre foster father and set about trying to locate her grandparents (what, I wonder, would be the popular reaction to the kidnap of a little girl from her heterosexual guardians by two men who lived together if it occurred off the screen?). Tracing her grandparents proves problematic – they only know their surname: Smith. This provides the entrée into a series of gags.

The first Mr Smith they locate turns out to be a boxer. When the door opens Ollie cheerily announces, 'We've got your son's child!' 'Blackmail, eh?' replies the boxer and punches Ollie on the chin with a bonecrushing right hook.

In another 'Smith' confusion they bring mayhem to a bourgeois wedding ceremony leading the father of the bride to think that the little girl belongs to the groom. The wedding cancelled, the bride rushes over to Laurel and Hardy and thanks them effusively for saving her from an unwanted marriage. Once again our lovers manage to upset the heterosexual applecart in heroic fashion, offering a moral contrast in their understanding of love to that of the cynical male characters they encounter who are sadistic, violent, selfish and callous. It is instructive of Laurel and Hardy's relationship that a film that begins with a declaration of war and conscription quickly devotes itself to a sentimental storyline about children.

Alas, the parody of masculinity and the example of another kind of loving that our boys provide us with is dependent, finally, upon the exclusion of women. This is shown in *Their First Mistake*: the problem Ollie and Stan are debating is how to get the women out their life. Any femininity entertained by them in the form of their frequent dragging up, for example, is a mere semblance (although it has to be said that Stan is *unnervingly* convincing in a frock). Real femininity, in the shape of their knuckle-dusting wives, is something to flee from (however, in contrast to the tradition, these fearsomely strong women are also very attractive).[16]

But this exclusion of women is an almost universal tradition in male comedy. From the sleeping habits of Jerry Lewis and Dean Martin or Morecambe and Wise to the drag extravaganzas of *It Ain't Half Hot Mum*, any transgression of masculine standards is predicated upon the maintenance of a boys-only environment including even the 1990s out-of-the-closet comedy of *Terry and Julian*. *Red Dwarf*, a comedy set in space, takes this maxim to the cynical extreme of having the only female character played by a computer – i.e. femininity literally disembodied.[17] (This is why Dawn French and Jennifer Saunders' all-female comedy is so refreshing and why their vengeful impersonations of men, complete with ball-scratching and fat arses escaping from jeans, is so shockingly hilarious.)

However, it is Adrian Edmonson's and Rik Mayall's double

act that must be the direct inheritor of the Laurel and Hardy tradition in Britain; like our defunct duo they are utterly 'crap' men, and for them everything exists to be destroyed. Of course, *their* relationship is depressingly up-to-date. They sleep in separate beds and are spectacularly cruel to one another without respite in an almost ritualistic fashion; they are not allowed any of the tender moments that Ollie and Stan enjoyed in between the nose-twisting and foot-stamping. Nevertheless Rik and Adrian remain together and their tainted, twisted 'love' survives an equally tainted, twisted world. And, as with Laurel and Hardy, the rectum is both an exclamation and a question mark hanging over them – a fact freely acknowledged in the title of their latest incarnation: *Bottom*.

It is not, as some would have it, an age of innocence that has been lost, but rather an impossible tenderness between men.

In an interview towards the end of his life, Foucault suggested that the rise of homosexuality as an identity has coincided with the disappearance of male friendships: 'the disappearance of friendship as a social relationship and the transformation of homosexuality into a social, political and medical problem are part of the same process'.[18] Perhaps what we have seen in the period since Laurel and Hardy is an *increase* of the presence of homosexuality *as a thing to be disavowed* in male-to-male relations, rather than its sudden arrival. If male-to-male ties were once taken to be 'the symbol of innocence itself' then perhaps this was only through a suspension of disbelief that is no longer tenable in an era when homosexuality is so much more visible.

In Ollie and Stan's day the audience's anxieties/interest in queerness could be titillated and the joke could safely be substituted for its actual expression: their behaviour could be 'funny' in a sense that *was* 'peculiar' but disavowed by *being* funny. But nowadays this mechanism, even with infantilization and the exclusion of women, seems unable to cope with *any* tenderness between our male comics. Looking back, contemporary audiences can enjoy the antics of the fat man and the thin man because, like Barr, they place them in a pretended pure and innocent past – 'the Great Good Place' – that never existed.

Finally, perhaps Laurel and Hardy are regarded with such fondness because they represent an impossible contradiction: innocence *and* queerness; they are men who are in every sense 'impossible' – then, and especially now: impossibly 'funny' and impossibly touching. Reports that Stan was 'inconsolable' after Ollie's death only heighten our own sense of loss at the passing of their screen affair.

Notes

1. 19 October 1992.

2. 19 October 1992.

3. 22 October 1992.

4. 22 October 1992.

5. 24 October 1992.

6. 22 October 1992.

7. 21 October 1992.

8. 20 October 1992.

9. *New Statesman and Society*, 6 November 1992.

10. *Observer*, 3 January 1993.

11. Vito Russo, *The Celluloid Closet* (New York: Harper and Row, 1987), p. 73.

12. Charles Barr, *Laurel and Hardy* (Berkeley: University of California Press, 1968), p. 57.

13. Leslie Fiedler, *Love and Death in the American Novel*, p. 350.

14. Stan and Ollie by their own behaviour reveal that they are not so innocent after all: why else would they display shame when discovered trying to swap their pants?

15. Judith Butler, *Gender Trouble: Feminism and the Subversion of Identity* (London: Routledge and Kegan Paul, 1990), p. 122.

16. Given this, it is perhaps unsurprising that the popular international Laurel and Hardy fan club is called 'Sons of the Desert', after the film of the same name where the boys can go to a convention of their men-only Sons of the Desert club in Chicago only by tricking their wives. (Of course their wives find out and there is hell to pay.)

17. The manner in which *Red Dwarf*, a *modern* boys' club comedy series (written by Rob Grant and Doug Naylor), negotiates the threats of femininity and homosexuality amongst its all-male crew is very telling. There is only one human crew member, Lister; the others are a cat-creature, an android and a despised hologram called 'Rimmer'. As a hologram, he is as disembodied as the female computer. This is because, as the name might suggest, he is the nearest thing to a homosexual threat to Lister, who is marked as unimpeachably laddish and heterosexual. So it is Rimmer who is Other (rather than the cat-creature and the

android) and the target for most of the jokes, homophobic and misogynistic. In one episode Rimmer catches a 'holovirus' from another *female* hologram that threatens to kill the crew. It turns him into a psychopath in a plaid skirt and Dutch-girl wig who tries to murder the others. In another episode the crew meet their 'bad' selves: Rimmer is a gay transvestite sado-psychopath complete with fishnets, leather harness, bull-whip and feather boa.

18. *Advocate*, August 1984.

Index